REAL EXPERIENCE

REAL
EXPERIENCE

THE TACTICAL FIELD GUIDE FOR
BUYING AND SELLING A HOME

BEN WALKLEY
AND KEVIN WASIE

LIONCREST
PUBLISHING

REAL EXPERIENCE

The Tactical Field Guide for Buying and Selling a Home

ISBN   978-1-5445-1565-6 *Hardcover*

        978-1-5445-1564-9 *Paperback*

        978-1-5445-1563-2 *Ebook*

Dedicated to my wife Kelly, who has been the real trooper, sticking with me through thick and thin. You've walked with me through all my highs and lows and have shown endless support and patience. Thanks for all the ways you care for me and our kids. You bring love and beauty to our home.

B.T.W.

Dedicated to my mom and dad for making our house a home. Dedicated also to my kids, Adelaide and Nolan, for all the fun you bring to my life.

K.W.

Finally, thanks to Greta and the Scribe team for endlessly helping us put this book together and getting these thoughts on paper. Thanks for believing in our project.

CONTENTS

INTRODUCTION

Imagine standing at the edge of a large forest. Your new home is waiting for you on the far side, but you're uncertain how to get there. Between here and *home*, there are countless winding paths that might lead you in the wrong direction. Guides step forward, offering you help, but you're not sure if you can trust them. You don't know this forest well enough to navigate the hidden dangers, and you sense that a single misstep could cause a disastrous fall. You need to get through this forest if you want to make it to your safe haven—but how can you make sure you do so successfully?

For many, this sums up the anxiety that arises when you prepare to buy or sell a home. You'd prefer a straight path through that forest, but that's rarely the norm. You want transparency from the people you deal with, and you want to be alerted if you're about to make a bad move. Is that too much to ask?

No, it's not—which is why we've written this book.

DANGERS ON THE JOURNEY

Unfortunately, it's easy to get lost or hurt in the world of real estate. Navigating all the various steps requires tons of information and expertise—much of which you likely don't possess. The real estate industry can feel opaque and full of barriers: banks, loans, title work, contractors, inspections—it's no wonder most people experience general confusion. There are plenty of people eager to "guide" you through the forest, but how many of them actually know the best paths? How many of them are wolves dressed in sheep's clothing, eager to make a buck even if it's at your expense? The pressure is high, too; we're talking about the place your family will create a home and one of the largest financial decisions of your life.

If you've never bought or sold a house before, you may feel hopelessly naïve. For those who have, your experience may have been negative, which can exacerbate the fear, suspicion, anxiety, or bitterness you might be feeling. You may not feel like you know enough, and you're not confident about who to trust. As a result, you might feel stuck from ever stepping forward—or plagued with anxiety every step of the way.

HELP ALONG THE WAY

Now: imagine if someone handed you a tactical field guide to navigate this forest. Inside is a map highlighting the different routes available. There are descriptions of the pros and cons of each different option, along with insider tips alerting you to hidden dangers and directions to discover the best views. You'll also get recommendations on how to choose guides who know the intricacies of the forest, will advocate on your behalf, and look out for your best interests.

With the guidebook in hand and trusted guides at your side, the scenario ahead would seem radically different. Instead of feeling plagued by fear, you'd be able to *relax* and open your eyes to the beauty around you.

That's what we want to give you with this book. We know this industry inside and out, and we're ready to guide you through it. Why? We've realized that one of the best ways for us to live meaningful lives is by using our professions to bless others. As we'll share in a moment, we've both experienced the soul-sucking emptiness of doing real estate in a way that focuses on making money as the sole priority. We've also experienced the incredible privilege of guiding people through the home-buying or home-selling experience that blesses everyone involved. At heart, we are educators—and we're eager to equip our readers so that they can have the fulfilling experience we all want.

WHAT YOU'LL LEARN

We've divided this book into two sections: **Part 1 is for people preparing to *buy* a house, and Part 2 is for those preparing to *sell*.** You may need the information in both parts simultaneously—such as if you're preparing to sell your current home and immediately buy a new one—or you may find these two sections relevant at two totally different stages in your life.

We invite you, therefore, to use the book as best suits your needs. You can skim the highlights, or you can read it cover to cover, gleaning every last nuance from the stories we've provided. You can read Part 1 now, as you prepare to buy your first home, and read Part 2 years later when you're preparing to sell it. We've tried to provide you the flexibility you need to reap the maximum benefit in your circumstances—whether you need to absorb this information in a hurry or are ready for a close read.

Still, regardless of where you are in the process, you'll find that the experience of home-buying and selling contains a journey: there's a beginning, when you first decide to buy or list your home. There's a middle: if you're a buyer, that's looking at homes and making offers; if you're a seller, that's preparing your home for the market and effectively listing it. And finally, there's an end: contract to close. Along the way, you need good people beside you who will actively work for your best interests. With all that in mind, here is what you will learn from this book:

- **Buy, sell, or rent?** For buyers, we'll discuss key points to consider about whether you *should* buy or if renting makes more sense. For sellers, we'll discuss the pros and cons of selling your property versus leasing it out as a rental.
- **The importance of mindset: homeowner versus investor.** Some people only evaluate a property in terms of how it might feel to live in; that's the "homeowner" mindset. Others view properties only in terms of their potential profit; that's the "investor" mindset. In order to make a wise financial decision that will bless your family, you need to think like a homeowner *and* investor. We'll explain why and how.
- **Find your guides: choosing a good real estate agent and mortgage lender.** Having the right people around you makes a world of difference as you navigate home ownership. We're going to provide recommendations about the qualities you should look for to ensure you choose good guides for the journey.

- **Financing: understanding the tools and timing.** As a buyer, there are a number of financial tools you'll want to be familiar with to maximize the opportunities available to you. As a seller, it's critical that you "tee up" your financing so you can sell your current house *and* also buy your next home.
- **Evaluating the property.** We're going to walk you through how to closely examine a house and property, so you know exactly what kind of property you're dealing with, its relative quality and condition, and how those variables should impact price.
- **Evaluating the price.** In addition to the quality of the property, there are other major factors that impact a list price, like interest rates, market inventory, timing, comparative market values, and so on. We'll explore each of these and explain how these factors can impact your negotiating power.
- **Negotiate: it's not just about money.** To negotiate well, it's critical to consider the motivations of the buyer *and* seller. With some, you should be shrewd and hard-nosed; with others, you should be affirming and gentle. We'll teach you how to use the information you have to create a win-win scenario for everyone involved.
- **Contract to close: navigating the final hurdles.** After a contract is agreed on, buyers and sellers still need to leap over three hurdles: the inspection, the financing, and the title transfer. We'll discuss what needs to happen for each hurdle and reiterate the importance of having good people on your team.

We want to empower you with information so that you find a clearly marked path through that forest. We want you to have clarity about what *you* need to do, and what your team members need to do. The end result: you'll feel protected and informed. Rather than fearing a venture into the unknown, we want you to enjoy the journey and successfully get to where you want to be.

REAL EXPERIENCED

The real estate world is full of suspect guides—so how would you know we're not two of them? We'll give you a few reasons.

One: unlike a buyer's or seller's agent who stands to make a hefty commission off your real estate transaction, **we're not financially entangled in your situation.** We simply want to pass along the best advice so that you can make wise decisions for your own personal situation.[1]

Two: **we feel genuine pain and frustration when we see real estate professionals lead consumers astray.** Unfortunately, it happens all the time—mostly due to simple inexperience on the part of the real estate agent, but sometimes it's worse. It's not uncommon to see clients being taken advantage of because their supposed "guide" stands to financially benefit from their naivete. On the flip side, we've both experienced joy and fulfillment by teaching consumers how to be savvier as they navigate the real estate process. This book is a passion project for both of us to spread that education more widely. We believe it will make the real estate world better for everyone.

Three: **both of us have years of experience working in the real estate world.** We've both bought, owned, and sold houses; we've

---

1   Granted, if you live in northeast Ohio and decide to pursue working with us in a professional capacity, we *would* stand to profit from your real estate transaction.

both invested in properties; we've dealt with countless real estate practitioners; and we've guided thousands of consumers in and out of their homes. We've been exposed to all kinds of properties, all kinds of people, all kinds of problems, and all kinds of variables. Because of our experience and our reputation for truth and transparency, we're some of the most highly respected practitioners in our area.

Lest you think that's an empty boast, we'll share a little more of our personal stories. Once upon a time, Ben could *not* have been considered a trustworthy guide—in fact, he was one of the wolves hiding beside the path through the forest. That's exactly why he knows the tricks a wolf might pull—and the emptiness that comes from doing so.

BEN'S STORY: A ONE-TIME WOLF

As a kid, as a teen, and as a young man, my life was driven by a single goal: to make money. To me, money felt like the key to a fun and fulfilling life. I didn't really care how I got it. In fact, during high school, I literally almost died while running a tree-cutting business—but it made me lots of money, so in my mind, it was worth the risk. I valued money more than my own life.

After graduating from college with a degree in accounting and finance, I took a job running the title company side business of my dad's law firm. I was in charge of transferring real estate titles for the law firm's estate customers. Was this in my area of expertise? No. I had no idea what I was doing. Was this a good way to make money? Initially, no. The job appealed to me because

I knew I stood to eventually run my own business, but I started making just over minimum wage and work was slow.

So, I started hustling to make more money. Whenever a transaction would come to me, I learned as much as I could from each person involved, and many of those professionals then sent me more work. This was before the 2008 financial crisis, and there were many shady mortgage loans being made. I regret to say, I gravitated toward the subprime lenders giving out bad mortgages—and they gravitated to me. Unfortunately, I closed whatever deals they brought me.

Under my leadership, the title company started booming. By the end of my first year, I had taken the annual gross revenue from $40,000 to $100,000. By the end of year two, it was $200,000; the next year, it was $400,000. But mentally, I was slipping further and further into a dark hole. Over time, I accumulated an attitude that I needed to win at all costs. Life was divided into two categories: winning or losing. I believed I was the most important person; I believed that *I* should win, which meant *other* people should lose. As I kept "winning," that ugly attitude kept growing.

I closed a property where the mortgage company was charging their client an exorbitant $26,000 in fees (normally, these fees would only be a few thousand dollars). Most clients would have recognized this as a ludicrous cost, but this particular client had suffered brain damage from a traumatic injury. He assumed that the mortgage company was doing right by him, even though he was massively being taken advantage of. I can still recall sitting there, having to sign these papers, knowing that he was being taken advantage of. But I stood to make money from it—and I wasn't willing to own up to him that he was being taken advantage of. From a legal standpoint, I was simply doing my job, but from an ethical one, I should have refused the work.

I told myself that my actions weren't so bad; after all, *I* wasn't the one making the bad loans; I was just bringing them across the finish line. But deep down, I knew it was wrong. I was being passive at best, and complicit at worst.

I wish I had stopped there, but I didn't. I also began buying and selling houses, restoring them for a profit—but restoring them poorly. I masked holes in the foundation with drywall mud. We put tiles down with bad methods—they looked good in the short term but would crack in the near future. One house had fire damage, which we just covered up. When it came time to sell, I helped the buyers find mortgage bankers that were willing to give loans to people that probably had no business getting a mortgage.

All my work paid off: I became incredibly wealthy. But at what cost? I sold rotten houses, in rotten ways—and frankly, I felt rotten on the inside, too. I started having suicidal thoughts, and my marriage was deteriorating. On the inside, I was this ruthless, ugly, angry man who would cut corners for profit, then went home and unraveled. My actions led me to a dark, empty, and lonely place.

One Sunday morning, I went to church, and the pastor said something I'll never forget: "Whatever you think about, whatever you talk about—whatever is most important to you, that's your god." The truth of his words cut me to the heart, and I couldn't stop thinking about them.

As I showered the following morning, I fell to my knees in prayer and wept. For the first time in my life, I realized how selfish I was. Money was my god, and I worshiped it at the expense of everyone else. I told God that I was so sorry and asked Him for a new life. In response, I felt overwhelmed with love—more deeply and profoundly than I'd ever experienced in my life.

The weeks and months that followed were insane. I gave away hundreds of thousands of dollars. I wanted to give *all* of my money away because it all felt tainted. (You can ask my wife how she felt about that!). And yet, one of the most surprising effects of rejecting the god of money was, incredibly, enormous financial success.

Customers came out of the woodwork—it felt like I ran into a new customer everywhere I went. When one of the city's top title companies went under, many employees came to work at our company because they were attracted to how we were now doing business. I told people *exactly* what I thought about their real estate decisions—the good and the bad. I expected my honesty to upset people, but more often than not, it caused people to weep with relief. It was unreal. However, my drastic change in approach caused a rift between my business partner and me. I was learning to speak truthfully but hadn't yet learned the importance of speaking with love. We eventually agreed to part ways, and he bought my share of the company.

I bought a dilapidated apartment building and slowly began restoring each unit—this time using quality methods and materials. The experience felt personal and humbling. As I cleaned and fixed these apartments, it felt like God went through all the chambers of my heart as well—cleaning out the bitterness and anger, healing the addictions and pain. I was doing the restoring, but *I* was the one being restored.

The experience made me realize that God is in the business of restoring people's lives, which was the kind of business I wanted to do, too. I wanted to treat clients the way that I wanted to be treated. I wasn't going to let others take advantage of me, either. But moving forward, I wanted to conduct myself honorably, gently but firmly, standing up for what I believed to be true.

Since 2003, I've owned three different title companies. Between the second and third companies (Fireland Title, which I currently run as CEO), I took a three-year pause to honor a non-compete agreement. During that time, I worked as a real estate agent and was disappointed in the breadth of knowledge among agents in the field. In 2015, I thus launched Fireland School, which teaches continuing education courses to real estate agents and investors. Seventeen years into my career in real estate, I currently own eighty-three units of property, have worked on thousands of real estate transactions, and have personally bought and sold close to a hundred properties. Thanks to the example of some great friends and the many lessons along the way, I've finally learned how to speak truth and act with love.

I spent seven years learning the shady side of doing real estate and spent the next decade seeking to honor, bless, and help people through my profession. Although I regret hurting people during the first seven years, I don't regret the knowledge I gained. I learned all the dirty tricks people can pull—and that makes me more effective now as I advise people, focusing on truth and transparency, highlighting the pitfalls they may not see. I believe real estate transactions should result in a win-win situation for all parties involved; it's good for business, and it's good for the soul.

KEVIN NARRATES: A NOVICE TURNED EXPERT

Like Ben, I started my career obsessed with making money, and like Ben, money ultimately let me down. In my twenties, I worked as a corporate executive for one of the country's largest retail chains. I was promoted quickly, performed well, and brought home impressive paychecks. I also regularly worked eighty to ninety hours a week—and felt absolutely miserable. I didn't know exactly what I wanted out of life, but I was increasingly sure my executive job wasn't it.

I also didn't know where to begin with buying a house. As a young husband and father making good money, I felt ready to become a homeowner—but I was suspicious of everyone in the business. Mortgage lenders were encouraging me to take out loans for homes worth more than a million dollars, which was way more than I needed. Real estate agents were ready to push me into the nicest homes in the area, but I wasn't ready to trust someone I had just met with such a massive life decision.

I tried learning as much as I could on my own. Although I made good headway, I was still houseless after looking for two years—and still miserable at work.

I needed a mentor—someone a little older, ahead of me in life. Someone who had found success doing something meaningful, and who was a family man. Through a mutual connection, I was put in touch with Ben. We made plans to grab dinner.

On that Tuesday in 2012, I woke up and hit my limit with my current job. I knew if I quit, everything might fall apart—but I was past caring. At two o'clock in the afternoon, I told my boss I was done. Four hours later, I sat down to dinner with Ben and giddily informed this brand-new acquaintance that I'd quit my lucrative executive job earlier that afternoon. Ben was not so giddy.

"You did *what?!*" he asked me.

"I quit!" I told him.

"And you've got a young daughter?" he asked. I nodded yes. "And you have no plan for what's next?" I shook my head no. "Man, you need to go beg your boss to get your job back!"

I didn't—but I stuck around for six more months to give my company time to transition. In the meantime, I tried to figure out what the heck I was going to do with my life. In spite of rejecting Ben's initial advice, I kept calling him—and he kept answering. He helped me work through some of the major questions I'd ignored for too long, guiding me through the dark soul-searching that he'd already travelled. At one point, Ben made the comment, "Why don't you get your real estate license? I think you would be good at this."

Ben's suggestion resonated with me. I'd been fascinated by all the research I'd already done into the real estate world. Also, my childhood hero and best friend, my grandmother, was a rock star real estate agent. She was successful, professional, wealthy, and she used her career as a platform for activism. She was one of the first real estate agents to help racially integrate the wealthy neighborhood where she specialized. Even as she got threats, she pushed forward with the sale. My grandma's example made real estate seem like a vehicle for success, financial achievement, and *calling*. That's what I wanted.

So, lo and behold, I became an agent. My education in economics from John Carroll University, combined with my experience running a multimillion-dollar business turned out to be a combination for dynamite. I started off at Keller-Williams and won their award for "Rookie of the Year." Success came quickly—in large part, I think, because I finally felt passionate about what I was doing.

As a real estate agent, I helped people handle something sacred: a home. Home is the one place where we should feel free to be ourselves—spiritually, emotionally, relationally. It can serve as the safest place we have, the place where we feel most at rest. In real estate, if people didn't have that safe place already, they wanted it—and they trusted me to help them. Given that I'd spent years feeling inauthentic, that felt profoundly meaningful.

Now that I was a practitioner, I did everything I could to present facts to my clients with transparency so that they didn't need to feel the same distrust I had felt as a consumer. In my former corporate job, I had saved my company millions with a computer program I'd written; now as a real estate agent, I developed new methods to enhance efficiency, clarity, and transparency for my clients. My pricing methods were so effective that I even became

Ben's go-to person for determining the price on all the different real estate transactions he was involved in!

Seven years in, I've continued to build my knowledge base, experience, and expertise. I started my own brokerage firm, called Exactly, which specializes in taking clients through a real estate experience that gives them the data and information they want up front. We make a point to provide the information that normally gets handled away from the consumers' view. We're 100 percent consumer-centric, technology-driven, transparent, expectation-meeting real estate brokerage—and it's amazing. I love what I do.

TRUTH AND TRANSPARENCY

Truth and transparency: those are the values we each arrived at individually in our careers and then strengthened through our friendship. We want to pass the truth of our experiences on to you and provide you the necessary transparency you need to make good real estate decisions.

After all, it's not just our experiences we're talking about here—at the end of the day, it's about the kind of experience *you* end up having while buying and selling your home. Each chapter we've written is aimed at making *your* experience easier, better, more meaningful, and more well-informed. The information provided in the pages that follow will help you more clearly see where you're at, what you need, and how to understand what's happening around you. Like a tactical field guide, this will be high-level. We can't guarantee that every variable will work out perfectly in your particular situation—but we are going to optimize your chances of setting yourself up well and getting great people on your team.

A lack of knowledge causes a lot of fear—but there's power in knowledge. There's security, there's protection, there's assurance, and there's a lot less stress. That knowledge opens you up to enjoy an experience that was formerly defined by fear.

That knowledge is what we've compiled here. It's based on our experiences, and it's for the benefit of *your* experience. It's meant to lead you home.

PART 1

THE TACTICAL
FIELD GUIDE
FOR *BUYING*
A HOME

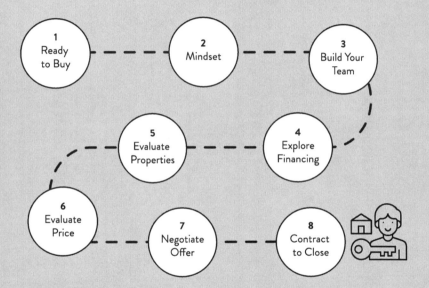

1
Ready
to Buy

2
Mindset

3
Build Your
Team

5
Evaluate
Properties

4
Explore
Financing

6
Evaluate
Price

7
Negotiate
Offer

8
Contract
to Close

CHAPTER 1

ARE YOU READY TO BUY?

THE PROS AND CONS OF RENTING VERSUS BUYING

A TALE OF TWO BUYERS

When Jana moved to a new city to complete her two-year medical residency, she was determined to buy. She sought out a desirable neighborhood and was incentivized to buy a more expensive property than she would have otherwise because the property had a tax abatement—in other words, for the next two years, she would pay almost nothing in property taxes. Two and half years later, when Jana had completed her residency and was preparing to move, she found out the tax abatement law had expired. That meant any new buyer would have to pay roughly $600 a month in property taxes.

She was forced to list her house for far lower than she'd bought it. Ultimately, she had to sell for $60,000 *less* than what she'd purchased the home for. On top of losing all that money, Jana also had to deal with the stress, complications, and endless paperwork of selling her home during an incredibly busy season of life. Although Jana's medical career will set her up to be fine financially, she knows her mistake could have bankrupted many other families. In retrospect, she wishes she had made the decision to rent—she could have afforded an even nicer place in the same area and saved herself a lot of stress and financial trouble!

Aaron took his time finding a home after first deciding he might be ready to buy, spending that time educating himself. He was meticulous in gathering information—sometimes to a fault. He took our classes and peppered us with questions about each new property he looked at. Finally, he found a winner. The house was in a great location, had good bones, and was listed at an incredible price—it was a no-brainer. He was able to make an immediate decision to buy the home because he was so prepared. Aaron spent the next year or so fixing up the house beautifully—once again, asking us for advice every step of the way. He spent five years there, enjoying his home and periodically making updates. When he eventually sold it, he got multiple offers on the first day it was listed and sold for a significant profit.

One person lost money on her home and endured a huge amount of unnecessary stress. The other person restored a house with pride, enjoyed his home, was able to stare his eventual buyers in the eye, trust that he was blessing them with a great home, and successfully made a great profit. One thought she was ready to buy—but wasn't. The other made sure he was ready to buy—and then nailed it.

Myth: Buying real estate is guaranteed to be a good investment because it's always better to build up equity than "throw money away" in a rental.

In no way are you *guaranteed* to make money when buying a house. If you buy a terrible house or one that's overpriced, you are far more likely to lose money on it. Also, it's important to remember that there's a time and place for renting—it gets you flexibility and may enable you to invest your money in financial tools that may be more conducive for your current season of life. Do not assume that it's always better to buy than rent. This is a complicated question and warrants reflection on several points.

What was the key difference between Jana and Aaron? It wasn't age or location or finances—it was knowledge. Jana was in a hurry, overly optimistic, and assumed that buying would always be a better decision than renting. But in her hurry, she missed out on some crucial information that would have saved her a lot of stress and money down the road. Aaron, on the other hand, collected as much knowledge as he possibly could. He was patient, realistic, and deliberate—and it paid off.

Buying a home is one of the most significant financial decisions you'll make in your life. Particularly if you plan to live in the home, **it will also be one of the most emotionally significant decisions you'll ever make.** Choosing to buy a home before you're ready can result in a bad housing situation that could negatively affect your life for years. If you *are* ready and you make a great real estate decision, that housing investment has the power to catapult you into improved life scenarios across the board, potentially leading to financial profit, better community for your family, better schools, a restful home, and so on. The house you buy today is going to impact the kind of home you end up in five, ten, twenty years from now—for better or for worse.

> **Tip:** If you buy a home before you're ready, the consequences could affect your life in negative ways for years to come. However, if you buy well, your property can serve as a catapult to launch you into higher echelons across all areas of your life.

However, that doesn't mean it's "game over" if you make a mistake. What matters most is not a single success or failure, but your *trajectory* toward either end. If you made a mistake and determined that you're going to learn from it, then you've shifted your trajectory toward growth and success. If your first home buying experience didn't go well, don't worry—you get to try again. You'll do it better next time! And here's some good news: the fact that you've sought out this book and are reading these words is a sign you're already thinking about how to improve. You've got the right attitude, and you're on the journey to learn. Keep going!

You want to get it right—which means you need to start by answering this fundamental question: Are you *ready* to buy? You'll be able to answer that question confidently by thinking through four different areas of readiness: **strategy, emotional readiness, finances, and knowledge.**

ARE YOU READY WITH A CLEAR STRATEGY?

Start with why. *Why* do you want to buy a home? Do you want to find a comfortable home for your family to settle down in? Do you want to buy a property as an investment, with the intention of selling it later for a profit?

Once you determine your *why*, you can then determine the *how*. The *why* informs your strategy. For instance, if you're looking for a home for your family to live in for the foreseeable future, it's less important to find a killer deal and more important to look for a home in a neighborhood you like, with a layout you'll enjoy, good amenities, and so on. On the other hand, if you're buying as an investor, that's going to require a different strategy. You might look for a house in a good area with a below-market-value price that you could easily flip.

Here's the point: you need a clear, well-informed strategy. Buying a home is not an area of life where you want to wing it.

STRATEGIC POINTS TO CONSIDER

If you think you're ready to buy, consider all of the angles. If you're buying with a spouse or someone else, make sure you get on the same page about key questions:

- Why do we want to buy now?
- Where exactly do we want to live, and what neighborhood characteristics matter most to us?
- How long do we want to live there?
- Why do we want to live there?
- What do we really care about in a home? What are our "non-negotiables"?
- What is the style that we like? What are our preferences?

Particularly if you intend to buy with a significant other, we recommend both partners play an active part in these conversations. We often see one member of a couple resort to passively going along with what the other person wants, but this can easily lead to problems down the road. If the husband, for instance, pushes to buy a smaller house in a more expensive area, then the wife may feel frustrated with him every time she feels cramped in that space. If the wife pushes to buy the home with the beautiful willow tree out front, the husband might feel angry every time the root system of that willow tree causes a major plumbing issue. "I never liked this house anyway." "I knew you were wrong." "Great, another problem!" You don't want those statements to be part of your future!

If you and your partner don't agree on what you want, that's a sign you are not ready to buy. Once you both are in firm agreement about where you want to live, then you're ready to move forward with a shared strategy.

> **Tip:** Location is *the* most important question to answer. Once you come to an agreement on what neighborhood you want to focus on, you can start educating yourself about that particular housing market, which will be instrumental to ensure you make a good buy.

ARE YOU READY EMOTIONALLY?

We know of a couple who experienced a mold issue shortly after they moved into their new home. They moved backed in with her parents and hired a team to come get rid of the mold, but even then, the husband didn't feel good about moving back in. They spent tens of thousands of dollars, doing more tests, looking for more mold, but still wouldn't move back into this house.

Finally, we learned that this mold issue had emotionally triggered the husband because of an experience from his past. When he was growing up, his parents divorced, and his mom struggled to make her mortgage payments. The roof had a leak that she couldn't afford to fix, which meant his childhood house had a ton of mold in it. Now, as an adult, the mold issue in his new house had been dealt with, but the trauma from his childhood meant he couldn't let it go. He'd been paying for this house for two years, didn't live in it, and eventually considered getting a foreclosure, which would seriously damage his future with home ownership—largely because of this emotional weight from his past.

> **Tip:** A good real estate agent will help you navigate many of the challenging emotions that will be stirred up in the home buying process. (In fact, Kevin's clients tell him all the time, "I didn't realize I'd hired you to be my agent *and* my therapist!") A good agent will be neutral. They'll tell you the truth about a property without thinking of what they stand to gain or lose. Especially if they notice concerning signs about a property, or find that you had a bad experience with a property in the past, they can make recommendations that you get the home inspected for that particular issue. They'll help you learn the truth about the property so that you can make an informed decision—and enjoy peace of mind.

Emotions play a much bigger role in real estate than most people realize, and the home-buying process is likely to emotionally trigger you in a number of ways. There's stress. There's excitement. There's anxiety—it's a roller coaster. Emotions *are* part of the journey, and it's okay to expect that you may get freaked out at times. However, you'll ideally get to a place of neutrality and objectivity when you're making this huge decision; you don't want to make this purchase in the heat of an emotional moment.

RED FLAG REASONS

When we meet with clients, we talk with them about their reasons for buying. Some of these reasons immediately raise red flags for us:

- They want to own a home because they think it will impress their friends and family.
- They think owning a house will solve their marital, familial, or personal problems, not realizing that buying and fixing up a home is stressful and could actually put *more* strain on a relationship.
- They see owning a house as a crucial threshold to cross before they can feel like they've "made it" as an adult.

Myth: Owning a home is a sure sign that you've "made it" as an adult.

You can be a fully fledged adult in a great rental apartment, and you can also be a childish homeowner of a broken-down wreck. Your possession of property has nothing to do with your status as an adult.

We would caution you from letting any one of these reasons act as your primary motivator for buying a home. For instance, if you want to own a home mainly to impress people, you might choose to buy the most impressive house the bank will let you buy, even if it stretches your budget far beyond what you can comfortably afford. That could introduce a lot of unnecessary stress into your life.

Another red flag pops up when we see people buying in a way that works against their personal timeline. What do we mean by that? Let's say someone decides to buy a house knowing they're likely to move again in the next two to three years. The costs of getting into and out of a home are so substantial that—unless you plan to flip it or the housing market is appreciating much faster than normal—you're unlikely to make money unless you stay in a home for longer than a few years.

Beware of buying a property for your ego. Beware of buying a property to solve your problems. Beware of buying a home with the assumption that "owning" is always better than "renting." You're likely going to create complications for yourself, and you may end up losing money.

But if you're ready to be a homeowner because it's an appropriate time to put down roots and it makes sense for your family, that's a great sign that you're ready to buy. If you're a real estate investor and you intend to buy smart—and you intend to turn a property into a home that will bless families in the future—that's a great sign you're prepared to make a good decision.

ARE YOU READY FINANCIALLY?

We've got an entire chapter in this book devoted to money—the loans, the down payment, the closing costs, and so on. We'll get to these big chunks later. For now, we want you to think about the smaller chunks of money required to be a homeowner.

Everything in this world is in a state of deterioration—just ask Einstein and his laws of thermodynamics. What does that mean, practically? It means repairs! Whatever property you buy is currently deteriorating and will continue to deteriorate as long as you stay there.

Houses have electricity and water running through them. They have wind buffeting them. They have birds making nests on the roof. They have bugs trying to get in through the windows. There are roots growing up into the plumbing. Everything in nature is actively working to tear homes down! You could go into home-ownership with the best building at the best price, but you still cannot predict what might go wrong.

We know a woman in Tennessee who bought a beautiful crafts-man home in a great neighborhood—we'll call her Stella. Several months in, she started hearing squirrels in her attic, so she called pest control. They informed her that the squirrels would prob-ably continue to get into the attic until she replaced her roof—a cost of around $10,000. Given that price tag, Stella decided she could live with squirrels in her attic a little while longer. Sev-eral months later, she discovered snakes in her yard and called pest control again. "The snakes aren't so bad—they'll take care of any rats and mice," the same pest control man told her. "But if you've still got squirrels in your attic, the snakes are gonna get into your house."

Stella paid the $10,000 to replace her roof. A year later, she had to go one step further and take out the squirrels' tree. She's still figuring out what to do about the snakes.

The point? You *may* get a great house, and you *may* have it easy. But you might also get a crazy property where stuff is constantly breaking down. Financially, you need to be prepared with a steady flow of side money that is available to handle these problems. If you don't have that reliable income and savings, you should think twice before taking on the potential liability that is homeownership.

Myth: Homeownership is a financial asset.

Actually, there are many ways it can be a liability!

When you consider buying a home, keep in mind that while you're living in it, that home will function more like a liability than an asset. The money that you put toward repairs will be substantial, and there's no revenue coming in from it—no one's paying you to keep up your home.

However, we don't want to be complete Debbie Downers. There are a few ways for your home to produce financial gain:

1. You buy a property way under market value and restore it.
2. You buy in an area where there is steady appreciation, and you're able to invest the money required to keep your property well-maintained. You stay in it for five years or longer.
3. You start with a solid first house, and eventually turn your first house into a rental property. For this to work out as an investment, your income in rent needs to be enough to cover the mortgage costs *and* any needed repairs required to keep the house in peak condition. At that point, your first house will turn into a financial asset that can help you accumulate wealth for your family.

Tip: If you decide to become a landlord, make sure you actually know how to manage a rental property. Bad renters can end up ruining what you have and can make your house worth less. Investing in rentals can be a double-edged sword.

DON'T FORGET ABOUT THE TIME FACTOR

When you're renting, you're not responsible for the landscaping or upkeep—but as a homeowner, you are. That takes time. You're the one mowing the grass, cleaning the gutters, and calling around to find a good contractor for the kitchen remodel. Your kids get older and want to change the paint color in their rooms—you're the one doing the painting. You decide you want to install a shade awning over the back patio—you're the one doing the research on the right one to buy.

As a renter, it's far easier to disconnect from a space and live with it as-is, because the property isn't yours. You wouldn't spend your money on improvements because you'll eventually move. But as a homeowner, it's *yours*. You'll come to take pride in your space, and you'll desire to have it the way you want. That's a good thing—but it does take time, creativity, energy, and money.

Will you be financially prepared to invest in the maintenance and repairs of your home, as regularly and ceaselessly as those needs will come? If you're in a position to take those on, and you're ready for the challenge they'll present—that's good. Keep reading.

Tip: Still wondering if you're ready financially? Look up the **"Buy Rent Calculator"** offered through the New York Times' website. You can plug in a series of numbers, which will help you determine if it makes more financial sense to buy or rent. Keep in mind that this is only one piece of advice and should be factored into your big picture with all the other aspects of home ownership we've just discussed.

ARE YOU READY WITH YOUR KNOWLEDGE?

Finally, if you're thinking about buying, be prepared for the steep learning curve that comes with homeownership. There's a lot to learn. Much of it, we're going to teach to you in the following chapters. We want to equip you with all the knowledge you need so that by the time you sign the dotted line, you can be confident you're committing to a great property, and you've gone about the purchase in a great way.

But that's only the beginning. You'll continue to learn about your particular property's quirks and issues. You'll continue to learn more about the financial tools you've committed to—their benefits and drawbacks. You'll learn DIY repair tricks from YouTube videos (some will work; some won't), and then you'll learn even more when you eventually hire the expert to come out and fix your mistakes. If, down the road, you decide to turn a home into an investment rental property, you'll need to learn a lot about how to be a good landlord. And still—these areas just scratch the surface.

If you're ready to sign up for all that learning, then we have good news: establishing a home can be an incredibly meaningful process, especially when you're doing it alongside people you love. We've tried to sober you in this chapter by sharing some of the bad news. We want you to be clear-headed and to dispel any romanticized ideas about home ownership that might lead you to make a decision you're not ready for.

But if you *are* ready—then get excited. Making a property your home can be a profoundly beautiful experience.

YOU'RE PROBABLY READY TO BUY IF...

- You're strategically ready: you know why you want to buy a home, you're well educated about your ideal location, and you're in agreement with your partner about real estate goals.
- You're emotionally ready: you recognize that you're pursuing home ownership for reasons that are in line with your and your family's larger goals, which make sense with your future timeline.
- You're financially ready: you understand the financial risks of home ownership and have the financial scenario to take on this liability.
- You're ready with your knowledge: The experience of home-buying and homeownership feels clear (we're going to help you with this), and you understand the challenges that will come with owning a home.

If you're able to affirm all four of those points, you can feel confident that you're in a good position to move forward in this journey toward home ownership. Now, let's make sure you've *got your mind* right as you start browsing listings and popping into open houses.

CHAPTER 2

COACH YOUR MINDSET

THINK LIKE A HOMEOWNER *AND* INVESTOR

BEN NARRATES: WE'RE WORTH IT AND SO ARE THEY

I grew up in what I can now identify as a very "investor-minded" household. Thinking about profit was a way of life. My grandparents owned multiple investment properties and my parents were both entrepreneurs. As an adult, when I set about to buy real estate, I had profit on my brain. I wasn't thinking about what it would be like to *live* in a home; I was thinking about how I could profit off that home by flipping it and selling it.

My wife, Kelly, on the other hand, grew up with a strong "homeowner" mentality. For her family, house meant home. They invested in their home with meticulous care, often going the extra mile in their improvements, just because they knew they would enjoy it. Kelly has a great eye for design, and in our early marriage, she enjoyed the home restoring process with me—she played a huge part in their transformation. But after living in eight homes for over eight years, she started to get tired of my ruthless investor drive. We had kids by then, and Kelly wanted to settle down somewhere.

I'm embarrassed to admit how long it took me to really listen to her, but once I did, our life—and my approach to real estate—transformed. Kelly helped me realize the value of *beauty* in a home. I'd always thought that, if I put $1 in, I should be able to get $2 out; Kelly made the point that sometimes spending $3, even if you know you'll only get $2 back, can be worth it for the *experience* it adds. I began to understand that "good enough" isn't actually that great. Families want to live in homes that are beautiful; they want details that make the home feel spatially restful, or great for their kids, or ones that can enhance their lifestyle. And *our* family needed to experience the safety and peace that comes from treating a house as a home, not just a source of profit.

As I began to think with more of a homeowner mentality, Kelly and I were able to work together to build a home. We began to understand one another better and are experiencing the joy of building a life together. My new homeowner mentality has also—ironically—helped me make greater profits off my rental properties! In fact, I found that often when I spent $3, I was able to get *$10* back, because people so highly valued the experience I'd added. As I've added details and touches that I know will make the homes nicer to live in, I've found that renters are willing to pay more to live in them! I'd been on the extreme end of the investor mindset, but I've found that my personal and professional life both radically improved when I *balanced* my mentality by thinking like a homeowner as well.

In every stage of real estate—as a seller, as a buyer, as an agent—it's crucial to think like both a homeowner *and* investor. Buying real estate is a huge financial investment so you *do* need to keep practical numbers and investment considerations in mind. But it's also where someone is going to live—either you, or your future renters, or your future buyers. You can make sure you're creating a win-win situation for everyone by getting your mind right. You're worth it—and so are they.

HOMEOWNER VERSUS INVESTOR MENTALITY

If you're looking to buy a home with a **homeowner mentality, your main question is: "How would this home feel to live in?"** You're thinking about comfort and convenience. You're paying attention to aesthetics—paint colors, cabinets, countertops, closet-size, square footage. You're thinking about the schools in the district and the size of the backyard. But beware! There's a danger in only considering your home as a dwelling place. **If you've got the homeowner mentality, here's what you may *not* be thinking about:**

- The actual cost of owning that particular piece of property.
  - For instance: what are the property taxes? What will it take to insure that piece of land?
- The cost to maintain the home and property.
  - For instance: the inspector said the furnace is running okay even though it's thirty years old. You *will* have to replace that furnace in the next few years.

- The cost to repair it.
    - For instance: The foundation is cracked and there are signs of rot. Those are major issues and extremely expensive to fix.

Your new home may *look* like a dreamy place to live, but if you don't stop to think of the financial and emotional burdens that will come from some of its related costs, your home will quickly become a source of stress. Therefore, it's not enough to *just* think like a homeowner.

Now, if you're looking to buy a home with an **investor mentality**, **your main question is: "How much can I profit from this transaction?"** You're thoughtful of all cost-related issues—the location, the needed repairs, the taxes involved. If you're planning to rent it or sell it, you might be thinking about how you can make those needed repairs as cheaply as possible. If you're planning to live in the home for a while, you may not consider making any improvements that wouldn't ultimately increase the value—even if those changes would benefit your family.

So once again—beware! There's an equal danger in considering a property only as an investor. **Here's what investor-minded people may fail to consider:**

- The amount you could sell the home for.
    - For instance: if you fix the home on the cheap, you may need to lower the price during negotiations. If you made solid repairs, you can more confidently hold a higher price.
- The reputation you'll gain over time.

- For instance: you'll gain a dishonest reputation if you consistently sell homes with lots of hidden issues.
- The emotional factor.
  - For instance: it's hard to avoid a sense of guilt if you know you're ripping people off. On the other hand, it feels great when you know you're blessing someone with a good home.
- The family stress you might cause.
  - For instance: your spouse might get angry with you if you're ignoring your family's comfort by just focusing on the bottom line. It's also extremely stressful to carry out renovations *while* living in the house you're renovating.

So, it's not enough to *just* think like an investor either. To make a smart real estate purchase—one that will pay off financially and one that will be a restful dwelling place—you need to think with a balance of *both* a homeowner and investor mentality.

THE YIN TO YOUR YANG

Once you're able to recognize your bias, seek out partners who can help you balance your own buyer's perspective. We often see this happen naturally between spouses: one partner might be inclined to think like a homeowner, while the other thinks like an investor. That couple might feel some tension when they're discussing the pros and cons of any given property, but they're actually a winning team! They do each other an incredible service by helping balance out their consideration of each property.

If both spouses have the *same* buyer's perspective, however, they may plunge headlong into a bad real estate decision. If they're both thinking like homeowners, they might get so excited about the curb appeal of the 1920s craftsman that they stretch themselves to buy it and completely ignore that all the plumbing needs to be updated—which, now, they can't afford to do. They become burdened by the financial stress of taking care of their home; they're in a great area, but they can't enjoy it.

If both partners think like investors, they might jump at the chance to buy cheap property in a good location, even though it's fifty miles away from their places of work and will be a nightmare to renovate. They might do a bad job restoring it, because they're doing it on the cheap. Their lifestyle takes a hit with their new long commute, which means there's a ton of stress and tension. It's frustrating to live in a house that's currently being renovated, which adds to the stress. They got the deal they wanted, but they can't enjoy it.

The point? Couples get into trouble when they both agree on a bad idea. You need someone to help balance your bias. If you're not married—or if you are, but you recognize you and your spouse have the same bias—seek out another teammate for needed balance. Consult a parent or other relative, a savvy friend, or a good real estate agent who can help you consider points you might miss.

THE CONSEQUENCES OF BUYING BLIND TO YOUR BIAS

We're going to share two stories to illustrate the importance of maintaining both the investor and homeowner mindset, and what can happen if you don't.

HOMEOWNERS' MENTALITY MISSTEPS

Greta and Jeff bought a home in the heat of emotions. They attended an open house, packed with other would-be buyers, and fell in love with the craftsman architecture, the beautiful built-in cabinets, the backyard patio, and the picturesque ivy climbing up the walls. Determined to beat out their competitors, they made an offer that went above the upper limit they'd identified for themselves—and they got it.

During the inspection, they found out that the ivy Greta loved so much was compromising the structure of the walls and would eventually need to be ripped out. They were also told they would need a new furnace soon. Still reveling in their "win" and determined to see the glass half full, they went through with the deal.

When the furnace started acting up only months after moving in, they debated how to replace it. Because of their huge monthly mortgage payment, they couldn't afford to put several thousand dollars into buying a new furnace outright, so they hunted around for a decent used furnace. Because of their relative inexperience, though, they couldn't tell who -if anyone—was being straight with them. They started to feel anxiety and stress, suspecting that people were trying to take advantage of them.

Finally, they sought out Joe from their church, who worked as a contractor once upon a time; they felt they could trust him. Joe agreed to help them find and install a new furnace, but it had been years since he was in the contracting business, and he was a little rusty. He found them a furnace that he assured them was good quality and a good deal, even though it was more than some of the other contractors quoted them. Joe took his time installing the furnace, but Jeff and Greta didn't feel like they could urge him to hurry up because he was their friend and doing it for a deal. September arrived and then October; the house kept getting colder.

> **Tip:** Don't hire the church guy to do your repairs! Or your uncle, or your bartender, or your friend from high-school—*unless* they're an expert in their craft and you get costs, timeline, and expectations mapped out in a contract. Neglecting to do this can strain an otherwise good relationship and put you in an awkward position. It might also mean your repairs are done poorly.

Meanwhile, the liquor store on the corner, which Jeff and Greta never even noticed when they bought the house, was creating problems. Transients wandered down their street late at night, inebriated and loud. One morning, they even found some-one asleep on their porch. They began to realize that this "up and coming" neighborhood wasn't as "up and coming" as they thought. They also suspected they way overpaid on their home. Now, they're looking into installing a security system, stronger locks, and new windows, preparing to go into debt since they can't afford it any other way.

What Could They Have Done Differently?

A number of characteristics about this home could have been caught before Jeff and Greta ever signed the dotted line: the furnace, the ivy, the corner liquor store, etc. In some of our future chapters, we're going to teach you how to closely evaluate the property value of a listing; Jeff and Greta could have avoided their mishaps by applying some of those tips before they made an offer. They also would have been wise to have gone into their home purchase with some money reserved for future repairs. Even if they couldn't have anticipated what they were specifically, they could have expected that *something* would come up.

Finally, Jeff and Greta would have been helped by thinking more like *investors*. More research into the neighborhood, repair costs, and contractors would have helped them enormously. It would have given them an open-eyed view of what they were committing to. Even if they had decided they still wanted to go through with the purchase, they would have had a much better idea of what to expect and would have felt less disappointed with the expenses that arose.

INVESTORS' MENTALITY MISSTEPS

Zack was getting ready to buy his second home with his wife, Mel. He'd seen how much they gained from their first house by doing some key updates, so they decided this time to pursue even bigger gains.

He bought a run-down property on a large lot in a desirable neighborhood. The neighborhood was far away from both of their places of work, but Zack decided the profit they'd make from selling a home in this neighborhood would make up for the inconvenience. Mel was not in favor of the idea but reluctantly went along with it. Their commute time doubled, and their time together was shorter. They also were often more tired and irritable by the time they finally got home.

To save money, Zack decided to do most of the updates himself.

However, since he was still working full-time, the updates went very slowly. Their only functional bathroom had no floor for three months. Mel became pregnant during this time and felt growing frustration every time she dealt with morning sickness on a bathroom with a plywood floor.

Myth: "I can get this done for less."

If you're somewhat handy, you might be tempted to take on your home remodels on your own to save money. We want to give you some cautionary advice: doing repairs on your own will usually take *much* longer than the time a professional would take and may not be that cost-efficient in the end. It's easy to make mistakes when you're doing the repairs yourself, which can cost extra money to fix. Also, keep in mind that the longer the repairs are underway, the longer you're feeling stressed and unable to enjoy your house—that can create spousal conflict. We often see people get 80 percent done with their project and then just leave it unfinished for years. It works for some people, but if you choose this route, expect it to take longer and cost more than you expect. There's a good chance that you'd be better off—financially, and in terms of quality and lifestyle—to just hire a professional.

Finally, Mel asked Zack if he would paint the nursery pink. He refused, explaining that it wouldn't add value to the house. He offered to paint it a trendier gray, but Mel didn't want a gray nursery—she wanted a pink one! They finally agreed to leave the room white but not until after they'd spent hours fighting about it.

Tip: It is *terrible* to live in a house that is undergoing renovations. Don't be fooled by your friends' dramatic "before and after" posts on Instagram. Living in a house that is being renovated is messy, inconvenient, and stressful.

The baby was due in May, but Zack felt the best time to list the house for resale would be June, since that's when there would be the most buyers—that resulted in another big argument. He decided to do "For Sale By Owner" so that they could save money on a seller's agent commission but made several mistakes in how he listed the house and felt increasing stress and anxiousness over fears that he was messing it all up. They finally ended up re-listing the house with an agent in August and made a modest profit when they sold. When they bought their next place, they chose a house that was move-in ready. After the experience they had, they never want to try to flip homes again.

What Could They Have Done Differently?

Zack and Mel first should have waited to buy until they were in full agreement about the investment strategy Zack wanted to pursue. Also, Zack would have benefited from listening more to his wife's "homeowner" perspective, which would have provided much-needed balance to his investor mindset.

Zack often tried to cut corners to save money, which cost him more in the end. Sometimes that was financially, such as when he tried to list the house himself (we'll discuss more about potential missteps sellers can make when they do "For Sale by Owner" in Part 2 of this book). Sometimes, that came at an emotional cost, such as when he tried to save money on the bathroom repair and ended up causing a lot of relational strain with his wife.

Here's the point: you need to think in financial terms *and* remember that you still need to live somewhere. When you're well-informed about both sides of the equation, you can pursue a situation that's good for everyone involved. It will end up being a better living situation and there's a good chance it's going to end up being more profitable as well.

THE BENEFITS OF BUYING BALANCED: BEN NARRATES

Just recently, I bought a beautiful brick ranch house that was next door to another rental house I owned. When I met with the owner to look at the house and discuss the price, we fell into conversation. He told me stories about his brother, who had recently died from cancer, and about his son, who used to own the house next door (the rental home I owned). As we talked, it became clear to me that this would not just be a business transaction; I wanted to buy this house in a way that would help bless this grieving man.

And it was a beautiful house—one I would have wanted to buy, regardless of who was selling it to me. It was well built and had a great layout. I walked through it slowly and carefully, looking for any red flags and ultimately concluding it would be a great buy.

I offered the owner $35,000 for it, but his bottom line was $40,000. I agreed to that; I knew this building would end up making me plenty of money after enough time because I'd always be able to find renters for it, and it was built so well. I outlined every additional expense he should expect to see through the selling process—all the different fees. When he realized that his ultimate take-home would be $5,000 less than he was expecting, he wanted to change the purchase price to $45,000. I held the line at $40,000 and explained my reasoning.

I thought about the homeowner—both this man and the future renters I expected to house there. I also thought like an investor. I made concessions on price where it made sense and held the line when I needed to. At the end of the experience, I'd bought a great house at a price I felt good about, and I knew I had helped this man make a great financial transaction and move through his grieving process. We both walked away feeling good.

We often see people buy properties with one heavy bias or another, thinking they're getting ahead in the world. Actually, they're getting further behind because they're investing money into something that they'll have to dig themselves out of later.

However, when you buy a home with a balance of both a home-owner and an investor mindset, you're heading forward in the right direction. You can create a place that serves as a safe haven, a place that accommodates your favorite pastimes and enhances your lifestyle. You make a calculated financial decision so that you're not burdened with the financial stress of the mortgage and maintenance payments. You're able to build equity in a property, so that you have more financial freedom to pursue other investments and the flexibility to move whenever you're ready. You live in a community that you enjoy and feel a sense of peace when you come home.

In other words, buying with a balanced mindset can enable you to create something beautiful, peaceful, and freeing—a home that will bless your family and others.

- 🔑 -

CHAPTER 3

BUILD YOUR TEAM

CHOOSING A REAL ESTATE AGENT AND MORTGAGE LENDER

REAL ESTATE AGENT FRENEMIES

Matthew and Julie were preparing to buy their first home. Julie's sister, Erin, had just gotten her real estate license, and it seemed like the obvious choice for Matthew and Julie to give her their business. That was a mistake. Because it was Erin's first real estate transaction, she was unable to advise her clients on all of the aspects about the home that would affect their long-term experience, such as crime rates in the area, cost of repairs, resale values, etc. In other words, the blind was leading the blind. When Matthew and Julie finally expressed enthusiasm about a home, Erin urged them to make an offer—even though a more experienced agent would have cautioned them about the neighborhood.

The home inspection revealed problems that would be expensive to fix, but Erin kept pushing them to buy. The truth is, Erin was tired. If she'd better understood the process, she might have been able to match Matthew and Julie with a great house within their first five to ten showings, but as things currently stood, Erin had already shown her sister and brother-in-law *thirty* houses. She didn't know how much more time she could afford to put in before getting paid. Meanwhile, Matthew and Julie were feeling increased concerns about Erin's lack of knowledge; if she hadn't been a family member, they would have found another agent long ago. Because Erin was Julie's sister, Matthew and Julie felt obligated to complete the transaction—even though they were having second thoughts about the home.

We heard about Matthew and Julie's almost-purchase when Julie came to Ben with concerns. When we found out the details of the sale, we told her the truth: it would be a terrible, terrible investment. They'd be hard-pressed to ever sell it, and they'd almost certainly lose money on it—likely a lot. Matthew and Julie made the wise choice to back out of the deal—but that, of course, created conflict with Erin. She was furious that her sister and brother-in-law had taken our advice over hers.

Myth: I should choose my friend or relative as my real estate agent because I can trust them.

It might feel reassuring to work with someone you know and love because you expect they will advocate for your best interests. Your friend or relative might genuinely have your best interests in mind—but can you trust their expertise? An inexperienced real estate agent might lead you, even with the best of intentions, into a terrible real estate situation if they don't yet have the expertise to do otherwise. That can put a lot of stress on a relationship. We encourage you to consider expertise first, and personal relationship second. If you have a match with both, that's great.

When you buy a home, you're making one of the biggest financial decisions of your life—and it will affect *every* area of your life. This is a time to go with expertise and skill, rather than emotional ties. Why? Because—as Matthew and Julie's story illustrates—relationships can become strained if your agent or lender lacks the competency your family needs.

SHOULD I HIRE AN AGENT?

Why not just do it yourself then? Serving as your own agent is a valid option. You can choose to look for homes by yourself, initiate all the paperwork, lead the negotiations, and handle the escrow process; if you are an experienced real estate investor, that can make sense. For the vast majority of people, however, it makes more sense to work with a professional real estate agent to purchase a home. A good agent will make the process more efficient, shed light on any potential blind spots, and provide helpful knowledge and experience.

As a general overview, a good agent will provide you with some of the following benefits:

- Educate you about all of your options when buying and selling.
- Connect you with competent affiliates, like a good mortgage lender or inspector.
- Coordinate showings and provide private viewings.

- Provide access to up-to-date information on properties.
- Advise you on the market value and appropriate price of homes.
- Write up the contract and negotiate in your favor.
- Communicate and coordinate all inspections and contingencies.
- Advise you on the needed repairs potentially found during contingencies.
- Coordinate and communicate with all outside parties.
- Be available to answer any of your questions and potential concerns.
- Provide support, encouragement, a shoulder to lean on, and help you see the process through.

We've seen hundreds of people try to avoid using a real estate agent because of the illusion of saving money, only to discover they're in over their heads and at risk of making a bad decision. Generally speaking, buyers don't stand to save money by doing everything on their own unless they've already been through a large number of transactions, as in the case of an investor. In most areas of the U.S.A., a buyer's agent's commission will be paid by the seller (when buying from a seller who's using a real estate agent), so for most people, there is not a financial benefit to completing the sale on your own. You would just lack representation—which could create unnecessary challenges and stress. If you've got representation from a good agent, on the other hand, you'll feel the benefits at every turn.

Every stage of your home-buying journey—from the initial search to the final days of the closing process—will be helped or hindered by the people you have on your team. In this chapter, we want to set you up for success to make a wise decision, saving you stress and potential heartache, by helping you choose the right team members from the start.

HOW DO PEOPLE CHOOSE A REAL ESTATE AGENT?

Choosing the right real estate agent and mortgage lender can be a tricky business—and the industry provides lots of flashy sales material, which can often confuse more than help. In many areas of the country, getting your real estate license is incredibly easy. The license is a start, but credentials don't tell you much about knowledge or skill. Most awards you see agents advertising are marketing ploys. You might think you'd be assured a good agent if you went with a well-known agency—but that's a gamble, too. Sometimes, the biggest agencies have the largest number of new recruits, and you might get assigned an agent or lender with very little experience.

So how do people typically choose an agent? Seventy-five percent of people hire the first real estate agent that they meet.[2] This statistic, to us, is terrifying! There are many wolves hiding in sheep's clothing in the real estate world, and you can easily be taken advantage of. A good agent can be a trusted guide to help you navigate a difficult and confusing process—but a bad agent can lead you directly into trouble. Even if they're well-meaning, they may not be able to guide you through the process because they themselves don't know it very well.

---

2   National Association of REALTORS. "2019 Profile of Home Buyers and Sellers." PDF file. Accessed 15 July 2020. https://www.nar.realtor/sites/default/files/documents/2019-profile-of-home-buyers-and-sellers-highlights-11-07-2019.pdf.

Here's how we typically see people choose their agent—see if any of these options sound like you:

- You have a friend/family member/acquaintance in real estate and start working with that person, or you get a referral from a friend/family member/acquaintance.
- You saw a house online you wanted to tour and called the listing agent to see it. The agent seems likable, so you work with them for your buying agent.
- You saw an ad on a billboard/grocery cart/magazine and call the person on the ad.
- You meet an agent hosting an open house, and they seem likable to you, so you start working with them.

Still, none of these options are guaranteed to lead you to a capable, trustworthy agent! So, what *should* you look for? We're so happy you asked.

WHAT TO LOOK FOR IN A REAL ESTATE AGENT

Between the two of us, we've spent a lot of years in this business. We know the qualities that great real estate agents have in common, and we've assembled them here. This list won't lead you to a guarantee, but it will set you up for success. When you start looking for an agent, have these qualities in mind:

- **Do they seem interested in genuinely getting to know you?** Good agents will often initiate a first meeting that primarily serves to establish a trusted relationship. They'll show an interest in getting to know your scenario, goals, and desires. Why is this so important? Knowing where someone is currently and understanding where they want to go should directly inform the search for a home. Many agents are eager to simply hop in the car and start looking at houses with you before taking the time to understand your goals. Look for an agent that wants to work toward *your* best interests as opposed to one who mainly seems concerned with pushing you through the process and getting paid.

- ○ *Hint:* See if the agent you contact suggests getting coffee or a meal together; do they ask you questions about your personal goals and plans?

- **Are they education-oriented?** Good agents will take the time to educate you about each step of the buying process. They're knowledgeable and take the time to answer your questions. You want a guide who will help empower *you* to make the best decision for your family—so you want someone with an eye to educate.

  - ○ *Hint:* When you first meet with an agent, ask them a few questions about the buying process—for instance, the steps to take when making an offer, or what to expect during the escrow process. Consider asking them questions about how they might help you evaluate the building quality or list price of a home. See how they respond. Are they knowledgeable? Do they seem interested in helping you learn?

- **Are they transparent?** Education and transparency go hand in hand. Many agents don't tell their clients how they get paid, but this can lead to conflicts of interest, which can work directly against the buyer (see box). Typically, buyers simply start working with an agent and may get all the way through their home-buying process before having a conversation about how the agent will get paid. Ideally, your agent will be honest from the start about compensation. They'll be upfront about where you're currently in the process, what you can expect from them, and what they should expect from you. Transparency up front is often an indication that the agent will continue to give you their honest feedback throughout your home-buying process.

- ○ *Hint:* Look for an agent who uses a **Buyer's Agent Agreement.** This is basically a contract that clarifies what you and your buyer's agent should expect from each other. The consumer always knows what to expect, what the real estate agent is going to do, and how compensation will work. With an agreement like this in place, an agent can feel free to dedicate more of their time and attention to you; they'll also be free to negotiate more effectively on your behalf. These agreements aren't commonly used, but if you find an agent who does use them, that may be an indication of their commitment to transparency. On the flip side, be wary of someone who tries to land you as a client right away without proving their own desire to educate.

How are buyer's agents paid? Most buyer's agents are paid only when their clients buy a house, and the amount of their commission is typically determined by the seller. That amount can vary—which can be problematic. Let's say that one homeowner specified that they would pay the buyer's agent 2.5 percent of the listing price, and a different homeowner said they would only pay the buyer's agent 2 percent. Other sellers, looking to sell quickly, may promise buyer's agents 3 percent. That difference in percentage could translate to many thousands of dollars, and these numbers are usually only visible to real estate agents—not their clients. Although many agents don't let those numbers sway their counsel, the uneven commission system could tempt a buyer's agent to steer people to buy one house over another, even if it isn't a great fit for their client's needs. **A Buyer's Agent Agreement** can get all of these numbers clarified ahead of time, which is good for the buyer and good for the agent. This agreement essentially brings more transparency to the process. It's worth noting that these agreements essentially function as a contract; once you sign them, you're committed to using that agent and no one else.

- **Look for someone who is full-time**: As a general rule, we do not recommend hiring a part-time real estate agent for the same reason you wouldn't hire a part-time lawyer. Buying property is a big deal. You want an expert—someone honing their craft day in and day out. Although there may be some stellar part-time agents out there, a full-time agent is more likely to be an expert. They also tend to have more availability because this is their full-time job, whereas a part-time agent will have competing responsibilities.
  - *Hint:* Most full-time agents also own multiple properties, which can be especially helpful for buyers. They'll be able to speak with personal knowledge about the cost of potential repairs and may even be able to recommend good contractors to you for your own home projects.
- **Look for someone experienced.** The longer an agent has been working in your area, the more knowledge they have. Experienced agents will be able to speak to the approximate cost of needed repairs, the fairness of a listing price, the various pros and cons of that particular neighborhood, and so on. They'll be savvy as negotiators because they will have already gone through many negotiations. They'll be ready to answer your questions and can guide you through potential potholes.

○ *Hint:* It's worth noting that some less-experienced agents may have valuable experience in a relevant field, like mortgage lending or home construction, which can provide them with valuable expertise and would make them a great agent to work with. Other agents may have years of experience but still may not be great at their jobs. Consider this factor in balance with all the others. Generally speaking, five years of full-time experience is a solid benchmark to look for.

Myth: You can feel confident about your agent if they're with a well-known real estate company.

Not necessarily! A new real estate agent can basically get hired anywhere. Just because they work for a familiar name says nothing about their competency and qualifications. Often, the people who are one-person brokers have been around longer, they're more educated, and they've handled a large number of transactions.

- **Look for someone who can balance your bias.** If you know that you and your spouse think like homeowners, look for an agent who can help you see the investor side of your purchase. On the other hand, if you tend to think like an investor, look for an agent who will help you consider the homeowner factor—what it's going to be like to actually live in that space. There may be friction with an agent who thinks differently than you, but that friction could end up helping you make a much wiser home purchase in the long run.
  - ○ *Hint:* Make sure you know your own bias (discussed in Chapter 2) so that you can seek out an agent who will help balance your thought process accordingly.

All of these recommendations should be considered *collectively*, and know that there will always be exceptions. For each of these recommendations, we could probably think of an outstanding agent who doesn't meet that particular qualification but has plenty of other strengths, which make them great.

Frankly, finding an agent who hits every one of these benchmarks would be tough! These recommendations are meant to be guidelines to help you make a thoughtful, wise decision—not a random one.

Here's the bottom line: **look for an expert *first*, then someone who is a good fit for your personality and mindset.** Remember, buying a home is one of the biggest financial and life decisions you'll ever make, so this is a time to prioritize expertise. Interview around and find the best person for you.

Afraid you'll get it wrong? Be reassured: the more *you* know, the more you will be empowered to navigate the home-buying process successfully. The chapters that follow will provide you with the knowledge that will equip you to make your own great decision about a home purchase. Although a good agent can be an invaluable resource, their expertise becomes less important as your own expertise increases.

DEBBIE VERSUS JACK

If you need any more convincing that you want to value expertise in a buyer's agent, consider our two acquaintances, Debbie and Jack. We're using Debbie Spencer's real name because she's a great real estate agent, and you should know about her. Jack is a fake name because he's a composite character of all the bad real estate agents we've known.

Debbie and Jack are both real estate agents with the exact same credentials. But they will give you a widely different experience.

Debbie was a corporate executive before she shifted careers to real estate, which gives you an indication about her intelligence, work ethic, and competence. She's been an agent now for well over a decade. She drives a minivan to all of her appointments, and her minivan is stocked with everything you might possibly need during a home-buying experience. She has paperwork, maps, flashlights for looking into dark corners during walk throughs, fruit snacks for cranky children who may need a boost—everything. She's thoughtful about what her customers may need and proactive to help them solve problems.

Debbie works with both investors and homeowners, so she understands the mindset of both. Debbie shows up to basically all of her closings—which is not a requirement or even an expectation for agents. She remains her clients' main point of contact throughout the process, until her clients sign their papers. If there's any disorganization or delays with the title company or a bank, Debbie will communicate efficiently with them to get the job done. From start to finish, she manages the experience that her customer is having. She's their guide and advocate.

Jack, on the other hand, has been a real estate agent for six months. When he approaches a transaction with a client, the paperwork isn't organized or filled out. He isn't familiar with all the pieces that need to be in place for a contract to close, so he can't advocate for the process to go smoothly. He often has to rely on other agents to clue him into what he needs to do, which creates tension, stress, and problems. Most dangerous of all, he only tells you what you want to hear; he won't warn you about a home's potential problems if he thinks there's a chance you'll make an offer.

Once Jack has a house under contract, he's essentially MIA. He doesn't remain available to his clients to help guide them through the emotional journey they're going through, or to ensure the process goes smoothly. He's just waiting for the news that the deal has closed.

You would pay these two agents the same amount of money, but you'd get a vastly different experience depending on who you hired. Debbie would smooth out every wrinkle and solve every problem before you even knew about it, whereas Jack could easily lead a family into chaos. When Debbie's clients encounter hurdles, she enables them to jump *over* the hurdles. Jack's clients smash right into them and get a mouthful of dirt.

Interview. Research. Ask around. *Then*, choose someone you are confident will be a trusted, competent guide on your journey home.

CHOOSING A MORTGAGE LENDER

It's also incredibly important to find a good mortgage lender and loan officer.[3] The loan officer, also known as the mortgage banker, functions as your main point of contact for the bank or lending organization. Behind that loan officer is a team of people, all of whom will be working on completing your mortgage loan.

Myth: It makes the most sense to go with a big-name bank for my mortgage loan.

Wrong! Often, the big-name banks are the worst at getting loans through in a timely manner because they handle so *many* transactions; they can easily get backed up. When you choose a mortgage lender, you're not just choosing a good individual—you're choosing a good *team*. Lots of people are involved in getting your mortgage financed. Smaller banks and/or lenders are often populated with more experienced teams and can move more nimbly through the process. This is not a hard and fast rule; plenty of people have had great loan experiences with big banks. However, don't just assume they'll be your best option simply because they're a big name.

The loan officer should talk you through the various financial products available through their lending organization. They should educate you about those products and help you find the best product for your particular situation—not just sell you a product that will be good for their own gain. That's step one.

Step two involves information gathering; often, this process begins during the preapproval process. A *good* mortgage lender will gather and process information in an organized fashion.

---

3   If you plan to pay cash for your home, you can skip this section.

They'll educate you on what's needed and why, and they'll be clear with their requirements. A bad lender will not communicate this information clearly and will be disorganized.

Why is preapproval important? Being preapproved means the lender affirms that they're ready to vouch for your ability to pay for a loan. The lender will give you a preliminary idea of the approximate mortgage amount they'll qualify you for and give you an interest rate. Being preapproved makes you a more appealing candidate to sellers who want to make sure they're choosing a buyer whose financing will come through. The numbers and conditions of your eventual mortgage loan may change once you select an actual property to purchase.

Once you're preapproved, you'll have a rough idea of what *interest rate* you're likely to get and what *loan amount* you qualify for; they should also tell you what they'll charge for their origination fee (the money they get paid for writing up the loan). The final numbers for your loan will end up being tied to the particular property you buy. Different lenders will likely give you different quotes, so it's worth shopping around a bit.

Step three in the mortgage lending process is the closing; this process begins after you've made an offer that's been accepted on a property. Some lending institutions will respect the closing dates and will work to get the financing completed by the closing date. If a customer has complications with their finances, a good lender will be up front about whether or not they'll be able to meet those closing deadlines. A bad lender will be vague about those details.

So, what, in a nutshell, should you be looking for in a mortgage lender? Here are our recommendations:

- **Good financing**: The biggest factor in determining your mortgage lender will be who gives you the best numbers. Banks will often qualify you for a higher loan amount than what you should responsibly be able to pay, so pay closer attention to the *interest rate* than the loan amount. We recommend you get quotes from several different lenders so that you have numbers to compare. This will be a bit laborious, because you'll have to provide a fair amount of paperwork to each one; however, shopping around could end up saving you a lot of money and stress in the long run.
- **Integrity**: Bad loan officers can be like bad salespeople—they're there to sell you something for their own gain. Good loan officers are there to *educate you* and help you get the best product. Look for someone who is education-oriented and transparent.
- **Knowledgeable**: The loan officer should tell you exactly what you need to do and what information you need to gather in order for the loan to be successfully processed and approved. Bad loan officers won't be specific about exactly what they need, which can cause the loan process to drag on, as they repeatedly need to collect more information from you. That's also a pain for you to deal with.
- **Familiarity with the products**: Good mortgage lenders are

experts in their craft. They should educate you on the different loan products you might qualify for and the pros and cons of each one. They communicate with transparency and clarity. They have the knowledge and wisdom to work with you as a guide because they know you need their expertise.

- **Good customer service**: Look for someone who returns your calls and emails in a timely manner and communicates well.
- **History of closing on time**: A good lending institution will respect the closing dates up front, and they'll know their customers' financing well enough to tell them if they're going to successfully meet the closing deadlines. A bad lender will have a history of failing to meet closing deadlines. They may tell you they can close in thirty-four days but have no intention of meeting that; they only want you to move forward in the loan process with them. Ultimately, that can cause a lot of additional stress in the home-buying process.

Tip: For a quick idea of which direction you want to go for a lender, you could call and ask the banker what the current rates are today and what the bank's associated fees are for those rates. Provide the lender with a ballpark of your credit score, income, and any outstanding nuances to your financial situation. A quick question could go like this: "I have a 700 credit score and make $50,000 annually as a teacher. I'm looking at buying a $200,000 house with 10 percent down. What are the current interest rates for someone in my situation and what are the total bank charges for this loan?" A conversation like this could be brief—around five to ten minutes. If you feel nervous having this conversation alone, feel free to recruit a trusted friend to weigh in or to even be the one to initiate the conversation with lenders. You want to look for the lender that will give you the best combination of a low interest rate and low fees. (This combination could translate to tens of thousands of dollars over time—it's worth doing your homework!)

LUCIA VERSUS DARRYL

Now let's get a clearer look at what your experience might be in real life with a good lender, versus a bad lender.

Lucia Alvarez is a great example of a good lender. She's incredibly knowledgeable of all the products available and can tell you exactly how the bank underwriting process goes. She knows what documents and information the closing department will ask for in order to get your financing approved.

Lucia is great at communicating clearly with customers and educating them. She's skillful at finding out a client's true financial state and then pairing them with the best loan option available to them. If she knows that you won't likely qualify for a conventional loan, she'd be upfront about that: "You probably wouldn't qualify, and here's why. If you *do* want to qualify for this type of loan, you're going to have to do A, B, and C."

She's at a mid-size bank and has surrounded herself with a great team; they're proficient at getting through the closing process in a timely manner and communicate clearly when something unexpected comes up that could impact the closing date. She's also great at calling people back.

We'll call our bad lender example, "Darryl." Darryl might seem good at first because he'll be very complimentary. He'll talk about how great you are and will want to say yes to any of your requests. That's actually dangerous, though, because, in all likelihood, you *can't* qualify for whatever loan product at whatever amount you want. Whereas a lender like Lucia will tell you honestly what you could and couldn't qualify for, Darryl will simply tell you that it's going to work out. When and if it doesn't, Darryl will fail to recognize that he created a lot of additional headaches for you because he wasn't transparent from the start. He makes you feel good, but it's not going to turn out good!

Darryl is unorganized, and he doesn't know what documents to ask for. His back-office team is disjointed. They haven't developed a smooth, organized processing system. He's used to dealing with people with bad credit scores, which means he's used to writing loans with higher interest rates and origination fees; as a result, he ends up charging you more because he's used to dealing with below-average scenarios.

> **Tip:** In general, it's better to work with a local mortgage lender when getting ready to buy a home, as opposed to an out-of-state lender. A local lender will be more familiar with state-specific loan products. They'll also know the nuances of doing loans in your particular area and have more experience with juggling the moving parts in conjunction with other local players, handling the time frames, schedules, and all the different people involved. However, if you're getting ready to refinance your home, an out-of-state lender could work well; in the case of a refinance, there are less moving parts involved in a property transfer.

GET YOURSELF A GOOD GUIDE

We get it: this sounds like a lot of work. You work a full-time job, you've got to get the kids to soccer practice, you've got your volunteer obligations—who has time to do all this interviewing, paperwork, and all the rest?

We're encouraging you to *make* time for this. Buying a house is a massive financial investment, and it's where you're going to make your home for the indefinite future. It's a big deal! This is a time to prioritize *expertise*. Do the hard work of interviewing people and shopping around to ensure you commit yourself to people who will do an amazing job on your behalf.

We also want you to keep in mind that, at the end of the day, you are responsible for your final decision. You are responsible for your loan and the home that you buy. The more *you* learn, the better decisions you'll be able to make—and the better you'll be able to recognize true expertise in others. That's why we've written this book for you. By building up your own knowledge and choosing experts to help guide you, you'll be able to move forward without fear and make a great decision for your family.

CHAPTER 4

EXPLORE FINANCING

FINDING THE TOOL YOU NEED

THE $5,000 FERRARI

Imagine someone approached you and asked if you'd be interested in buying a Ferrari.

Maybe you laugh: "There's no way I can afford a Ferrari right now."

The person insists: "No, no—I'll give it to you for a deal. I've got to offload it. $5,000."

Now: if someone offered to sell you a Ferrari for $5,000, let's hope your response would be an immediate YES. Even if you weren't in the market for a sports car, you'd find a way to buy that Ferrari. Even if you didn't have an extra $5,000 lying around, you'd find a way to get that money.

Why? Because of its *value*. A new Ferrari is worth far more than $5,000; because the value is so much greater than the cost, any sane person would determine it was an investment opportunity that couldn't be passed up.

But what if you don't have the cash on hand? You might decide to get creative about how to drum up $5,000. Maybe you'd ask your wealthy friend or relative to give you a short-term loan; maybe you'd make a withdrawal from your retirement account. Soon, you'd be the owner of a Ferrari for a killer deal. At that point, you might choose to keep the car and pay off your loan over time—enjoying your incredible ride in the meantime. Alternately, you might re-sell it for a more accurate price of $350,000 and make a huge profit.

What does this $5,000 Ferrari story have to do with buying a house? We're trying to make three points here:

1. **It's possible to get very creative about what you can afford.** You might assume you can't afford to buy a home yet, or that you might only be able to afford a home that costs "X" amount of dollars. We want this Ferrari story to remind you that, actually, there are many financial tools that exist that can help you buy a home. In fact, there are tools out there that you may not even know about! Here's a hint: when people think of affordability, they often think in terms of what they can afford via a fifteen- or thirty-year loan. But more financial tools become available if you shorten the time period—for instance, many people could afford a higher monthly payment if they only had to pay it for three months and then shifted to a different financial tool.

2. **"Affordability" is far less important than *value*.** If you go to a car lot with $5,000 in hand and say, "I can afford a $5,000 car," the salesman may very well take you over to a beat-up Buick and say, "This is for sale for $5,000!" You'd end up paying top dollar for a car with little value. That Buick might have a price tag of $5,000, but its *value* might be closer to $1,000. On the other hand, a Ferrari's value is far higher than $5,000. In real estate, homes are priced incorrectly all the time—which means you need to focus on value more than price. If you get a chance to buy something of great value for a low price, which beautifully suits your needs, do it! And conversely, don't buy a crappy house just because its price tag falls within the range of what you think you can "afford."

3. **Learn about value so you can recognize it!** Buying a new car is scary enough; buying a home is even scarier. These are not purchases people make every day, and they're *enormous*. Most people just want to make a wise financial decision. To do that, you need to learn about value. In other words, what does a Ferrari look like in the real estate world? What homes are more like an overpriced, beat-up Buick? What are the standard market costs in your desired location? What are your needs and desires, and what are those worth to you? If you educate yourself about value, you'll have the eyes to spot a $5,000 Ferrari when it pops on the market—and you'll be able to recognize when some questionable character is trying to sell you a beat-up Buick for more than it's worth. That's how you make a wise financial decision.

Myth: Money is a barrier to entry in real estate.

Not true! Just about anyone can find the right financial tool to own a home. However, this doesn't mean that everyone *should* pursue home ownership. We've previously outlined a number of considerations to help you determine if you're ready to buy a home. The advice in this chapter is for people who have concluded they're ready on a number of fronts.

So: let's say you find the equivalent of an amazingly affordable Ferrari, in house form. You love it. It's a great value. It will beautifully suit your needs and desires. You know it's a great investment. Now, how do you actually buy it?

There are a wide array of financial tools that can enable most people to buy a moderately priced home. We're going to acquaint you with many financial tools in this chapter so that you understand what opportunities may be available. If you know those opportunities exist, you're in a position to take advantage of them if a $5,000 Ferrari comes along.

Warning: this stuff is about to get complicated. We're going to go into detail in this chapter because we know that the money stuff is often one of the most intimidating and confusing areas of buying a home for most people. We want to give you enough information here that the money stuff feels less opaque so that you feel empowered in moving forward. However, you should also feel free to skim and only read the sections thoroughly that you know apply to you. **Use this chapter as it will best serve your needs, reading as deeply as you are comfortable.**

FINANCIAL TOOLS

First, a word of advice: know your financial literacy level before you take one of these tools and start waving it around. For instance, it would be reckless to let a four-year-old handle a power saw because most four-year-olds would not handle that saw responsibly, and there's a high probability they'd get hurt. If you recognize that your financial literacy is at the level of a four-year-old, you're going to want to be careful, seek advice from trustworthy experts, and do your best to strengthen your knowledge and understanding before you try using one of these tools.

Also, remember that the financial tool that you select should be based on the real estate product you want to buy. You don't base your construction project around the fact that you have a hammer; you tailor your tools to the nature of the project. In the same way, you shouldn't *start* with your financial tool and go looking for a real estate opportunity that fits that particular tool. You should find the home you want, then figure out what tool will be best for that particular property.

Here's one smart way to order your process:

- At the beginning of your real estate search, **get a general idea of what financial tools may be available to you.** You can do this by meeting with a mortgage lender (or several) and having a discussion. If you have bad credit, you may not be eligible for certain financial tools; however, that doesn't mean you're barred from entry. Some borrowing tools depend on the property, not the buyer's credit.
- Once you get an idea of what's available to you, then stick a fork in it: wait. Go look at properties and **build your**

knowledge about *value.* Look at pricing, construction quality, market trends, and so on.

- When you know you've found a property worth investing in, *that's* when it's time to **return to the financing table and figure out your best tool to move forward.**

So, what are some of those tools? Let's dive in.

CASH

Not everyone has this tool in their tool belt, but if you're lucky enough to have enough cash on hand to buy a property outright, it can open up a wide variety of opportunities. You might have this cash literally sitting in your checking account, or perhaps you could make cash available with a little more legwork—like pulling it from your IRA or your stocks. If you're already a homeowner, you might have a Home Equity Line of Credit (HELOC) with an available balance that you can use like cash. If you've got it, this is a great tool to have on hand.

- *How it works:* There's not a lot of complicated stuff to understand about buying a home with cash. You take all the dollars, and you wire them to the relevant parties.
- *Pros:* Cash enables you to move fast and get a killer deal. No bank inspections are required for cash buys. This means cash is especially helpful if you want to buy a property that is dilapidated in some way, which wouldn't get approved for a bank loan, but which you know you could turn around as an investment. Paying cash also enables you to avoid paying interest, which could end up saving you lots of money in the long run.

- *Cons:* There aren't a lot of cons to buying a home with cash, other than the potential opportunity cost (explained below). Generally, cash buyers are seen as highly appealing to sellers, and you have the most flexibility about what you can choose to buy.
- *A Word of Caution:* If you can pay cash, consider your risk tolerance and the opportunity cost. If you're wealthy enough to buy a $400,000 home outright, you're guaranteed to save whatever you would have paid on interest—say, 4 percent. That would make sense if you have a conservative risk tolerance and want to play it safe. But let's say you *could* have chosen to finance that home and invest your spare $400,000 into stocks, which might give you an 8 percent increase. That might be a better investment for you; you'd have to pay the 4 percent mortgage loan interest, but you could earn 4 percent *beyond* that by having your money in a more aggressive investment tool.[4]

PRIVATE FINANCING

Okay, maybe *you* don't have hundreds of thousands of dollars on hand, but you know someone who does—and they would trust you to spend it. That's a prime scenario for someone to use the **Private Financing tool.** Private Financing means you're using someone *else's* cash, who is in your network. For example, your dad is willing to give you his cash to help you buy a home, and then you will owe him money.

Here's an example of how this could work: let's say Sharon finds

---

4   Disclaimer: this is a hypothetical scenario and may not be best for your particular set of circumstances. You should talk with a financial advisor before making any major financial decisions.

a great house in a great neighborhood, but there's no kitchen. It turns out the former owner had to foreclose and was so bitter about losing the house; he demolished the kitchen before he left. The bank won't approve a loan for a kitchen-less house, but a friend agrees to loan Sharon the cash to buy it for $300,000; that's **Private Financing.** Sharon puts $50,000 into installing a great new kitchen and then refinances with the bank for $350,000, paying her friend back the $300,000, plus interest. Sharon now has a fixed-rate mortgage that matches her goal of long-term homeownership.

- *How it works:* You can set up Private Financing in a number of ways. For instance, you could borrow cash from an investor via a short-term loan, use the cash to ensure your offer on a house is chosen and close quickly, and then refinance that property with a bank loan.[5] You then pay off the short-term private loan and move forward with the refinanced mortgage.
- *Pros:* Private Financing boasts all the same pros of buying with your own cash: you have more flexibility, you can buy any property you want, you're seen as a more appealing buyer, and you don't have to deal with getting an inspection or appraisal. Private Financing can also pose some benefits to both parties: the financer has the opportunity to make a relatively stable investment (provided the property purchased has good *value*), and they get the satisfaction of knowing they're helping out someone they care for. The buyer might have a chance to get into a home that would have otherwise eluded

---

5   If you want to pursue this option, make sure you *will* qualify for a refinanced bank loan. There are also rules and stipulations for doing refinancing; for instance, some banks will only lend 80 percent of the home's value, which might mean you can't fully pay back your investor friend. Make sure you know the rules and have a clear strategy in place before pursuing this option.

them, and the cost of borrowing the money (interest rate and fee) is likely to be low.

- *Cons:* Two words: relational tension. In spite of all the pros of Private Financing, there are many ways that this tool can put stress on a relationship. ("Dad, I know I'm three months behind on paying back that loan, but it's Christmas time, and I won't be able to afford presents for the kids if I pay…") Also, whereas a bank might expect you to pay back a loan over thirty years, private financers usually want their money back sooner than that, which can put pressure on buyers to pay off their mortgage quickly.

- *A Word of Caution:* In order to mitigate the potential for relational strain, make sure to put everything in writing when doing Private Financing. Don't do anything on a handshake. The loan should be written out in exact terms and recorded at the county; in fact, it would be wise to have a lawyer's help in drafting the final document. Also, given that you're risking your loved one's money, be that much more diligent in making sure you're making a good investment.

If you don't have ready cash on hand to buy a property or know someone willing to privately finance your home purchase, then these tools aren't in your tool belt, and that's okay. There are other financial tools to use. However, before you dismiss this option entirely, give it another thought. Most people don't realize that there may be several people they know with the available cash to invest in real estate. It may be hard to imagine someone "sponsoring" you in an investment opportunity like this—but remember, if you're bringing them a $5,000 Ferrari that has a resale value of $300,000, they'd be making a great investment with you. If you find the right property at the right price, you might be doing a cash-investor a service by presenting them with the opportunity!

OWNER FINANCING

Mrs. Smith is in her eighties, has paid off her home, and is ready to move into a retirement community. She knows her grandson is looking to buy a house for his family, so she offers to owner-finance her house to him; in other words, she acts as the bank. They draw up a mortgage contract, agree on the money her grandson will pay for the down payment, and Mrs. Smith finances the mortgage. She's able to move into her retirement community, gets a mortgage payment check from her grandson every month, and feels happy about the fact that she's been able to bless her grandson's family with her beloved home.

- *How does it work?* Owner Financing means the owner of a property finances a loan to the buyer. There's still a formal mortgage agreement written up and a title transfer, but no appraisal is required. It's important to note that this tool works best when the buyer and seller share personal and/or professional trust. This can be a useful tool for several situations:
  - **Two people with a relationship want to help one another**. Take the Mrs. Smith scenario: Mrs. Smith ends up procuring a steady income for herself by owner financing her house to her grandson and doesn't have to worry about upkeep or property taxes. Her grandson gets a house at a deal with a low-interest rate.
  - **Investors who want to avoid capital gains taxes.** If you have a property and don't want to pay all the taxes up

front, you might owner finance it to somebody else. You'll still eventually get all your payments over time with interest, but then you don't have to take all of that gain in one year.

- **A distressed property scenario.** Because no inspection or appraisal is required with owner financing, an owner is more likely to do owner financing if a property is in bad condition. For example, let's say Jane inherits a property from her mom, can't fix it up, but doesn't want to dump it, either. You could ask Jane to owner finance the property to you for the next year for $100,000, and the title would transfer to you. You'd invest your down payment money into restoring the house, and once it was fixed up, you'd get a traditional loan to pay back Jane. Jane has to wait a year to get her money but still collects your monthly mortgage payments in the meantime. You're able to fix up a house without going through the complications of taking out a construction loan.

- *Pros:* There's less hassle. You can often save money on real estate agent commissions, inspection fees, and so on. The state of the property won't slow down the title transfer. Also, when owner financing goes well, it can create a win-win situation for everyone.

- *Cons:* This tool wouldn't be as appropriate for a seller with a beautiful home, who would be better off selling their home on the open market and getting top dollar for it. (An exception would be in a Mrs. Smith scenario, where the owner doesn't care to get top dollar and would rather do a favor to someone she loves.)

- *A Word of Caution:* Similar to private financing, owner financing can create relational tension and frustration if one person doesn't hold up his or her end of the bargain. For instance, if Mrs. Smith's grandson starts missing his mortgage payments, she has the legal right to take back the house, but that would be a hard and stressful situation. If an investor's buyer fails to restore the property in the quality way they promised to, they might end up causing the property to decrease in value rather than increase. For these reasons, again, it's best for two people to share trust if they use this tool.

BANK LOANS

The most common way to finance a mortgage is by getting a loan from a bank.[6] (You probably know this already.) The three most utilized types of bank loans are Conventional, FHA, and VA loans. As opposed to using cash, which requires very little oversight, bank loans come with a lot more paperwork and a lot of red tape. That's not necessarily a bad thing—a bank loan can still be a great financial tool. Let's talk about each one, and the kind of person who would be ideally suited for each tool.

Conventional Loan

Kelly and Nate both earn steady paychecks and have a good credit rating. They've saved up enough money to pay 20 percent in a down payment. They expect to live in their home for the indefinite future. Kelly and Nate are prime candidates to take out a **conventional loan.**

---

6   As a general note, specific laws relating to loans will vary state to state; lending laws and conditions also vary over time. When researching loans for your home purchase, we recommend doing your homework to learn about the nuances of your lenders' practices.

- *How they work:* Conventional loans are given to people who have good credit and can pay more than 5 percent down. The mortgage is usually assigned to be paid in either fifteen or thirty years; a conventional fixed-rate mortgage means your interest rate will be locked in for the duration of your mortgage. The more money you can put down, the more money you'll save in the long run: you'll get a better interest rate and a better bank charge (see side bar). If you don't have 20 percent saved for a down payment, you'll likely be required to pay private mortgage insurance (PMI) for whatever amount would catch you up to 20 percent. So, if you put 8 percent down, you'd have to pay PMI on 12 percent of the mortgage.
- *Pros:* If you've saved your money and paid your bills on time, a conventional loan will generally reward you for that good financial behavior with a good interest rate. In terms of bank loans, conventional loans will usually be the most cost-effective. You'll also be treated like the savvy financial dealer you are; real estate agents expect people with conventional loans to negotiate well and will take you seriously.
- *Cons:* A conventional loan is more cumbersome than cash, but it's still a great option. Conventional loans are given to borrowers who have a track record of financial stability: you must have good credit, need 5 percent or more to put down[7], and they'll also require an inspection, appraisal, etc. The good news: if you can qualify for a conventional loan, that's an indicator most other financial tools will also be available to you.

---

7   Banks in different areas may offer different products. Some conventional loan lenders may require just 3.5 percent down; others may require more than 5 percent. Check with your local lenders to get a better understanding of what percentage for a down payment they require to finance a conventional loan.

- *A Word of Caution:* If you get a conventional loan, you're treated like a savvy financial dealer—so follow through on that. Be shrewd when you look at buildings. Make sure that you're investing in a good property. Don't take out a loan that's too large to comfortably pay down. Your good credit may get you a better interest rate by a half percent, but you can still tank the investment by purchasing a bad house. Make sure to read about how to assess property value and the Comparative Market Analysis (CMA) in the chapters that follow.

FHA (Federal Housing Administration) Loans

Sarah makes a modest income as a teacher at a school in an expensive area. She wants to buy a home in her school's community but can only put 3.5 percent down. She might decide to pursue an FHA loan.

- *How they work:* FHA loans are meant to help people with lower credit scores and less money to put down. Because the government is backing the loan and because the bank is taking on more risk, the inspections will be more rigorous than with a conventional loan.

Tip: With FHA/VA inspections, the bank will mainly be concerned with whether or not the house is *functional*. If there's a major issue with functionality (like there's no working furnace), the loan won't get approved. You might assume that if a home passes an FHA inspection, it's in top condition—but that's not the case. The inspection won't tell you whether you're buying a junk functional house versus a quality functional house. You still need to do your homework.

- *Pros:* This government tool can be a big help for many middle-class families to get into a house. If you don't have a lot of money to put down and/or a low credit score, the FHA loan might be your best tool to get into home ownership.
- *Cons:* Typically, FHA loans make you pay more money somewhere because you're considered a riskier borrower; often, that translates to a higher interest rate and/or higher lender fees. An offer from an FHA buyer will be less appealing to a seller than a cash or conventional loan buyer because the home inspection will be more rigorous. (Translation: "more of a pain" for the seller.) FHA buyers will also have to pay Monthly Insurance Premiums (MIPs) to insure the loan against default. Additionally, because of the rigorous requirements for the home inspections, buyers are much more limited to what kind of building they can buy—no fixer-uppers, unfortunately.
- *A Word of Caution:* FHA loan buyers are often perceived as being less savvy than a conventional loan buyer, and they can become easy prey for the wolves in the business. Home flippers who have created a shiny, pretty house with terrible quality materials and methods (a pig with lipstick) may look for FHA buyers. Oftentimes, FHA buyers will buy a property at max price. This can happen for a couple of reasons: if the inspection is approved, they may (wrongly) assume they're getting a great house and pay top dollar. Some FHA buyers don't negotiate shrewdly because they're putting less money down and feel less attached to a difference of several thousand dollars; or, perhaps they're less informed. If they have a history of credit issues, they may feel so happy about getting a house, they don't think to push back on price. There's also the "wolves" issue—the people on the other side of the

negotiating table may try to take advantage of the FHA buyers' perceived weaknesses. The FHA loan can be a great tool—but make sure you know your stuff if you're going to use it! Don't get taken advantage of.

VA (Veterans' Administration) Loans

Gordon and Courtney are a military family who has just been transferred to San Diego from Guam. They decide to purchase a home with a VA loan, part of Gordon's benefits as a member of the military.

- *How it works:* VA loans are reserved for current members of the military and veterans. The government backs a VA loan with 100 percent financing; in other words, families are required to put *zero* percent down. Like an FHA loan, buyers with low credit can still qualify. There's also no maximum purchase price on a VA loan.
- *Pros:* The VA loan is an amazing benefit that the government offers to veterans, for all the reasons just listed. They do look at debt-to-income ratios, so they will take your monthly income into the equation in determining how much you can borrow. There's no barrier to entry because you're not required to put any money down. You're also not required to pay PMI.
- *Cons:* VA loan holders must pay a VA funding fee, which may be financed into the loan. VA buyers may not be seen as appealing to sellers for the same reason that FHA buyers are sometimes met with skepticism. Finally, VA loans are specifically reserved for primary residences, not investment properties.

- *A Word of Caution:* The VA loans can compound the potential issues of an FHA loan. Because the barrier to entry for home-ownership is *so* low, and because these loans are *so* easy to come by, many people make fast, reckless decisions. Often military families are in a hurry to move because of an abrupt transfer, which can worsen the problems. We have seen some military families buy a house in a hurry at max price—they do not do their research or negotiate shrewdly. They often forget about the additional monthly costs that they'll need to pay on top of their (potentially huge) mortgage, like their loan insurance premiums. Unfortunately, we've seen many veterans struggle to maintain the payments on their home or the needed upkeep; their homes may be underwater in value if the market doesn't quickly appreciate. However, we've also seen plenty of smart veterans use this tool to great advantage. The VA loan can be an amazing tool, provided it's used with care and caution.

Myth: Easy is good.

Actually, when things come easily, they may cause you to be careless. The harder you have to work at home ownership, the more you are incentivized to learn and be smart about what you buy. More skin in the game usually means you've got more of a game-face!

LESS COMMON TOOLS

A few more financial tools are worth mentioning but are less likely to fit the most common scenarios.

- **Hard Money Lending:** Some people are in the business of doing private financing but not in a particularly benevolent way. Hard money lenders will issue a private loan at a high-interest rate (often 10–15 percent), with a high fee. Usury laws in our country prevent loans from being issued to individuals at too high an interest rate, so hard money lenders only work with LLCs, where those usury laws don't apply. It's a short-term product that can make sense if there is a big margin that's going to be made on the house, like in the case of a home flip—but it's very unforgiving. If your schedule drags on for any reason, the high-interest rates and fees could take a serious bite out of any potential gains you're working for.

· **Equity Financing:** This tool works well if you want to buy a new home before selling the one you currently live in, and you've earned substantial equity in your current house. If you have paid off your house, you can go to the bank and get a Home Equity Line of Credit (HELOC) for most of what your home is worth; for instance, if your house is worth $500,000, the bank might extend you $400,000 in a HELOC. Once that process is completed, you owe zero dollars on that line of credit, but you have the ability to write a check anytime you want, up to the available balance. In this scenario, you can make offers as if you are paying cash, even though you're drawing the money from your HELOC. Once you use the HELOC, you'll need to start making payments, but you have a lot of flexibility about how to make those payments. For instance, you could choose to do interest-only payments to keep the payments low while you complete the transaction of buying a new house; then, later, you can sell your first house and pay back the HELOC entirely. HELOCs have adjustable interest rates, which can be both a pro and a con.

- **Rehab Financing**: If you find a house with great potential but is distressed enough that a bank wouldn't approve a conventional loan, you can ask the bank for a Rehab Loan. In this case, the bank agrees that the property can be fixed up and will eventually be worth more than it currently is; for that reason, they'll loan you more money than the current building is worth, enabling you to take some of that extra money to put toward the building's rehabilitation. Although Rehab Financing can be a useful tool, it's extremely cumbersome to use. There are many rules and regulations surrounding it; for instance, you have to use a contractor from a preapproved list, and they usually charge higher fees. If you want to fix up a run-down house, it's much faster and easier to pursue private financing or owner financing. However, if those tools aren't available to you, this tool might be worth pursuing.
- **Construction Loans**: Constructions loans can be a good tool if you want to build a *new* home. Over the course of the year that the home is being built, a construction loan's payments are interest-only at an adjustable rate. Once the home is complete and you move in, the loan will convert to a more standard, fixed-rate mortgage.

BUYING MONEY: INTEREST RATES AND LENDER FEES

When you take out a loan, you're basically paying to use someone else's money. There are two costs to use someone else's money: the interest rate and the lender fee (aka, origination fee or bank charge). Let's take a closer look at both.

INTEREST RATES

When arranging your financing, you'll be assigned an interest rate by the lender; that rate will be determined as a percentage of the overall loan, and you'll pay it over the duration of your loan. Essentially, the interest is what you pay to use the lender's money. If you've shown that you're trustworthy in handling money and have a good credit score, your interest rate will generally be lower. This interest rate is determined by several factors:

- Your credit score and debt-to-income ratio.
- The current interest rates determined by the federal government.
- The loan product you're taking out.

How much do interest rates matter? Well, it depends on how long you're going to be paying the loan.

For a **short-term loan, interest rates don't matter much.** If you were to take out a loan with a 10 percent interest rate and do a home flip over six months, you could probably muster up the additional cash to pay that high-interest rate for six months. If you end up increasing the home's value by $50,000 and can sell quickly, that's still a great investment.

However, **interest rates matter a great deal for long-term loans.** Here's a comparison of how an interest rate would play out over the course of a thirty-year mortgage:

- $100,000 mortgage / thirty-year loan / fixed *4 percent* interest
  - Monthly payment: $477

- Over thirty years, you'd end up paying $71,870 in interest, on top of the principal.
- $100,000 mortgage / thirty-year loan / fixed 7 *percent* interest
  - Monthly payment: $665
  - Over thirty years, you'd end up paying $139,509 in interest, on top of the principal.

At a 7 percent interest rate, after thirty years, you would have paid $139,509 *just* in interest—that's more than your original principal! Your monthly payment would also be significantly more expensive—in this example, nearly $200 more. If you're pursuing a long-term loan product, you want to do everything possible to negotiate for the lowest interest rate possible.

What's the deal with **adjustable interest rates?** Adjustable interest rates do just that—they adjust, usually based on a market index rating. At regular intervals (six months, to a year, to two years), the market will determine the new interest rate. Again, for short-term loan products, an adjustable interest rate is not a huge deal; you could fix up a place then refinance and get a fixed-rate mortgage loan. However, for long-term loans (over five years), an adjustable interest rate can wreak havoc on your finances and budget. We would strongly encourage you to get a loan with a *fixed* rate if you plan to maintain a loan for the foreseeable future.

LENDER FEE

A **Lender Fee** is also called an origination fee or bank charge. Basically, it's the upfront cost that you pay to a lender to set up the loan. The interest rate and lender fee will be inversely related to each other: the higher one is, the lower the other will be. Here are a few examples to illustrate how this inverse relationship can work:

- 3.75 percent interest rate; $7,000 bank charge
- 4 percent interest rate; $5,000 bank charge
- 4.5 percent interest rate; $2,000 bank charge

See? As one number goes up, the other goes down. You want to look for the lowest combination of interest rate and bank charge. You can negotiate for a lower interest rate by offering to pay a higher upfront fee; that may be a worthwhile investment. For example, you might elect to pay an extra $500 for your upfront lender fee in order to drop your interest rate by an extra 0.25 percent. Let's say that equaled $20 less for each monthly payment. In approximately twenty-six months, you would have made up for that $500 fee. For every payment made after that twenty-sixth month, you're saving money. If you plan to stay in your house for a long time, you could end up saving quite a bit of money.

Want to shop around? You can ask banks to provide you with a **Good Faith Estimate** for any given property, and they'll provide you with a standardized sheet listing all the prices, rates, and costs associated with that loan. Then, you can compare sheets from different banks side by side and pick your best lender. However, this process can take time. If you expect you'll need to move quickly with buying a home, this may not be the right strategy.

THE COSTS OF BUYING A HOME

You've found the property you want; you've figured out the appropriate financial tool to buy it—but what other financial considerations do you need to make? There are a number of costs and fees required to get into a new home, and we want to make sure our readers have a clear idea of what they are. Be sure to consider these costs so that you're prepared to pay them; if you're not prepared to pay them, you're probably not ready to move forward with your home purchase. (Remember, you'll also want to expect a steady stream of expenses for maintaining your home!)

UPFRONT COSTS

These are payments you would make upfront after your offer is accepted by a seller. Let's define each one.

Upfront Fees
Paid for at the Beginning of an Accepted Contract

Purchase Price	$150K	$300K	$450K	$600K	$750K	$900K
Earnest Money	$1,000	$3,000	$4,500	$6,000	$7,500	$9,000
Appraisal	$450	$450	$450	$450	$750	$750
Home Inspection	$350	$350	$350	$450	$550	$650
Termite Inspection	$75	$75	$75	$75	$75	$75
Total	$1,875	$3,875	$5,375	$6,975	$8,875	$10,475

- **Earnest Money:** This is a cash deposit you put down as a "good faith" indication to the seller that you're serious about buying their property. Depending on market considerations (like whether it's a buyers' or sellers' market), earnest money is typically 1–10 percent of the purchase price. If you want your offer to get the seller's attention, you can offer more earnest money. Provided the contract goes through, the earnest money will eventually be applied toward the buyer's down payment. Depending on how the contract is written, the earnest money may be refundable if an issue with an appraisal or the inspection comes up; however, a buyer may try to make their offer more appealing by identifying their earnest money as non-refundable. If a seller terminates a deal, the earnest money will always be refunded.

- **Appraisal:** This cost pays for the bank's appraisal of the home's value, which will impact their decision to finance a loan. The cost of an appraisal varies by state and location but is typically around $500.[8] More expensive homes may cost more to appraise.

- **Home Inspection:** This fee pays for a professional property inspector to evaluate the condition of the home. It usually costs around $500, though the price can vary with the size and complexity of the property.

- **Pest Inspection:** Usually, a separate pest inspection is warranted to evaluate the home for issues with termites, critters, etc. A pest inspection costs around $75. You may also decide to do additional inspections, such as a sewer line scope or hiring a specialist to look at the foundation, HVAC system, wiring, etc. Each additional inspection will come with its own costs.

CLOSING COSTS

These fees would be paid when you're ready to close on your new home. It's important to note that many of the closing costs can serve as a point of negotiation between buyer and seller in terms of who pays them.

---

8   Cost estimates are based on standard market prices in the year 2020.

Expected Closing-Day Fees
Paid for at the Time of Closing

Purchase Price	$150K	$300K	$450K	$600K	$750K	$900K
Real Estate Agent Fees	$495	$495	$495	$495	$495	$495
Title and Escrow	$1,750	$2,500	$3,250	$4,000	$4,750	$5,500
Lender Fees	$1,250	$1,250	$1,250	$1,250	$1,250	$1,250
Homeowner's Insurance	$263	$525	$788	$1,050	$1,313	$1,575
Total	$3,758	$4,770	$5,783	$6,795	$7,808	$8,820

- **Real Estate Agent Fee:** This is the amount you may pay to the real estate agent who helps you find your home. These are typically minimal costs, sometimes called Transaction Fees.
- **Title and Escrow:** This money is paid to the title company for researching the property's title information and handling the escrow money. Title companies can easily provide you with an accurate cost if you call and ask. The amount you'll pay will vary according to the purchase price.
- **Lender Fees:** Also known as the origination fee, this money is paid to the bank for processing your loan. The cost is agreed upon between the buyer and lender when the loan is drawn up and will be inversely related to the interest rate.
- **Homeowner Insurance:** You'll typically pay a portion of your insurance premium as part of your closing costs, often somewhere between three and six months. You could anticipate paying somewhere between $700 per year (for a $100,000 home) and $2,000 per year (for a home between $500,000 and $600,000). The insurance cost will be based on the property's value and perceived risks, along with the coverage plan you select. (The numbers in our chart reflect estimated costs for three months' payment.)
- **Down Payment:** This is the money you agree to pay in cash

toward your new home, typically between 3.5 and 20 percent of the purchase price.

Want to get a ballpark idea of what you're looking at? Your real estate agent or your bank will be able to provide you with some estimates based on a certain sales price or property.

Example of How These Costs Play Out

Since it's much easier to consider numbers when they apply to a real-life situation, let's consider an example of how these figures could realistically play out.

Total Costs Associated with Purchase

Purchase Price	$150K	$300K	$450K	$600K	$750K	$900K
Upfront Fees	$2,375	$3,875	$5,375	$6,975	$8,875	$10,475
Closing Day	$3,758	$4,770	$5,783	$6,795	$7,808	$8,820
Earnest Money Credit	–$1,500	–$3,000	–$4,500	–$6,000	–$7,500	–$9,000
Down Payment						

Don and Sue buy a $300,000 house. Shortly after they get an offer accepted, they pay these upfront costs:

- I percent earnest money: $3,000 which goes toward their down payment.
- Appraisal: $450.
- Home inspection: $350.
- Termite inspection: $75.

Their upfront costs to get into their home total around **$3,875**, and that's all paid within days of their offer being accepted.

On the day of closing, they wire a great, big sum of money to the escrow company, which covers the following costs:

- Their Buyer's Agent Fee: $495.
- Title and escrow fees: $2,500.
- Lender fees: $1,250.
- Homeowner's insurance: $525.

Before paying the remainder of their down payment, Don and Sue pay **$4,770** in closing costs. They still need to pay the rest of their down payment, which subtracts the earnest money they already paid, working out to an additional **$27,000**.

In sum, their total closing costs work out to about **$31,770**.

All told, it costs Don and Sue close to **$35,645** out-of-pocket to get into their $300,000 home, when paying a 10 percent down payment.

Tip: Depending on the type of financing you're using, **buyers can request that the sellers pay some or all of your closing costs.** The reason you would do this is to decrease your total *out-of-pocket* costs when you're purchasing a home. For example, say you buy a $100,000 home and need your $5,000 closing costs covered. You could offer to buy the home for $105,000 and ask the seller to pay $5,000 toward your closing costs. There are pros and cons to doing this; you should discuss with your lender to determine whether or not this option makes sense for you.

YOUR FINANCIAL SCENARIO

Now, how should you apply all of this information to your particular scenario? First, complete some of the necessary steps we've recommended already: make sure you are strategically, emotionally, and financially ready, as well as committed to learn quickly as you buy a home. Get your mind right, with a balance of a homeowner and investor mentality. Gather expert, knowledgeable team members who can give you good recommendations and referrals and help you navigate this process.

> **Tip:** The financial tools we've discussed here only begin to scratch the surface. Enlist your expert team members to further understand how these tools can be used and applied to your particular situation. Your mortgage lender (and, if you have one, your financial advisor) may be especially helpful in understanding these financial tools.

Consider also:

- What kind of homeowner do you want to be? Do you like the idea of restoring a distressed property, or would you prefer to buy a move-in ready house at a higher list price?
- Do you know people who might be willing to owner-finance a loan to you?
- Do you have sufficient funds to cover the upfront and closing costs, in addition to your down payment money? Will you have the necessary income to help cover future maintenance costs?

These questions will help you identify your motivations, goals, and financial readiness. Considering these points will also help you determine the best financial tools to use.

Once you're ready to dive into the money stuff, we recommend you take the following steps, roughly in this order. This certainly isn't the only way to approach buying a house, but it's a solid way:

1. Establish the general parameters of your financial scenario. Go through the pre-approval process with one or several lenders and see what tools might be available to you.
2. Learn about those different financial tools and how they work.
3. Determine the area you're most interested in buying in and start learning as much as you can about that particular market. Get an idea of the high and low ends of that market. In other words, educate yourself on *value*. What's a bad deal? What's a good deal? What's a great deal? What amenities are you willing to pay more for to increase your quality of life?
4. Understand your motivation and goals. What kinds of properties make the most sense for your particular homeownership goals? What financial tools apply to those kinds of properties?
5. Understand the different types of sellers you might be able to work with (e.g., a Mrs. Smith versus a Housing Urban Development property) and consider their motivations and goals. What financial tools might be most relevant to those types of sellers?
6. Once you've selected a property, and learned about the seller, work together to apply the best tool for that purchase.

Remember: you most likely have more financial tools available to you than you think. Consider what tools might make the most sense for you but also be willing to explore options outside of your comfort zone. Who knows what's going to come up? Once you learn what's within your realm of possibility, the sky's the limit.

KNOW WHAT YOU BUY

Too often, we hear people describe their home-buying search in terms of what they can afford. We want to encourage you to *end* your search process with the money; don't *start* with the money. Remember: money is a tool applied to a process. Build up your understanding of what's possible so that you can identify the project and then pick your tools to achieve that project.

These financial tools will only help you make a wise investment *if you get the right building*. Remember that beat-up Buick some salesman was trying to sell you for $5,000, that we discussed at the start of the chapter? You should never take that deal! You would be sinking $5,000 into a terrible investment and would never make that money back.

A clear understanding about what you're buying is the key to good financing. If you understand the product well, you won't have any fear about whether or not to finance it. If you don't understand what you're buying, you will finance something inappropriately and can get yourself into a lot of trouble. That's why we're now going to discuss how to assess a property's *value*—so that you can be smart about what you buy.

CHAPTER 5

EVALUATE PROPERTIES

HOW TO CONSIDER PROPERTY VALUE

KEVIN NARRATES: SO YOU CAN SLEEP AT NIGHT

I once worked with a doctor who had just been transferred to our area for his residency. Although he was only planning to be in our area for a short time, he and his new wife were determined to buy—and they wanted to buy in a hurry. They gave me a timeline of one week. We found them a cute house—a recent flip. It was listed at max price, but the couple wanted to move forward.

Unfortunately, the inspection revealed massive issues with the house. The roof was in terrible condition, and broken plumbing meant that there was water pooled behind one of the walls. In spite of that, the couple still insisted on moving forward.

I remember standing in the driveway of this home, baring my soul to this guy. "Listen, I need to tell you everything that's wrong with this house so that I can go home and sleep tonight." I spelled out all the problems, named the estimates of the needed repairs, and reminded him that he could simply rent during his residency. He still wanted to proceed forward—but at least I was able to go home and sleep that night.

Unfortunately, the situation turned out as badly as I'd feared. The couple discovered even more problems with the house after they'd moved in. They got involved in a stressful, expensive, and time-consuming lawsuit with the former owner. They had to sink thousands into doing the needed repairs. A few years in, they sold the house at a loss.

I'm not sure why they were so determined to buy at that time, or why they were so set on buying that particular house—but I hope their story gives caution to us all. When you buy, you want to be fully aware of all of a property's potential problems. If it turns out to be a pig with lipstick—or just a pig—we want you to have the clear-mindedness to walk away. We also want you to be able to recognize when you're purchasing a gem.

The information we give you in this chapter is meant to help you make a wise, open-eyed decision about the home you buy—so that you can sleep at night.

THE MOST IMPORTANT THING TO GET RIGHT

Hear this: **all of the money that you will gain or lose in your property happens in the purchase.** You may come to own a solid investment or you may commit yourself to a life-sucking money pit—all of that happens in the moment you purchase the home. This will also be the building that you live in, the building that you maintain and fix and enjoy. So, how do you make sure you get a good one?

Here's how: you make sure you're getting a great property. Being able to effectively evaluate a property is the most important thing to get right in your entire home-buying experience because the quality of the property will determine whether you end up purchasing a Ferrari for a steal, or a beat-up Buick for a fortune. In this chapter, we're going to teach you what elements of a property to examine when walking through a building so that you can ensure you're making a great investment.

> Being able to effectively evaluate a property is the most important thing to get right in your entire home-buying experience. The quality of the property will determine whether you end up purchasing an asset or a liability.

And speaking of investment: we want you to once again be ready to trade hats between Investor and Homeowner while reading this chapter. We're going to talk a lot about building construction, like what signs on a building indicate wear and tear, which will correlate to dollars and cents. That's important to think about. But we also want you to remember to ask yourself, "Would this house work for me as a homeowner? Would I enjoy living here?" That's an equally valuable consideration.

Remember that the natural world is constantly battering any structure and slowly causing its deterioration. Water seeps into cracks, roots invade a foundation, critters chew holes in the siding. A building's purpose is to keep all those elements *out*. You want a solid structure that you can depend on so that you can live comfortably within. The points we're going to discuss in this chapter will help you spot all the hidden ways the natural world is attempting to overrun the place you might choose to call home.

Those signs are easy to miss—especially because there are often shiny, pretty things to look at during a walk-through, which can easily distract you from much larger problems lurking. Don't get distracted by the shiny, pretty things! **Cosmetics on a home should be considered secondarily; focus instead on the "bones" of the house.** Aesthetic features are usually relatively easy to change and less expensive than, say, an issue with the foundation. The bones of a house pack far more weight in determining the value of your investment.

We want to help you recognize those danger signs—and we also want to teach you how to recognize a beautifully built and maintained home. Remember that you'll have help from a home inspector in evaluating a structure's physical property. Good agents can also help you better understand the quality of a building. Still, we believe that building up your own knowledge in evaluating property value is vital. It will give you confidence to push hard on a good deal, and the necessary wariness to hold off on a bad one. You'll feel empowered, informed, and that much more excited when you commit to what you know is a truly great investment—and home.

HOW TO EVALUATE A PROPERTY

Imagine that you've found an appealing property on Zillow, and you want to take a closer look. The first thing you're going to do is drive to that property and get out of your car.

The location is the main driving factor of the overall price that you pay for a home. However, the main factor which will affect your daily life is the quality of the building and the work that needs to be done. The same building, in two separate areas, may be priced drastically different, but your experience of living within the home can be the exact same. It's important to keep both location and building quality in mind as you take a closer look.

STANDING OUTSIDE: WHERE TO START

As a general rule of thumb, **start by considering the PROPERTY'S AGE.** Newer properties tend to have fewer issues. They're often more efficient and built with technologically advanced materials. A home nearing the twenty-year mark, on the other hand, can be a ticking time bomb, even if they look like they've been well taken care of—we call those "well-maintained crappers." Due to the expected lifespan of many major home systems, everything in that house will need to be replaced soon—unless they were already. If you find that many of those major systems have been upgraded, that's a win. If not—proceed with caution.

There also may be important clues from the decade in which the structure was built. For instance, where we live in Northeast Ohio, most homes made in the 1950s are practically built to withstand a bomb—they're typically incredibly solid. On the other hand, many of the homes that were built during the 1970s were made with flimsier materials. You can usually get information about a building's age from an online posting or your real estate agent; your agent might also be able to tell you something about the original builder and their reputation.

CRAFTSMANSHIP is important. The better something was done to begin with, the longer it's going to last. If you can tell that the general quality of craftsmanship is high—installations were done well, all the seams are perfectly aligned, the materials are high quality, and so on—that's a sign that this property has great longevity. If you can see signs of poor craftsmanship on the other hand, there's a good chance this property will experience frequent problems or breakage. All of the following signs will give you clues about the property's general level of craftsmanship.

> **Tip:** Craftsmanship is crucial! You want a house that was built by experts. The better something was done to begin with, the longer it's going to last.

It's time to start using all your senses. Stand at the curb and start making the following observations.

- **Look at WHAT SURROUNDS THE BUILDING.** What do the neighbors' properties look like? Are there sidewalks? What kind of a street is it on? Are there any structures nearby that are appealing or—even more important—unappealing? Use all your senses. Can you smell a bad odor from a nearby paper mill or waste treatment plant? Listen: what do you hear? Can you hear the sound of a nearby freeway, a buzz from power lines, or roars from planes flying directly overhead? All of these factors can add to or subtract from the property's value.

- **Look at the LANDSCAPING.** Have the plants been trimmed, or are they overgrown? Has the yard been left to gather weeds, or are there plant beds and clear signs of cultivation? These will give you clues as to the owner's general habits of maintaining the rest of the building. If there's nice landscaping, that's a great thing. Landscaping creates lifestyle value. Great outdoor spaces, like a nice patio, will regularly enhance your experience living somewhere and may be worth paying extra for.

- **Look at the TREES**, if there are any. Will they drop debris or seedlings? How close are they to the house? A tree too close to the house is a big deal: its root systems could put pressure on the foundation and/or create issues with plumbing and wiring. If the canopy hangs over the roof, that will increase the rate of the roof's deterioration and potentially create critter issues. A large tree close to the house could also pose a danger during storms.

- **Consider the WOW FACTOR.** Is it a cute building? Does it have some unique qualities, or does it look like a standard-issue row home? Was it made efficiently, like a box? Or do you see curves and angles and special windows, which indicate attention to craftsmanship? Will this property have a resale appeal? Generally speaking, if the house is unique or special, it will be viewed as more charming and hold more appeal for resale. If it doesn't have the WOW factor, consider if changes could be made to get it there. Some homes just need a few updates to get the WOW factor, but other homes are just ugly.

Now, walk right up to the building.

> **Tip:** We recommend arranging one of these walk throughs with a real estate agent or with the owner. If you go by yourself, don't be nosy. Be respectful if there are current residents.

Take a closer look at each of the following:

- **Look at the ROOF.** Are there shingles blown off? Does it look faded and worn? Can you see moss growing? Are there signs of deterioration? What kind of material is it made of? A slate roof in good shape will last nearly a hundred years, but a three-tab shingle roof will last for a maximum of thirty. If you plan to live in a house with a three-tab shingle roof for several decades, you'd probably have to plan to replace the roof. Consider the replacement cost of this particular roofing material.

- **Look at the WINDOWS.** Windows come in a wide range of quality and are not always installed correctly. They may look good from a distance, but if they're made of poor quality material or installed wrong, you'll have major insulation issues. Start by considering the age of them. Do they look old or new? Are there signs of them breaking down? Are the seams coming apart? Do they look like the wood is rotting or peeling away? Is there fog in the glass, indicating a bad seal? How thick are they?

- **Look at the SIDING.** Consider the material and look for signs of deterioration. If it's vinyl, does it have holes in it? Is it faded and brittle? Are there signs of pests getting in? If it's aluminum siding, are there dents? If it's stucco or brick, do you see cracks, indicating a foundation issue? Many homes with wood siding may distract you with their appearance. They may look freshly painted or may be dirty with peeling paint—but the paint condition is not what you're looking for. Dirt can be easily washed off, and repainting is quick. You're looking for signs of *damage*. It's possible the siding might look shabby but actually be in great shape. Look closely enough that you can determine whether there are signs of deterioration.

- **Look at the GUTTERS.** Are the gutters working properly? Do you see stains where the water overflowed onto the siding? If the gutters have seams, what condition are they in? Are the gutters hanging off the house or full of debris and growing plants? The quality of the gutters is often a sign of whether or not the owner consistently did the required maintenance on this property—that should give you a preview of either more disrepair or more quality to come.

- **Look at the GARAGE (if there is one) and DRIVEWAY.** Is the garage door insulated? What's the condition of the driveway? Generally, gravel is the cheapest way to do a driveway (and lowest quality), then asphalt, then concrete. However, if you notice that the concrete driveway is full of cracks, that could point to other issues. Are the cracks right by the house signaling a potential foundation issue? Do they seem to be caused by tree roots, indicating potential issues with roots in plumbing or wiring?

- **Look for the AIR CONDITIONER unit.** Usually, these units have a sticker with a date of installation on it. How old is the air conditioner? Does it look like it's in good shape?

By the time you've finished walking around the outside of the building, you should feel *worse* about the property than when you pulled up. At a distance, it's easy to miss many of these potential issues. However, if you've done your job and looked closely at all these building elements, you should have discovered signs of deterioration: all buildings have them. The question is, how many issues are there, and will any of them be a deal-breaker? If you've discovered some of these issues, pat yourself on the back! You should have a more sober understanding of the building as you prepare to go inside.

WALK THROUGH THE INSIDE

When you first enter in, allow yourself to **put the HOME-OWNER HAT back on.** At a basic level, do you like it? Does this building strike you as a place where you would enjoy living? Does the layout seem like it would generally work for you? Could you see yourself enjoying life as a family here?

If there are no glaring issues and you feel you could enjoy living in this space, then **put the INVESTOR HAT back on**, and continue to scrutinize the building.

· **Head to the BASEMENT.** (If there is no basement, go to

wherever the "guts" of the house are.) This may be the least interesting area of the house to you from a homeowner's perspective, but it's the most important part of the house from an investor's perspective. The basement is the epicenter of all the mechanicals in the house: it usually contains the plumbing, the hot water tank, the furnace, the sewer, and the majority of the electrical wiring. Take a look at those different mechanical units. Do they look well-cared for? Do you see signs of wear, or do they look well-maintained? How old are they? (Your agent or the seller's agent may be able to tell you.)

- **Look at the BASEMENT WALLS.** You're looking for foundation issues—the most expensive issue to fix in a house, and foundation issues will be most evident in the basement. Do you see any cracks in the walls? Do the walls slope or bow out (bad), or are they straight (good)? Are there water stains on the walls or in the corners, indicating gutter issues? Does the basement feel moist or dry? Was the basement recently painted? This could be an indication of something being covered up. You can also look for signs of mold or mildew on the basement ceiling, which would look like the same mold you would see on old bread. Mold could indicate plumbing issues, foundation issues, or some other source of water damage.

Once you've gotten a clearer idea of the condition of the house's "guts" and foundation, head back upstairs.

- **Go to the KITCHEN.** How's the general style of the kitchen? Does it look dated, or is it up to HGTV standards? Do you like the layout? What's the general quality? Don't be shy about trying out the appliances or opening the cabinets. Get a sense of the general workability of the space. Are there any signs of pests in the kitchen—droppings in a drawer, for instance? What's the condition of the flooring? Will the kitchen require some updates?

- **Check out the BATHROOMS.** Consider the quality, layout, and general design. Do you like the style? Do the fixtures look new, or is this clearly a dated bathroom? Look at the flooring—what kind of condition is it in? Consider the condition of the tile and/or countertops; does the caulking look clean and tight? Do you see any signs of mildew on the ceiling or walls? If you're in a downstairs bathroom, those signs of mildew could indicate leaks from a bathroom above, which will mean repairs.

- **Is there a FIREPLACE?** A wood-burning fireplace can be a wonderful addition to a home, but you'll want to get a chimney inspection before using it for the first time, to ensure it's clean and safe.

- **Walk through the rest of the GROUND LEVEL.** Now you're making more general considerations, looking at flooring, paint colors, room size, and so on. If there's carpet—what is its condition? If it's hardwood, do you see warping, or are there creaks? If you don't like the paint color or flooring, not to worry: those are relatively easy and less expensive changes to make.

- **Go UPSTAIRS,** if there is one. Try to get a look at the underside of the roof; if there's an attic, check out the attic. You're looking for any signs of leaking, critters, and general condition. Is the attic insulated? After looking at the attic, walk through the rest of the upstairs. Once again, make those aesthetic considerations: do you like the size of the rooms, the flooring, the lighting? How would this building feel to live in?

A FEW MORE CONSIDERATIONS

Before you come to any final conclusions about the property you just walked through, there are a few more points to consider.

Look for Signs of Deferred Maintenance

As you do this walk-through, you'll start to get a sense of how much **deferred maintenance** may be represented in the property. People put stuff off—like repairing the roof, for instance. It's expensive and inconvenient to do big repairs, and many people would prefer to kick that can down the road and let the next owner deal with it. Other owners are different—they consistently take care of their home.

Take a lesson from the cockroaches: if you see one cockroach, you know there's a thousand more in the wall. Similarly, if you notice a few glaring maintenance issues during this walk through, you can assume there are probably more. It's likely this owner has deferred a lot of their needed maintenance and would prefer to pass most of those problems onto you.

On the other hand, someone who has holistically and diligently cared for their home won't have a bad roof; they've likely done a great job maintaining all aspects of their home, including the hidden issues. That's a property you can feel more confident about pursuing.

Remodels Are a Pain

Another consideration: know that **remodels are hard and expensive.** If you walk through a house and think, "I don't love the kitchen, but we can just remodel it," or, "We could improve the flow of the living area by knocking out this wall," you may be right—but those remodels might also make you miserable for as long as they're in process!

Put on your homeowner hat again: would you be willing to sign up for that? Many people think they want to remodel and/or flip, and HGTV has glamorized the idea. But in the real world, remodeling is much harder than it appears to be on those shows. Also, those home-remodel shows take place in homes *no one is living in*. If you plan to live in your house while undertaking a remodel, you're signing up for a long duration of stress, mess, and inconvenience. Consider the value of your time: what would it be worth to you to move into a home where everything was already done?

One additional factor to understand about remodels: often, remodels are done poorly, especially when people are living in the home. People often want to do their remodels as cheaply as possible and/or do it quickly. As a result, the quality ends up being sub-par. Those mistakes come back to haunt you when you eventually go to sell.

Consider the Cost and Difficulty of Needed Repairs

Which house would you rather buy: a house with great bathrooms in need of a new roof, or a house with a great roof but dated, ugly bathrooms?

Don't answer immediately. This question requires some thought—and you're going to need to think like a homeowner *and* investor to answer it adequately.

Consider: how big is the roof, and how much would it cost? Although a new roof is a major and likely expensive repair, it would also cause almost *zero* disruption to your daily life. Roof repairs can happen over the course of several days, and nearly all the work happens outside. It's quick and relatively easy—assuming you hire professionals.

On the other hand, remodeling the bathrooms may seem initially like a smaller endeavor, but that would have an enormous impact on your daily life. How many times a day do you use your bathroom? Multiply that by the number of people living in your house, and you'll get a sense of how constant the inconvenience would be. If you plan to do it yourself, the remodel will probably stretch on far longer than if a professional did it. If you hire professionals to do it, that means you'll be doing life alongside construction workers for a time.

When considering the needed repairs of any property, think of these three factors:

- **What will the estimated cost be?**
- **How long would the repair take?**
- **How much would it interrupt and inconvenience my life?**

For instance, a house that needs a new furnace might seem like a deal-breaker, but you could find a decent furnace for around $3,000. That repair would be quick and likely cause very little disruption to your life. A foundation issue, on the other hand, is one of the most expensive repairs to make, would take a long time to fix, and would probably cause huge disruptions in your daily life. Houses with major foundation issues, therefore, are probably ones to avoid.

GENERALIZED PRICING, DURATION, AND INCONVENIENCE FACTOR OF COMMON REPAIRS

Note: These numbers are meant to provide a *generalized* idea of what a repair or replacement might entail when working with a skilled professional. However, every home is unique, and your repairs might either go over or under these estimates, depending on your scenario. Take these numbers with a grain of salt and use them as a basis of comparison; we encourage you to do your own additional research into specifics of the particular repair you're considering.

These estimates were made for a 1,500-square-foot, three-bed/two-bath ranch-style house with twenty-five squares of roofing and fourteen windows, choosing to do affordable but tasteful updates.

Repair:	Cost Range:	Average Duration:	Inconvenience Factor (on a scale of 1 to 10; 10 being *most* inconvenient):
Furnace or A/C unit	$2,500 to $4,500	1 day	1
Roof	$7,500 to $10,000 ($300 to $350 per "square")	1 to 2 days	2 to 4
Replacing all windows	$3,000 to $5,000	1 to 3 days	4 to 6
Replacing electrical panel	$750 to $1,250	1 day	1 to 2
New gutters	$1,500 to $2,000	1 day	1
New siding	$10,000 to $15,000	3 weeks	5
All new pipes for plumbing	$3,500 to $5,000	3 to 4 days	4
Pest treatment	$500 to $1,000	multiple weeks, for multiple treatments	4
Painting (Tip: many people choose to paint their home themselves, but a professional's work will make a noticeable difference)	$3,000 to $4,000	8 to 10 days	7
New flooring throughout the home	$5,000 to $10,000	3 to 4 days	6 to 8
Bathroom remodel to totally redo one full bath	$4,000 to $7,000	2 to 3 weeks	9
Kitchen remodel	$10,000 to $20,000	4 to 6 weeks	10
Foundation repair to replace a bowed out wall	$5,000 to $10,000	2 weeks	7

Most houses will need at least *some* repairs. Consider what you, personally, are willing to sign up for. You can often ask sellers to take care of some of them before you move in, but it's just as common to negotiate the purchase price down with the expectation that you, the buyer, will fix them. If you decide as a buyer you're willing to do those repairs. You might be able to get a decent house at a cheaper price. But consider the home-owner factor as well: how challenging might it be to live through those repairs?

THE MORE YOU KNOW, THE BETTER OFF YOU'LL BE

Let's say you find a house you like, but the plumbing is missing. It's bank owned, and they drop the price by $30,000 to compensate for the missing plumbing. You know you could probably replace the pipes for less than $30,000, but that would delay your time for moving in. Should you go for it?

Or what if you find a phenomenal house that's listed far under the standard price for its area, but you discover there's a foundation issue. If everything else about that house was in great shape, should you go for it?

Here's the thing: evaluating property value is an art and a science. You need to weigh the numbers in your head—the costs, the duration of the repairs—and you also need to consider the less tangible factors: the homeowner experience of living through the repairs, combined with the relative appeal of this particular house, in this particular location. There's no one formula you can fill with numbers that can tell you whether or not the buy is worth it for you. It's nuanced. It's personal.

So how can you know if you're making a good decision? Learn, learn, learn. The more you know, the better off you'll be. As you visit homes and do these thorough walk-throughs, you'll learn more every time. If you can, bring friends along who can help build your knowledge, like contractors, architects, inspectors, or even friends that have had to live through remodels in their own lives. Ask your real estate agent to share their knowledge about repair costs and comparative market value.

When you're evaluating a property, the art of it is to be able to put together all of the variables. **To sum it all up, these are the general questions that we answer when looking at a property:**

- What is the quality of the original construction?
- What are the current updates and their value?
- What deferred maintenance will need to be fixed soon, and what is the cost of it?
- Are the needed repairs going to disrupt your life? To what extent?
- Will the location justify your improvements? (For example, it wouldn't make sense to invest $100,000 into a house in some parts of Akron, OH, because people can buy an entirely new house for $100,000. However, in a location like southern California, you could invest $100,000 into updating a building and make all that money back when you resell.)

Do your homework. Research your preferred neighborhood so you can start to collect a knowledge base of the spectrum of costs in that area. What streets are best? What streets are worst? What elements of a home add value? What elements should lower the price?

Finally, be honest with yourself about the kind of person you are. Do you need to buy a house that's move-in ready? That's okay to admit, and it's okay to pay more for a property that will provide you with that convenience. Do you like the idea of flipping a home, even knowing it will create some stress and inconvenience? That's okay, too—look for a house that's below market value and buckle up for the ride.

The more you know—about the market, about the building construction, about yourself—the better off you'll be in making an open-eyed decision that's right for you. You'll feel more confidence and excitement when you do finally sign on the bottom line. And speaking of that bottom line—you'll also be in a better position to analyze the property's list price, which is what we're talking about next.

CHAPTER 6

EVALUATING THE PRICE

HOW TO ASSESS A FAIR PRICE

KEVIN NARRATES: REAL ESTATE RUBBER-NECKING

About four years ago, Ben and I were driving through a nice neighborhood when we passed a "For Sale" sign in front of what looked like a great house. We immediately pulled a U-turn. Unbelievably, we discovered the list price was roughly half of what would be typical in that area. Was it a mistake? Was there some glaring issue that was not apparent from the outside? We scrutinized the house together, half expecting Big Foot to loom out of a window. Nothing. It looked like a cute home.

It turns out, the real estate agent *had* made a mistake. The home needed some cosmetic work, but all other aspects were solid—good bones, quality roof, new windows, and so on. I decided I wanted that house.

I knew that the house was worth way more than its list price. I also knew I could further increase the value by giving the home the TLC it needed. I made an offer for $13,000 over the list price because I was determined to get it. My offer for $55,000 was chosen, I fixed up the house, and now it provides me with a great source of revenue as a rental.

I knew the house was quality, I knew what it was worth, and I knew it was listed way underprice. That enabled me to pull the trigger quickly, feel confident about my offer, and rest assured that I'd made a good investment. All told, I put $35,000 into improving the house for a total investment of $90,000. After those repairs, the home was worth about $140,000.

Myth: You can assume that a list price is an accurate reflection of the property's value.

Wrong! Houses are listed at inaccurate prices *all the time.* If you know how to assess a property's value and how to understand pricing, you can learn to recognize what's overpriced, what's fair, and what's a screamin' deal.

WHY PRICING KNOWLEDGE MATTERS

Imagine that someone came up to you today and said, "Hey, I'll sell you my Apple stock for $1,000 a share." You might think this sounds like a good move—you've heard all about how great Apple stock is. However, you'd be foolish to go for that sales price before checking the current market value of Apple's stock. If Apple stock is currently selling for $500, then buying the stock for $1,000 per share is a bad deal. If it's selling for $1,000, then the offer is fair, and you should feel free to take it. If Apple stock is currently selling for $2,000 a share, grab the opportunity! The market value of a stock share is a moving target—which is why it's so important to **do your homework before buying.**

Knowing the current market rates is equally important when buying a home. You might find a place that seems as sensational as Apple stock—but if you're paying above market value, you could end up with a bad investment. By learning how to assess real estate pricing, you give yourself the ability to recognize whether a listing price is too high, too low, or fair market value. **Pricing knowledge will strengthen your negotiating power and your peace of mind over whether or not you've made a good buy.**

Tip: Don't think primarily in terms of what you can afford; think about what something is *worth*.

Here's the challenge: comparing the price of real estate is far more complicated than comparing the price of a share of stock. When you buy a share of company stock, you know exactly the price that you're paying for it and what other people are paying, but homes are filled with complicated variables, which make comparing prices very difficult. For instance, a three-bedroom/two-bath home will list for widely different prices in Akron, Ohio, versus New York City. So how do you know what's a fair market value? That's what this chapter is all about: understanding the analysis that goes into real estate pricing.

Like evaluating a building's structure, pricing a property is both an art and a science. Some variables can be easily quantified, but many can't. For instance, a website like Zillow has algorithms to automatize their estimates of a home's value, but Zillow can't tell you if the home smells like cat pee. These algorithms *start* with the science, but a savvy buyer needs to finish with the art: "This home smells like urine, and I will therefore offer less."

You can begin to understand the *science* by learning some of the property evaluation tools we discussed in the previous chapter and the main pricing factors we're about to describe.

The *art* comes through practice. Visit homes. Read countless listings in your target area so you can hone your familiarity of that particular market. Learn as much as you can from your real estate agent—if they're good, they'll give you a gut sense of what elements in a home should impact the price.

This chapter *isn't* about how to find the best below-market deals, although you could take it that way; we're simply trying to help you understand how the market works so that you can make the best decision for your life and your wallet. In the end, you may decide to pay $300,000 for a home worth $250,000 because you want to live next door to your mom. That's okay, so long as you're making that decision with your eyes open.

So, let's do some eye-opening. In this chapter, we want to teach you about six major pricing factors, including how to form a Comparative Market Analysis. All these factors should be considered when evaluating property value. Learning them will strengthen your ability as a negotiator and help you make a wise, objective choice.

Keep this in mind: Remember to *end* with the money, not *start* with the money. Focusing on "what you can afford" in a monthly payment is often where people start their housing search. However, we'd rather you think of this *after* you consider other factors, like the quality of the investment.

SIX MAJOR FACTORS THAT INFORM A PRICE ANALYSIS

Each of these factors taken by itself won't get you very far, but they become incredibly informative when taken together. We're going to start with a wide focus, looking at something as general as current market interest rates. Each step will help us narrow our focus and sharpen our understanding of a property's worth.

First of all, understand that the adage of "location, location, location" is true. Location is the most important factor in real estate! The six factors of home pricing we're about to discuss should be done within a defined geographical area. For instance, a home in Manhattan is always going to be worth more than the same home in rural Indiana. When considering these factors, make sure your comparisons are done within a certain area with similar characteristics.

1. INTEREST RATES

"Interest rates are historically low." "Interest rates are predicted to climb." We hear reports like these in the news—so how do they impact a listing price?

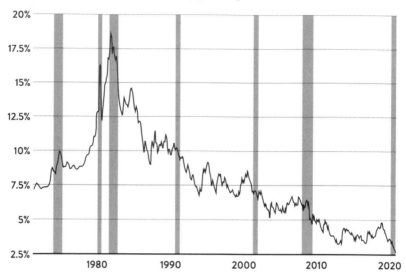

30-Year Fixed Rate Mortgage Average in the United States

Shading indicates US recessions; the most recent one is ongoing. Source: Freddie Mac

Generally speaking, when mortgage lenders are issuing higher interest rates, listing prices have to drop. Why? Because people still need to afford a monthly payment. If they're going to have to pay more in interest, they won't afford as high of a mortgage principal.

On the other hand, if interest rates are low, listing prices can go up. People can afford to pay a higher mortgage principal payment because they're not paying as much in interest.

For instance, let's revisit our example from Chapter 4 of a thirty-year fixed mortgage loan of $100,000, at two different interest rates:

- A $100,000 thirty-year mortgage, at 7 percent interest, is $655 per month.

- A $100,000 thirty-year mortgage, at 4 percent interest, is $477 per month.

The difference between 4 percent and 7 percent interest ends up translating to a difference of roughly $200 in a monthly payment. That's significant. So how does it translate to buyer behavior?

If interest rates are at 7 percent and you know you can't afford to pay more than $600 a month on a mortgage, you need to look for a less expensive house. On the other hand, if you get a loan with a 4 percent interest rate, you could afford a more expensive house. Now, what happens when *all* buyers come to the same conclusions for the same reasons? When interest rates are high, and buyers conclude they need to look for lower listing prices, that response *en masse* drives down listing prices across the market.

Side note: Lending trends have a big impact on pricing. If money is easy to access, list prices go up. If money is more constricted, then list prices will drop. In fact, this is one reason why there was a housing bubble in the early 2000s that burst in the housing crisis of 2008: loans were incredibly easy to come by, which drove up listing prices.

When considering this first factor of pricing analysis, consider what's happening in the world with interest rates. If interest rates are *low*, there are probably a lot of people buying properties right now. You can expect to compete with many other buyers for houses listed at high values, but there's also probably more inventory on the market because sellers know they can ask for a high list price. If interest rates are *high*, that might drive down inventory as potential sellers decide to wait a couple of years in their current houses until the interest rates decrease.

2. TRENDS IN THE LOCAL AREA

After you've identified the main area you're interested in buying in, pay attention to what's happening in that local area, and consider how that could impact pricing.

Prices in a neighborhood should go up if: a brand new school is going in on the next block. Amazon is creating an extension campus in your city. The nearby main street is getting trendier all the time, with new restaurants and an upscale grocery store.

Prices in a neighborhood should go down if: unemployment is increasing. A major corporation that employs thousands of people just announced that they are shutting down. There's been an increase in criminal activity.

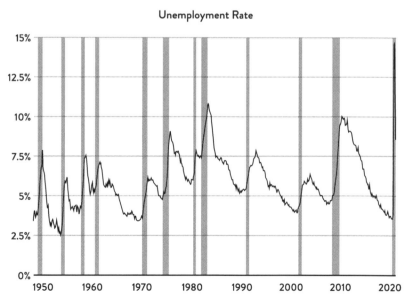

Shading indicates US recessions; the most recent one is ongoing. Source: US Bureau of Labor Statistics

Take, for example, the issue of unemployment. When unemployment is low, people tend to feel secure about the future. That often results in lots of competition among buyers who are willing to spend money, which drives list prices up. On the other hand, as the unemployment rate increases, the market changes. There may be less market demand as potential buyers feel fearful about the future and decide to rent another year. There also might be more inventory on the market as homeowners decide they need to get out of their mortgages. If unemployment in an area goes up, list prices should start to lower.

When considering this pricing factor, **watch for outliers and dramatic variations in pricing within a neighborhood.** Some neighborhoods will remain steady in their reputation and value; a $100,000 house in that neighborhood will probably maintain its value and steadily appreciate over time. But other neighborhoods might hold more flux. If a manufacturing plant suddenly closes down, for instance, the surrounding homes may quickly drop in value. If a home is on the fringe between a popular area and a more depressed area, you might see a wide variation between home prices. That could be an opportunity—but it's also a risk. A home stands to increase in value quickly if its surrounding location starts to improve. On the other hand, if the area falls into greater disrepair, its value may drop.

Spotting these outliers should cause you to scrutinize the price big time, because they're especially hard to price accurately. You might be able to negotiate a list price down significantly or find a great deal on a home that's been undervalued.

Tip: Out-of-town buyers are in danger of spending more than they should for a house simply because they're not familiar with what's happening in that particular neighborhood. Out-of-town buyers would be wise to hire a local real estate agent who will be candid about local trends and movement.

3. TIME OF YEAR

Imagine trying to load a piano into a moving van in December in the Midwest, with sleet falling and ice on the walkway. There's a reason people prefer to move in the summer!

The time of year has a significant impact on real estate pricing. **During winter, inventory tends to be low, and there are generally not as many buyers in the market.** Curb appeal is almost non-existent, and there's a general lack of enthusiasm during those dark winter months. As a result, properties are sometimes listed at lower prices, and sellers tend to be more flexible. The properties put on the market during the winter are usually listed by sellers who have unusual circumstances or who do not care about market trends. For this reason, investors often try to snatch up houses in the winter. They can often find good deals and may not need to move into a property right away (which removes the sleet and ice factor).

If sellers have the flexibility, they'll usually hold off on listing their homes until the flowers start to bloom in March. It's around that time that market inventory increases—and prices start to increase as well. June and July tend to be the busiest real estate months: the kids are out of school, everything looks great, moods are cheerful, inventory is high—it's a great time to move! That convenience comes with a price increase: **homes listed during the summer months will typically be listed at the higher end.**

2019 Home Sales in Northeast Ohio by Month

Source: Yes MLS!

The time-of-year pricing trends will be impacted by the type of property and the area's general climate. For instance, condo prices tend to be more stable throughout the year; ugly winter landscaping is less of an issue in a condo complex than it is for a single-family home. The nicest homes are usually listed in the summer and fall because owners want to make sure they get top dollar for them. Also, there's a geographical factor here. If you live in southern California and can generally expect a sunny day any time of the year, seasonal trends in real estate will be less of an issue. In Ohio, however—we can tell you, a foot of snow on the ground does not make people want to drive around to open houses. People would rather hibernate.

4. COMPETITION: WHAT'S CURRENTLY ON THE MARKET

This one is pretty straightforward. **If there are plenty of buyers competing for not-as-many houses, prices will go up.** Sellers are in the position to call the shots.

On the other hand, if there are eight condos for sale in the same area and they've been sitting on the market for months, the prices of those condos will be driven down. When there's a surplus of similar inventory on the market, buyers shift to the power position. **When supply is high, and buyers have more choices, prices will necessarily decrease.**

Let's say you're looking for a three-bedroom/two-bath home in a certain school district, and you want an acre of land. If there are only two or three options available that fit that criteria and you've got a limited time window—like, you need to move your family during summer vacation—you don't have many choices. Expect to pay more and flex more on your side of negotiations to ensure you get one of those few options.

On the other hand, if your target area has plenty of similar homes for sale, you have some opportunities. First, educate yourself about the standard pricing those homes tend to go for; that will make you a smarter buyer and savvier negotiator. You also can be choosier about what you buy because of the inventory available to you.

Will prices decrease when a new building development comes to a neighborhood?

This one is a little tricky. On the one hand, a new building development means lots of new inventory—like, *brand* new inventory. New homes are appealing to buyers (usually "new" equals "less problems"), and there would be plenty of them. Shouldn't a new building development mean neighborhood prices drop, giving buyers the power?

Maybe—unless you don't want to wait for a new house to be completed. In areas where new building developments are going in, nearby used houses often increase in value because they're already available. No one has to wait for them to be completed. Especially if the new homes are slightly more expensive than the surrounding older ones, demand might actually increase for the surrounding homes, driving their list prices up.

The time of year, as discussed, will play a major part in determining how much inventory is available to buy. Inventory is also determined by area and standard price-points. For instance, there might be enormous competition for a moderately priced home in a popular neighborhood with great schools. On the other hand, an expensive home in a run-down neighborhood may sit for months. Few buyers who could afford a house like that would want to live in a depressed neighborhood—there's less buyer competition, so the price would need to drop.

When evaluating a listing's price, consider: how many buyers might be competing for this property? How many other similar properties are available in that same area? Adjust your financial expectations accordingly.

5. COMPARATIVE MARKET ANALYSIS (CMA)

A comparative market analysis (CMA) is a way to compare the home that you're interested in buying to other similar homes. Let's say you're trying to compare a four-bedroom/two-bath on a half-acre to a three-bedroom/three-bath on a full acre. What should each property cost? How should they compare? It might feel like you're trying to compare an apple to an orange.

Because no home is identical, **the CMA assigns financial values for the differences in the homes**, and helps you arrive at what *this* home should be worth, versus *that* home, based on the financial differences. You end up with the ability to compare apples to apples, rather than apples to oranges.

Myth: Most real estate agents will know what a home should be worth.

Wrong! Inexperienced real estate agents rarely have the knowledge to quantify in dollars the various differences in homes. Usually, they don't have experience in CMA analysis (like Kevin) and they typically haven't seen enough properties to know, on a "gut level," how a price should increase or decrease depending on a home's unique features (like Ben). On the other hand, if you're working with a seasoned, experienced real estate agent, they will be in a good position to educate you about CMA data—and that will pay off.

Let's start with a simple example. Say you are looking to buy a three-bedroom/two-bathroom home in Akron, Ohio. One just sold for $300,000 with a three-car garage, but the home that you want to purchase has a two-car garage. Assume that, in all other ways, the properties are identical and located right next to each other.

??? | .5 Acres

$300,000 | .25 Acres

You need to determine: How much should you pay for the home you want to buy? How much of a deduction in price for a two-car garage would be reasonable? If you know that an additional garage bay, at the $300,000 price point, is worth $10,000, then you could reasonably pay $290,000 for your home and feel confident that you're making a good financial decision.

In essence, this example highlights how we compare properties with a CMA. First, we find similar homes to the property you want to determine a value for; then, we isolate the differences in the homes; then we assign a value for the differences; then finally, we add and subtract those differences to arrive at a justifiable price. Again, this is an art and a science, so we use about three to six properties to compare, and then draw a story out of the analysis.

A CMA price range could be done for any number of features—a mother-in-law unit, a pool, a covered patio, an extra bedroom, and so on. The more unique the feature, the more challenging it will be to price because there will be fewer examples to pull data from. It also gets harder to determine what a buyer might be willing to pay for that feature. For example, you might be willing to pay a premium for a house outfitted with handicap-accessible features because your spouse is in a wheelchair, even if, "officially," a CMA determines that a handicap accessibility feature has a lower value.

Keep in mind that the *condition* of a home will also impact how you evaluate a comparison. For instance, let's say one home has two bathrooms that have both been recently renovated, and another house has three bathrooms, but they're all nasty. That three-bathroom house should not necessarily be valued higher than the two-bathroom house, because of the difference in their condition.

Let's go back to the two-car garage versus three-car garage example we just brought up. The three-car garage house sold for $300,000, and you're trying to figure out what to offer for a similar house with a two-car garage. Suppose that, when you look a little closer, there are a few other differences that should be factored into a price analysis. For instance, the house you like is smaller, but it has a larger lot. The kitchen is average, compared to the three-car-garage house, which has a brand-new kitchen. With all that taken into account, what kind of an offer would make sense for the house you're interested in? We do the math with a CMA.

	Property You're Evaluating	Comparison Property	
		Data	$ Value
Sale Price			$300,000
Square Feet	2,000	2,500	–$15,000
Land Size	.5 Acres	.25 Acres	+$4,000
Garage Size	2 Car	3 Car	–$10,000
Fireplaces	1	1	–
Outdoor Living Space	15' x 15' Patio	15' x 15' Patio	–
Kitchen Condition	Average	Excellent	–$12,000
Bathrooms Condition	Average	Average	–
Total Adjustments			**–$33,000**
Evaluated Property's Adjusted Price			**$267,000**

When you line the features up side-by-side and assign dollar amounts, it's much easier to calculate what a reasonable sale price for a home would be. The adjusted price for the home you're evaluating would fall around $267,000. You can take that number and use it to inform some of the other factors, like market competition, time of year, your own needs, and so on. The CMA provides a clear base line from which you can choose to move up or down.

Given the variabilities present with each unique home, you'll want to consider a CMA in light of the home's "whole package" value. What is this particular home worth to you? What do you believe is fair? Factor in some of your other areas of knowledge: based on your close look at the property, is it a really solid home but listed toward the bottom of the range? It might be under-priced and, therefore, a great deal. Does it seem like a standard home but is listed on the high end of the range? It might be slightly overpriced.

It would be complicated and unnecessary to go through all the details of how a CMA is put together, but the point is not for you to become an expert. The point is for you to evaluate properties with a new lens of awareness. We want you to understand that **properties should be consistent with their comparative market value; if there's inconsistency, you should either pounce on a good deal or negotiate an inflated list price down.** Rather than comparing different homes with a vague sense of "that one felt spacious" versus "that one had nice furniture," we want you to think more critically. What features does this property have, compared to some of the others? What condition is this property in, and how does that compare to some of the others you've seen?

Kevin specializes in completing CMAs for his clients at Exactly, but unfortunately, it's not common practice for real estate agents to complete CMAs for their clients, even though the benefits are obvious. Still, we recommend you ask your agent for one. If you're not content with what they come back to you with, consider asking another agent or seeking out an appraiser, which will give you comparable knowledge. This CMA knowledge—whether it's statistical or coming from an experienced "gut" instinct honed from years of experience—is invaluable.

6. WHAT YOU ATE FOR LUNCH TODAY

We've just listed all kinds of statistical, objective, fact-based data to consider when you're evaluating the list price in your search for a home. But honestly, sometimes it all just comes down to what someone ate for lunch that day.

Let's say your daughter sent you off to work with a big hug, your boss complimented you on your project presentation, it's a gorgeous spring afternoon, and you just had the most delicious burger you can ever remember eating. You attend an open house at two o'clock, feeling awesome. It's a cute house. You like it. You imagine tucking your daughter into her bed in that sweet third bedroom. You imagine doing dates with your spouse at that nearby restaurant and having more of those fantastic burgers. Sold! Why not, right? You're feeling great!

As a buyer, **your emotions will play a significant role in your housing search.** We have often seen buyers make emotional offers in the heat of the moment—maybe they attend a crowded open house, and they see other people making offers. They want it, and they want their offer to win! They might put in an offer that's beyond what they can afford. Later—when the emotional high wears off, they might experience serious buyers' remorse.

Here's the truth: we want you to feel excited about whatever home you buy. We *hope* you experience elation, enthusiasm, and confidence when you find a home you're ready to make an offer on. We want emotions to *accompany* your decision, but we don't want your emotions to *drive* your decision. Keep that investor hat on. Do your homework and get a clear idea about what the home should be worth.

And once you've done that—enjoy the freedom to make the decision that's best for your family. The great-lunch factor isn't always a bad thing. If you wake up, get a promotion at work, your future's bright, and you find a home that's a block away from your best friends, it might be totally appropriate to pay more than the home is worth. You might say, "I'm going to buy this house, and I don't care what the price is. I love it. Today's the day we're making a decision. It's listed for $400,000, and even though I know it's only worth $350,000, I'll take it for $400,000."

You could take yourself through a little checklist:

- Do I have a clear idea of what this home is actually worth?
- Can I comfortably afford what they're asking?
- Do the lifestyle benefits of this property appeal to me enough to pay more than the home is worth?

If the answer to any of those questions is "no," you might want to hold off on making any offers—regardless of how good your burger was. But if you can confidently answer yes to those questions, go for it! Make an offer and feel good about doing so. You're knowledgeable about the property, and you're knowledgeable about what will be best for your family.

KEVIN NARRATES: KNOWLEDGE IS POWER

Years ago, when I was still a grocery chain executive and looking to buy a home for my family, I felt incredibly frustrated by my lack of knowledge in real estate. It wasn't like shopping for a dozen eggs at a grocery store, where I knew exactly what a standard price should be and when to recognize a good deal. I didn't know how to quantify all the different variables I was confronted with. I also didn't feel comfortable taking the word of a real estate agent I'd just met when dealing with so much of my family's money. For two years, I held off on making a real estate decision because I felt like I didn't have enough good information.

My solution was to learn the information myself. I dove into it head on, reading books, learning from experts like Ben, visiting countless properties, and learning the tools. Eventually, I got so into it that I developed an expert pricing method after *becoming* a real estate broker, which I use now with all my clients. Knowledge is powerful, and it's enabled me to make several strategic home buying choices of my own and countless others for my clients.

Recently, I worked with an elderly couple who were interested in buying an investment property. We found a duplex listed at $159,000, which they liked enough to pay the full list price. However, after doing a CMA, I determined that the house was worth about $20,000 less than what it was listed for. Given that data, my clients put in an offer for $139,000. In spite of its inflated list price, I found out the duplex still had multiple offers and went back to my clients to ask if they wanted to increase their offer. They said no. They were primarily concerned with making a smart financial investment and didn't want to commit to $20,000 more than the property was worth. Ultimately, they lost to another buyer—but they felt good about that. The data and knowledge gave them the confidence to walk away, content to wait for a different property that they could purchase for a fairer price.

I hope this knowledge empowers you as much as it empowered me and empowers others. You don't have to become an expert in pricing analysis to still benefit from it as a tool, but you should understand its importance and complexity. Solicit the expertise of your agent to help you understand whether or not a home is priced fairly. Just as a doctor could help you interpret an x-ray, an expert agent can help you see pricing factors and understand the life impact of needed repairs better than you could.

Pricing information will enable you to more effectively scrutinize a list price for its accuracy—not to mention determine if you're working with a savvy, knowledgeable, experienced real estate agent. Remember that buying a home is one of the most significant financial decisions you'll ever make, so it's important to consult expert advice and think through these pricing factors to help you make a good decision.

Pat yourself on the back: if you've made it this far in reading this book, you know *way* more than the average consumer! You're positioned to make a great home-buying decision.

CHAPTER 7

– 🔑 –

NEGOTIATING YOUR OFFER

THE IMPORTANCE OF UNDERSTANDING YOUR SELLER

BEN NARRATES: DO UNTO OTHERS

I met Chris Kim when Kevin took him on as a client to help him sell his family property. The property was stunning—a twenty-eight-acre farm with gorgeous grounds and a house built in 1882. However, it was an expensive property. It also needed a lot of work. Chris secured one buyer, but after the inspection revealed some new issues, the buyer backed out. Kevin knew I might be interested. I was—but not at that price, and not with so much work needed.

Still, I visited the property. I fell in love with it—the place seemed to breathe peace. I also connected well with Chris, particularly over our shared faith. Finally, the two of us got creative. I asked Chris if he would be willing to owner-finance the property to me so that I didn't have to deal with the bank's red tape. He agreed that he would be willing to serve as the bank in this transaction. When I asked him what kind of interest rate he'd like to charge, his response floored me.

"Well, in Deuteronomy, it says you don't charge an interest to a brother. So, the interest rate would be zero." I almost fell out of my chair. I told him, in that case, I wanted to pay the full price.

Later, we discovered that the IRS doesn't allow interest rates to be lower than 1.93 percent, so we revisited our terms. Chris insisted on *dropping* the price so that I would essentially still be paying zero interest. He also asked me what kind of changes I would want to make to the property, and he ended up fixing the barn's foundation before transferring the title to me. It's guys like Chris that have taught me what it means to live honorably. I had never had someone treat me so well in a business transaction. It's inspired me to look for new ways to bless the people I work with.

I now pay Chris a mortgage payment every month and am in the midst of restoring the property to its full potential. Chris and his sisters are gratified to have sold their beloved family farm to someone they knew would carefully restore it, and we continue to enjoy a friendship.

One of the reasons this transaction ended up working out so well for both of us is that **we both took the time to genuinely consider each other's motivations.** Chris knew that I wanted the property but without the complications of a bank rehab loan. I knew that

Chris had an emotional tie to his property and would want to see it restored. Both of us were in a financially strong position: he could afford to owner-finance, and I could afford to fix up the property.

If the situation had been different, the negotiation would have likewise changed. For instance, if Chris's property had already been perfectly restored, he would have been better off selling the property to a buyer with a traditional loan, at max value. Or if the property had been a foreclosure, I would have radically changed my offer, knowing that I was dealing with a bank and all their stipulations.

In Chapter 4, we made the point that the property you want to buy should dictate the financial tool you use. Different properties will require different tools. In the same way, understanding your seller should inform how you approach the negotiation. **Different sellers will require different negotiation approaches.**

All the pricing factors we discussed in the previous chapter should inform your offer—but you also need to understand your seller's motivations. Approaching a seller in the wrong way could actually cause them to drive up their price or result in you losing the property. On the other hand, you could secure a win-win situation for all by thoughtfully considering your seller's motivations when negotiating.

YOUR OWN NEGOTIATION PREP

If you've read our book up to this point and you're now ready to negotiate an offer, you should have crossed these items off your list:

- **You've got a good team in place,** and you can trust them to provide expert help during the negotiation process. Those good team members can help you with all the points listed next.
- **You have evaluated the property** and have a clear understanding of its condition. You know if it's in top condition or if it's in disarray; you know if there's been deferred maintenance and what kind of imminent repairs will be needed.
- **You have a clear idea of what you think the property is worth.** You've determined how the property fits within its current market compared to other similar properties. You understand where other pricing factors are at as well, like the other inventory available, the time of year, interest rates, and so on.
- **You've determined your own bottom line.** You know what you'll be willing to pay up to, and you're also confident about walking away at a certain number.

Why does this last point matter so much? **If you know your bottom line, you'll feel peace however the negotiation works out.**

Let's go back to the Ferrari example we discussed in Chapter 4. If you know a brand new Ferrari is worth $350,000 and you get the opportunity to buy it at $5,000, you would definitely take it. But if somebody offers to sell you a Ferrari for $275,000, you might pause. $275,000 would be a deal for a new Ferrari, but it's still a lot of money.

Maybe you decide at $275,000, you still want it, but at $280,000, you reach your tipping point—that's your bottom line. If you don't get it for $275,000, you can walk away feeling perfectly happy.

We don't want you to feel buyer's remorse. We also don't want you to feel haunted by "the one that got away." If you determine your bottom line and stick with it, you'll be able to bid up to that line for a property you know you want. Then, if you win the offer, you can feel great! But if you get outbid, you can feel peace walking away.

Myth: If I find the perfect house, I need to do whatever is humanly possible to make that perfect house mine.

Actually, there is no perfect house and this rationale could lead you to make reckless decisions. There will *always* be another property you will get excited about! Let us repeat: **THERE WILL ALWAYS BE ANOTHER HOUSE *THAT YOU WILL GET EXCITED ABOUT!***

It's common for first-time buyers to not have a clear internal sense of their bottom line. We sometimes see inexperienced buyers make an offer that's slightly less than their line, lose the bid, and kick themselves for missing out on the house. Often, those same buyers will end up overcompensating the next time and offer *more* than what they're comfortable with because they don't want that bad feeling again of missing out on something good—except now they have a *new* bad feeling of committing to something they can't afford or don't really want.

Before stepping up to negotiations, identify your own clear bottom line. If you're buying with a spouse or partner, make sure you're on the same page. You'll feel more confident and less stressed if you do so.

HOW THE NEGOTIATING PROCESS WORKS

Let's assume you're a buyer working with an agent. Your agent writes up an offer, then presents that directly to the seller or the seller's agent. If the seller is an entity, like the government (e.g., if the property is being sold by HUD, Housing Urban Development) or a bank, the offer is presented to their representative. If you're not working with an agent, you would negotiate directly with the seller or seller's agent.

Typically, an offer goes back and forth a few times until both parties agree on all the particulars and contingencies. (We'll talk more about contingencies in the next chapter.) At that point, there's a housing inspection, which usually ushers in a second round of negotiations as needed repairs are discovered. Usually, buyers have the option to either ask the seller to fix the issue, drop the price, or they can exit the deal if the inspection uncovers major repairs and a solution cannot be reached.

COMMON POINTS BUYERS CAN NEGOTIATE[9]

- **House price:** We recommend making an offer that reflects the work you've done evaluating the property and price analysis—not just starting with the list price.
- **Closing costs:** Sellers can pay a portion or all of the buyers' closing costs, dependent on the buyers' financing. This can reduce the buyers' out-of-pocket expenses. This is a negotiable item.

---

9   Dellitt, Julia. "5 Things To Negotiate When You Buy Your First House."
Forbes. Forbes Magazine, June 21, 2018. https://www.forbes.com/sites/
juliadellitt/2018/06/20/5-things-to-negotiate-when-you-buy-your-first-house/#2cf9e1d32d0e.

- **Repairs (negotiated after inspection):** Sellers can either make the repair themselves or offer to drop the price for buyers.
- **Home warranty premium:** Buyers can ask sellers to pay this for the next year after the date of purchase.
- **Prorations:** Buyers can ask sellers to pay the prorated cost of utilities, housing insurance, HOA fees, and so on, based on the date of possession.
- **Closing/Possession dates:** Flexibility on when the new buyer takes possession of the house can be helpful for both sellers and buyers. Sellers may need a few extra weeks to get into a new home, or buyers may want to finish up a lease or close on their former house first. Buyers can also ask sellers to pay the penalty for breaking their lease early.
- **Furniture, cosmetic updates, etc.:** Buyers may choose to buy some of the seller's furniture and/or amenities. They can also ask for certain cosmetic updates to be made, like paint colors or new flooring.
- **Title/Escrow Company:** Buyers can request that a specific title/escrow company handle the transaction. The title/escrow company handles all of the final paperwork and the money, so it's important to work with a good one. In certain areas, many real estate agents own title companies and receive money from those companies. If you know that the seller's agent owns a title/escrow company, proceed with caution—there might be a conflict of interest, and you should ensure the title/escrow company is good at what they do.

DON'T DO IT THIS WAY

Negotiations are often fast and dirty, which is not what we'd recommend. We often see buyers purchase a home in a fever-pitch of high emotion. Their agent eggs them on—"Go for it!"—and they write a full-price offer. Maybe they ask the seller to pay their $7,000 closing costs. If the seller counter-offers and asks to split the closing costs at $3,500, the buyers might think, "We got $3,500 off! We did such a good job negotiating." They're convinced they got a deal and saved money—even if they offered way more than they should have.

This is not a great way to go about negotiating. Instead, you should negotiate from a position of, "What is this house *worth*?" If that's your primary question, you'll be incentivized to get informed, be thoughtful, and hold your own bottom line. Instead, we often see buyers negotiate with the primary question, "How can I *get* this house?" If that's your leading thought, you're far more likely to be swayed by emotions and pay more than you may need to. People offer way more than they should all the time.

Myth: The most important consideration when buying a home is, "How can I get this property?"

Actually, that consideration is more likely to cause you to make a rash decision that you may later regret. Instead, consider, "What is this house *worth?*"

A RECOMMENDED APPROACH TO NEGOTIATIONS

Let's say you're sipping a beverage on your couch at night, looking through listings on Zillow. A new property catches your eye. You open it. Good square footage, decent price, it's in one of your top school districts, updated kitchen, and—oh my gosh, look at the back patio! You've just successfully completed Step One.

- **Step One:** Find a listing that appeals to you. (Check!)
- **Step Two:** Arrange a time to go look at it. Evaluate the property and form an opinion of what the house *is* and what it *isn't*.

> **Tip:** Remember to look at plenty of other houses along the way—it will help you enormously to have a strong basis of comparison! In addition, make sure that you are comparing "apples to apples" and looking at homes in the same area.

- **Step Three:** Try to get an idea of who the seller might be and guess at their motivations for selling the house. Understanding your seller will help you with Step Four.
- **Step Four:** Make a plan that considers your seller's motivations and determine if you should move fast or slow—we'll talk more about this in a moment.
- **Step Five:** Make a calculated offer that is mindful of your own bottom line.

If you determine a house is worth $475,000, then offer $475,000. If someone else buys it for $529,000, then that's fine: walk away.

Remember—**THERE WILL ALWAYS BE ANOTHER HOUSE YOU GET EXCITED ABOUT!** Always. If you have the time and flexibility to be patient, you will eventually find a great house at an undervalued price. Get preapproved, familiarize yourself with lots of similar properties, and learn what a fair pricing is for similar listings—then, you'll be prepared to jump quickly if a gem of a property comes along.

OTHER NEGOTIATION FACTORS

Our biggest advice to you when sitting down to negotiate is to understand your seller—we'll devote a lot of time to that topic in a moment. But before we get there, we have a few other preliminary tips for ways to understand the negotiation process.

First, **the list price is basically irrelevant.** It's useful in that it might grab your attention if it's within a certain range you're looking at, but then you should basically disregard the list price completely. Come up with your own estimate based on doing your due diligence and getting very familiar with your targeted area. You might notice that the pictures posted with a certain property don't seem to match their list price. Look into that: are you dealing with an outlier? Could this be an opportunity? When you come to the negotiating table, make an appropriate offer, and back up your number with data and facts.

With that said, though, **market conditions should be at the forefront of your mind when approaching negotiations, along with understanding your seller.** If it's a strong seller's market and a seller has ten other buyers they could sell their house to, you'll want to break out every negotiation trick in the book. You'll need to plan to meet or exceed their asking price. It will be even more important for you to consider the seller's motivations. You'll also want to use some of the other tools we've suggested, like non-refundable earnest money or flexibility on the date of possession. On the other hand, if it's a buyer's market, you'll have much more negotiating power and could ask for things like help with closing costs, etc.

Physical repairs will significantly impact your negotiation

style. The physical quality of a house will determine everything from the kind of buyers it attracts to the financial tools available, to the list price. If you find a house in great condition, you should expect lots of competing buyers and the need to pay more; with that extra money, you're buying peace of mind and quality of life. (No tedious bathroom renovations needed!) This house will serve you less as a financial investment and more as a dwelling that serves your lifestyle. On the other hand, if you're interested in a house that needs a lot of repairs, you might be able to buy it for cheap and turn that into a good financial investment, but it will also require much more of your work. You'll be more limited in terms of what financial tools are available to buy it, and it will require more of your time—likely throughout the buying process and afterward, as you begin to fix it up.

The time of year will impact your negotiating power. If you're buying a house in peak season, you'll have less negotiating power. If the seller doesn't like something about your offer, there will almost certainly be another buyer in line behind you who will snatch it up. If you find a great deal in a busy time, make sure you offer them the right price; otherwise, you'll miss out. On the flip side, if you find a house during the offseason, there's likely to be less competition, and you might be able to find a better deal. You can think of this in terms of booking a vacation: if you want to travel during the high season, you need to be prepared to pay higher rates. If you go in the offseason, you might have to deal with bad weather or other inconveniences, but you'll get lower prices.

Your ability to close fast could make you a more attractive buyer. Some sellers have flexibility in terms of when they close.

If you come to them with a VA loan (translation: will take a longer time to close because of the rigorous inspection) and offer \$420,000 for a house listed at \$410,000, that flexible seller might like your generous offer. They don't mind waiting forty-five days for your VA loan to come through. But let's say that seller is in a hurry to close. They might want the money as soon as possible so they can buy a new house. In that case, a buyer who's made a \$400,000 offer with cash who can close in two weeks might win the bid. This is one good reason to get preapproved before making an offer and making sure you've got a mortgage lender who can respect the timing of closing dates—you're in a better position to close quickly.

Offering a seller flexibility on your possession date could make you a more attractive buyer. Think of a family with three kids and a dog who's preparing to move out of the home they've been in for the last decade. If they get an offer for \$355,000, but the buyer wants to take possession of the house on the closing date, that might feel stressful for them. That would mean *they* have to be prepared to close on a new house on that same day, which is a lot to coordinate; if they can't do that, they might need to find a month-to-month rental to live at in the meantime, which means moving twice—big, fat pain. Those sellers might be more inclined to go with an offer of \$350,000 that gives them an extra month to stay in their house between the closing date and the date of possession. That extra time will better enable them to find a new house, pack up their stuff, and so on. They won't have to find a temporary dwelling to move to in between their two residences. That convenience could be worth a lot.

Asking for closing cost assistance makes you a less attractive

buyer. Closing costs cover the money paid to the title company, the bank, the appraiser, and so on. Buyers and sellers can choose to negotiate who pays for what service, or they can agree to split the costs. This is not uncommon, and many buyers genuinely need this help to see the deal through. However, asking for this assistance will make you a less attractive buyer.

Typically, if you ask for closing cost assistance, the implication is that you can't afford to buy the house if you *don't* get that assistance. That could cast doubt on your ability to get approved with your financing and makes you seem like a less savvy buyer. It also means the seller gets less money. On the other hand, if you don't ask for closing cost assistance, you present yourself as a buyer who can fully afford to see this process through. If you're looking for a reduction in price, you might be better off asking for a repair cost credit after the inspection. In that case, you'd actually be perceived as a more generous buyer, since you're making it easier for the seller to get through the transaction and move on, rather than needing to make a repair.

The more earnest money you put down, the more attractive your offer will be. Earnest money is basically a deposit on your down payment; it's a way to seal your status as the chosen offer. Earnest money is generally assumed to be refundable (in the event that the deal falls through for a legal contingency, per the contract) but can be designated as non-refundable. Non-refundable earnest money means guaranteed money to the seller, regardless of how the rest of the process goes. Now, if two buyers are competing for a highly desirable house, and one person offers $1,000 earnest money, and the other offers $5,000 non-refundable earnest money—which offer do you think the seller will accept?

They're going to take that $5,000 offer, especially because that non-refundable status implies the buyer is in a strong financial position and will come through on the rest of the financing.

If you know you're dealing with a hot market, are fully confident in the quality of a house's physical condition *and* your ability to purchase it, then you can use this tool of non-refundable earnest money to make your offer especially appealing. If your assumptions about the property are correct, you'll win the offer, subtract your earnest money from your down payment, and get a great house. There's a risk, of course, if the inspection reveals that the house is a lemon—then, you're either stuck with it, or you lose that earnest money. Also, if you cannot purchase it due to a financing snag, the seller keeps the earnest money. You're taking a risk when you offer non-refundable earnest money, but it's one that can pay off if you know your stuff.

But how do you know when to offer flexibility with possession dates? How do you know whether or not you should promise to close fast? How do you know if you should ask a seller to make a repair versus drop their price? All of that is determined by our final and most important point: you need to understand the kind of seller you're dealing with.

THE IMPORTANCE OF UNDERSTANDING YOUR SELLER

Imagine, for a moment, that you are a seller. For the last ten years, you've been living in your home. It's where you brought home all your kids from the hospital. It's where your dog is buried. You updated the kitchen three years ago and still can't get over how much you love it—especially that new backsplash. This house contains so many memories for you. You know it's time to say goodbye, but it feels like losing a friend.

Now, let's say a buyer makes an offer. It's a generous offer—but they mention plans to tear up the backyard. (The backyard where Murphy is buried!) They want you to paint the bedrooms gray. (Your kids' bedrooms!) Then, they ask that you lower the price so they can redo the kitchen. "I'm not going to be able to live with that backsplash," the woman quips. (GAH!)

Would you be tempted to walk away from these obnoxious buyers entirely? Ask them for more money? Recruit another buyer? Maybe not, but you sure wouldn't feel good about selling to them.

As a buyer, you do not want to put yourself in this position. If you're buying a house from a person, be thoughtful in how you talk about their home. Make that person feel good about selling to you! If you're buying from a bank, on the other hand—say whatever you want. They don't care. Understanding your seller will also help inform your strategy on how fast you should move and what kind of points you focus your negotiations on.

So how do you learn about your seller? Their property will give you clues. Often, the external condition of their property represents what is internal in the seller and can therefore help you determine your negotiation approach. We'll give you some examples.

COMMON SELLERS, COMMON MOTIVATIONS

Let's first take a look at some of the common sellers that fall under the category of "Real People." We'll talk about their common reasons for selling and how that should impact your negotiation strategy.

When You're Dealing with a Person

- **The Martha Stewart—a meticulous homeowner.** Martha Stewart's beautifully maintained home represents her high value for the quality. She will ask for an exact price for her home and will not suffer fools.
  - *Negotiation Strategy:* Don't mess around with the meticulous homeowner. Give her the price she asks. If the inspection reveals an issue with the furnace, ask her (politely) if she'll replace the furnace, but don't ask her to drop the price. Also—don't forget to wipe your shoes on the mat and mind your manners.
- **The Big Lebowski—sloppy homeowner.** Home ownership is not a big part of the Dude's value system, and that's reflected in his dilapidated property. He's going to be very willing to negotiate with you on price.
  - *Negotiation Strategy:* Make sure, first of all, that this is a property you actually want. Do your homework, identify the needed repairs, and negotiate the price down. You probably want to ask for a reduced price rather than ask the Dude to make the repairs. There's a good chance he might call in his buddies to give it the ol' college try and do it on the cheap. Best to take care of the repairs yourself.
- **The Taylors: Tim the Tool Man, Jill, and their three sons— family homeowners.** When you walk through this home, you see family pictures on the wall and lots of cute decorations. You're probably dealing with family homeowners. Assume

these sellers have spent many sweet years in this home and have worked hard to make it nice for their family. They care about the kind of person who buys their home—ideally, they'd like to sell it to someone they believe will care for it the way they have. They care about the money they get, but their emotions are also involved.

- *Negotiation Strategy:* Write a letter to Tim and Jill and rave about how much you love their home. Make a financially appropriate offer that recognizes the good condition of the house; your letter may lead them to take your offer over someone else's. Don't insult them or the house! (Tim the Tool Man Taylor would not stand for that.)

- **LeBron James—job transfer.** This house is empty when you walk through it, a sign that someone has already moved into a new place. If you find out that the house has been sitting on the market for a while, you might be dealing with a job transfer. These sellers are usually financially stable and more interested in getting the house sold than getting top dollar.

  - *Negotiation Strategy:* Particularly if the house has been on the market for a while, feel free to make a corrective offer. Job transfer sellers are more likely to budge; they've already moved on, and they have a good job—they're going to care less about a few thousand dollars. Sometimes, if a company has transferred its employee, the company actually buys the property. In those cases, an accepted offer will have nothing to do with emotions and everything to do with dollars and cents.

- **Brad and Angelina—divorce.** You're walking through a beautiful four-bedroom home that looks almost as though it's been converted to a bachelor pad—lots of rooms are empty, and it's a little messy. What's going on here? There's a good chance you're dealing with a divorcing couple. Negotiations with divorcing couples tend to go one of two ways. If it's an amicable split and they each have their own careers, they probably just want to move on quickly. They might be willing to sell it for a deal—in those cases, divorcing sellers can work out well for buyers. However, if it's a messy split, proceed with caution! Negotiations under normal circumstances are already challenging—the seller wants more, you want less, and so on. Disagreement is normal. But if you add a third voice of disagreement to the process, you could find yourself in the middle of a nasty, toxic extrication. Particularly if the couple refuses to communicate directly, the entire process can get bogged down as each point of negotiation is volleyed back and forth between lawyers. Yeesh.

- ○ *Negotiation Strategy.* Prepare yourself for a potentially long, frustrating process, or consider walking away and finding another house entirely. Do your best to keep the peace and be patient. If repairs are needed, don't ask them to do it—ask for a price reduction instead. There's a chance things might go quickly and easily; if that's the case, breathe a sigh of relief!

- **Yorick's Family Members—death:** Yorick has recently passed away, and this house is listed as part of his estate. Like divorces, estate sales can often go one of two ways. Most of the time, family members are agreeable. Often, they don't care about getting top dollar—they just want to liquidate the estate quickly so they can grieve and move on. Other times, however, the family is squabbling over money and they want to get max value for the home. In either case, they're unlikely to want to do any repairs.

- ○ *Negotiation Strategy:* Approach these sellers honorably. You might see that the property needs work; if so, communicate that in polite, factual terms. Explain that the property will take this much money to be restored, which is why you're offering a lower price. Offset those remarks by discussing the intangibles of the property—you love the location, you could see your kids climbing the trees in the backyard, and so on. Consider writing a letter explaining why you love the house, why you're making the offer you are, and what repairs might be needed. Remember that the family is likely to want to sell to someone who will take care of the property.

- **Chip and Joanna—flippers.** If you find a home that's been carefully flipped at a high-quality level, that's one of the only times you should consider paying full price. However, be wary of home flips. Since home flipping is a business, many home flippers are interested in maximum profit—which means doing the flip as cheaply as possible. In that case, steer clear: you might be buying a pig with lipstick. Home flippers will also be shrewd negotiators—remember, they're interested in making a profit, so they may nickel and dime you. Sometimes, a flipped home sits on the market for a while. If that's the case, you can assume that the home flipper is getting increasingly desperate to sell the property as it costs them money to hold onto it.
  - *Negotiation Strategy:* Your ability to evaluate property in a home flip scenario is going to be critical. If the home has been beautifully restored, make a full price offer. However, if you can tell the home flip has mostly prioritized the shiny, pretty things, either walk away or negotiate *down* and negotiate robustly. Often, home flips are listed at vastly inflated prices—the home flippers may easily try

to get an extra $40,000 if they can find a naive buyer who will go for it, so don't get taken in. Every so often, you'll find a home flip that looks halfway done. In those cases, you're usually dealing with someone who found a good deal, tried to flip it, got in over their head, and now they're desperate to unload it. In those cases, you might have found a viable option—you can probably buy the house for a deal and finish fixing it up the way you want to.

When You're Dealing with an Entity

Sometimes, your seller isn't a person but an entity—the bank, the government, or an auction. So how do you approach negotiations with them? With entities, it's far less important to consider emotions. Instead, it's mostly going to come down to math.

- **The Bank**: The bank has a collection of properties in its portfolio, which have usually been collected through foreclosures. They want to manage how much money they've extended in loans and credits versus how much capital they have in hand. The bank won't want to do any repairs, so if there are any problems, they're going to sell it at a below-market value; they'll ask any buyer to sign a form saying whatever problems exist are the buyer's problems and not theirs.
  - *Negotiation Strategy:* Successfully buying a bank property will often come down to your financial tool. Banks will be looking for a buyer that has a flexible tool—preferably your cash or someone else's. If the house has problems that prevent financing, a bank is unlikely to choose a buyer that's coming to them with a loan from another bank because they'll know the house is unlikely to pass that

bank's inspection. They'd rather offload the property to a cash buyer for a low price. If you fall in love with a bank-owned property, see if you can secure flexible financing for the short term, and then refinance the home with a traditional loan once you've made some repairs.

- **The Government:** The government sells properties (usually HUD properties) primarily via algorithmic tools. They use real estate agents who give an opinion of what the property's list price should be. They then use an algorithm for what percentage of that list price they'd be willing to sell that property for. If the property sits on the market, the government drops the list price and adjusts the algorithm. It's literally just about math for the government.

  ○ *Negotiation Strategy:* Like a bank, the government won't want to do any repairs, so don't ask for them; instead, ask for a lower price. You'll want to make an offer that's within their algorithm, which means you may need to stick relatively close to their list price. The government may be less flexible with closing dates/dates of possession.

- **An Auction:** Homes are put up for auction when someone wants to just get rid of them. The price is determined by the market represented by the other bidders who show up. They don't require an inspection; they're sold as-is. If you want to buy a house via auction, you might get a deal but make sure you do your homework ahead of time and learn what kind of a property you're really dealing with.

  ○ *Negotiation Strategy:* There is none! You're simply bidding against whoever else showed up. In our area, if an auction is scheduled on a day that happens to have a big snowstorm, you might only have a few people show up. Your chances of getting the property at a good price increase.

If many people show up and it's a competitive property, don't let your emotions carry you away in the heat of the bidding—remember your bottom line.

BEN NARRATES: DON'T NEGOTIATE ALONE

The two of us are experts in our fields and have years of experience buying and selling properties. In spite of that, we still regularly consult each other during negotiations. It's incredibly valuable to get others' insight, wisdom, and input into how to handle a deal. Kevin is often able to give me expertise on pricing, and I'm able to perceive details about the property or sellers that are also incredibly valuable.

So, don't negotiate alone. Lean on the expertise of your real estate agent. Get advice from other people you trust, especially people familiar with building construction, the real estate market, and financing. Even friends with good abilities to read people can help you better understand your seller.

Think of this as a team sport. For the last several months, I've been coaching my daughter's basketball team. It's been a slow learning process. Every practice, we work on the basics like dribbling, passing the ball, moving to an open place, and so on. They've progressed—when we first started, many of them never even had a concept of how to do offense. But at their first tournament game, they took all the elements of the game they'd learned and put them together. And they were dynamite! They dominated the other team. The girls could sense that they had put all the pieces together and had played a real basketball game.

That's the kind of synergy that can come when you put all these negotiation tools together and step onto the court. When you combine your skills in evaluating the property, the pricing, the market factors, understanding your seller, the appropriate negotiation strategy, and financial tool—that's a dynamite combination. When you bring in the strengths of your other team members, you're ready to play a hell of a game.

THE HEART OF THE MATTER

People matter just as much as finances when it comes to successful negotiation. Understand your seller's motivations and speak to those, pursuing a win-win outcome. Make sure you also know what your bottom line is and hold it; that way, you can feel peace with whatever outcome arrives.

CHAPTER 8

- 🔑 -

CONTRACT TO CLOSE

SUCCESSFULLY NAVIGATING THE EMOTIONAL RIDE

TO BACK OUT, OR NOT TO BACK OUT?

It was not the news they wanted to hear. The inspector explained to Gina and John that there seemed to be foundation issues—likely, an entire foundation wall needed to be replaced. They were crushed. They'd been so sure this was their perfect home. It was in the neighborhood they wanted, it was in their price range, and they'd already envisioned how they could turn the fourth bedroom into John's home office. Plus, they'd put down $2,000 in non-refundable earnest money.

"You've come this far," their agent said. "This foundation issue can be fixed. It's not that big of a deal." When Gina and John indicated that they might want to back out, the agent reminded them that they'd lose their earnest money.

"It would suck to just lose that money," John said to Gina.

Gina protested. "I don't feel good moving forward. And besides, how much money would we have to spend fixing that wall?"

That's when their agent got manipulative. "If you back out of this, the seller can sue you for specific performance. You're going to have to pay a ton in legal fees just to get it resolved, and you're still going to have to buy this house. It's really probably best to just go ahead."

We've seen and heard numerous stories similar to Gina and John's, many of which end with a buyer moving forward, even with major reservations. Maybe it's because they don't want to start the process over again, or maybe it's because they think they'll lose money. Sometimes, timing is an issue; if Gina and John are selling their current house at the same time they're buying a new one, they may feel like they *have* to move forward with this problematic house because they don't have time to get under contract with a new place before their current house closes. Or—yikes—maybe it's because their agent or the seller resorts to scare tactics and manipulation.

Myth: Once a house is under contract, you're locked in.

No. If you realize during the contract-to-close stretch that the property has significant problems, it's okay to back out; that's what the contingencies are there for. Even if you go outside the contingencies, you can often still exit the deal by giving up your earnest money (even if it was supposed to be refundable). It might be better to lose some money in the short term than commit to a bad house. Please note, this is contract specific; in some rare cases, if there are no contingencies in the contract, then you *might* actually be locked in. Although we have never seen any buyer be forced to purchase a house, we recommend getting advice from an attorney if you should find yourself in that unlikely scenario.

During the time period between the contract to close, circumstances can change. New information can come. There might be an issue revealed with the inspection or from the title company; the appraisal value might come in significantly different than your purchase price; some abrupt change might occur in the economy. Even your own finances can change. We knew one buyer who lost his job during the contract to close and didn't tell the bank; he assumed he could find a new job quickly or get hired back. Unfortunately, he didn't and ended up needing to foreclose on his brand new house. You don't have to be afraid to walk away if you know it isn't right.

Good news, though: *most of the time*, buyers successfully get through contract to close and are able to move into their new home. Any issues revealed during the inspection are minor enough to fix quickly. The appraisal comes through at the right number, and the title is transferred without an issue—it all works out! And frankly, if you've read this far and applied most of our suggestions, you're far more likely to sail through these last steps and have all your good decisions confirmed. (High five!)

Even in those best-case scenarios, though, buyers should prepare for an emotional roller coaster. Getting under contract is a little like reaching mile twenty in a 26.2-mile marathon. You've come a long way, but you're not at the finish line yet, and these last six miles will be draining.

By giving you a heads up about this emotional ride, we're hoping to better equip you to get through it. Think of us as cheering for you along the sidelines at mile twenty-one, passing you a cup of Gatorade and an energy gel. You can do it!

WHAT IT'S LIKE AND WHY IT'S STRESSFUL

First comes **excitement.** The sellers select your offer, and you sign the papers; the house is under contract. Pour the wine to celebrate!

Then comes **anxiety.** Within a week's time, you start to feel doubts. A new listing pops up on Zillow that looks like it might have been a better option for you. You wonder—did I really buy the right house? Will there be something wrong with the property? The inspection reveals needed repairs, which causes new waves of anxiety. This house has issues! Maybe not huge issues, but still—issues!

There might be a momentary pause where things **even out** a little. You negotiate with the seller over how to address the needed repairs brought up by the inspection and convince yourself you're still getting a good house.

Then comes **stress.** The realization hits: *I have to move.* You always "knew" that you'd have to move, but now you actually have to pack. Your kids start to freak out because you're freaking out. You're getting bombarded with calls and emails from various people associated with the transaction, asking for paperwork and documentation. Meanwhile, you're calling different moving companies for quotes and trying to keep everything straight. You and your spouse get into arguments over who needs to do what.

You feel **doubts and insecurity** approaching the appraisal. You think you're paying an appropriate amount for this home, but what if the appraisal determines the home value is worth way less than what you're paying for it? Are you making a bad investment?

There's often **impatience.** Once the inspection and appraisal pass, there are two weeks or more where you're simply waiting for the closing to happen. Sometimes a weird issue comes up, and it takes extra time; your stress spikes again, and you need to juggle new logistics with the change in timing. You're ready to get to your new place and move on. When will it end?

When it does finally end, you're **exhausted.** You've spent the last thirty to forty-five days uprooting your life and your finances. You're about to write one of the biggest checks of your life, and you don't even know exactly how much it's going to be. They've explained the million little fees, but even so, you don't understand what they're all for. You're not even sure if you *should* pay all of them—maybe you're supposed to negotiate again? It's hard to care at this point.

Finally, there's **relief.** The end comes, you sign the papers, it all gets filed, and you write your big check. You move into your new place, and life can start again. Pour another glass of wine!

At that point, it's not uncommon for the cycle to start again. First comes **excitement** over being in the new place, then **anxiety** as you discover new issues that weren't uncovered by the inspection, then **stress** with getting the house fixed up and furnished, and so on...

> **Tip:** Moving is supposedly one of life's top five most stressful experiences, right up there with job loss, major injury or illness, the death of a loved one, a new baby, and divorce.[10] Cut yourself some slack if you're on edge—this is hard!

Moving also has the amazing ability to trigger you on a deeper level, unearthing psychological stuff you may not have even known was buried. Was there financial stress in your childhood? There's a good chance that this huge financial transaction will stir up some of that ancient angst, making you sweat over whether or not you got a good enough deal. Did you grow up taking responsibility for things you didn't need to take responsibility for, like your parents' problems? You may end up feeling responsible for any hitches in the closing process, like an issue with the title transfer that has nothing to do with you. Big life events in your present tend to uproot the big life stuff from your past, causing new stress and conflict.

But believe it or not—this is normal. If you feel all of these emotions, it doesn't mean you're crazy or losing it: it means you're feeling exactly what you should be feeling in the midst of an incredibly stressful life experience. This *is* an emotional experi-

---

10 UHBlog. "The Top 5 Most Stressful Life Events." University Hospitals. The Science of Health. The Art of Compassion. University Hospitals, July 2, 2015. https://www.uhhospitals.org/Healthy-at-UH/articles/2015/07/the-top-5-most-stressful-life-events.

ence. Prepare to manage those emotions and do your best. That's all you can do.

THE CONTRACT TO CLOSE PROCESS: BEHIND THE SCENES

By the time you get a home under contract, you've already run those first twenty miles: you've found your real estate agent, gotten preapproved, looked at properties, made an offer, negotiated, and now—your contract has been accepted!

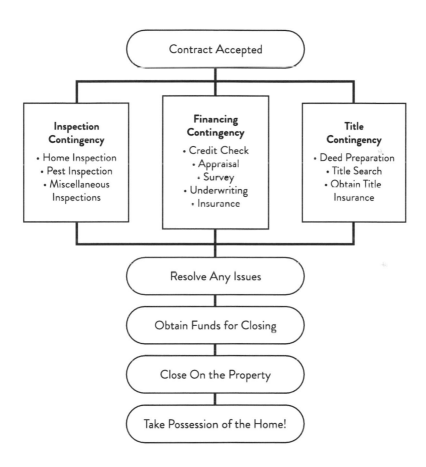

So, what happens next? About the point where this diagram explodes outward on both sides is where you're at now, once your contract has been accepted. There's a whole lot of people who get involved, moving a whole lot of pieces at once.

This nice little explosion can be summed up under the title "Remove Contingencies." What does that mean? In between contract to close, there are basically three areas where something can go massively wrong and tank the deal entirely:

1. **The Inspection Contingency** (e.g., There's a foundation wall that needs to be replaced, so you back out of the deal.)
2. **The Financing Contingency** (e.g., For some reason, your loan can't be approved as planned, and the bank won't go through with your financing.) NOTE: this financing piece is not relevant if you are buying with cash.
3. **The Title Contingency** (e.g., It turns out the seller doesn't *actually* own the house because of an issue with a title transfer on a previous sale, which means they can't sell it to you. Usually, these issues can be fixed, but it may take some extra time.)

Most buyers write their offer **contingent upon these three items.** In other words, they don't have to proceed forward with the deal if one or more of these items are not to their satisfaction. Sellers have the option to include contingencies as well for their own protection; the three just mentioned are the buyers' contingencies.

You could choose to opt out of any one of those contingencies. For instance, you might be so desperate to buy a particular house that you commit to buying it regardless of what the inspection reveals and opt out of the physical inspection contingency. You *could* do this—but why would you?

Generally speaking, we recommend having all three of these contingencies in place in your contract. That way, you commit to buying the house if, and only if, all three of those areas work out. These contingencies offer protection to you. It's rare that you would be in a position to not need the information and/or safeguards put in place by these three conditions.

If all goes well, you will see almost none of this bustling activity exploding on either side of the diagram and can simply focus on packing up your current life and getting ready for the move. If something goes awry, however, you can expect to hear about it. We want to give you a frame of reference so that you have a way of understanding what's happening behind the scenes during the contract to close process—just in case there's an issue, or you want to understand a delay.

THE PHYSICAL INSPECTION

You'll hire an inspector to *conduct an inspection* shortly after getting the house under contract. A third-party inspector will go out to the property and tell you everything that's wrong with it. You should plan to meet them out at the property, and if your real estate agent is worth their salt, they'll meet you there, too.

The inspector will walk through the house with you and give you a report of everything that's wrong. You should not be concerned if the inspector finds something that needs to be fixed because that's literally the inspector's job.

Tip: There will *always* be something wrong revealed by the home inspection. A home inspector will find issues with every single property, even on brand new houses.

However, you *should* be concerned if the inspector finds an issue that changes the property's value. Are there safety issues, structural issues, problems you couldn't see when walking through the house that will affect your ability to inhabit it? If significant problems like these are discovered, you can back out of the deal because of the inspection contingency.

If the issues revealed by the inspection do not change your desire to go forward, you should *resolve any issues* through further talks and negotiations with the seller. You have the option to renegotiate the purchase price and/or arrange for the seller to make those repairs. (Remember to consider your seller's motivations when having this conversation, as discussed in our previous chapter.)

Remember that certain loan products (especially FHA and VA loans) will require a more rigorous inspection focused on the property's functionality. If you're buying a property with cash, you don't need to get an inspection, but you may still choose to do so if you have questions about the quality of the property.

THE FINANCING

The bank is going to complete five main checks to obtain and approve your mortgage financing: your credit check, the property's appraisal and survey, the underwriting, and the insurance.

OBTAIN MORTGAGE FINANCING

1. Credit check
2. Appraisal
3. Survey
4. Underwriting
5. Insurance

As you can imagine, lots of the people bustling around doing work for your transaction are connected to one of these five tasks.

The bank does all this flurry of activity because they want to know two things: number one, are *you* safe to lend money to? And number two, is this *property* safe to lend money *on?* The bank doesn't want to lend to someone who will eventually default, and they especially don't want to get stuck with a house they can't sell in the unfortunate case the borrower does default. Hence, the bustling. The financing could fall apart on either issue (you or the property), which is why the contingency in the contract matters. You don't want to commit to paying a mortgage if the bank takes back their offer to give you a loan.

So, what are all these people doing? First, the bank will do a **credit check.** Essentially, the bank is going to look into your finances to make sure you have as much money as you've indicated and that you can be trusted to pay a mortgage loan. Is your income stream steady, or did you lose your job? Is your debt-to-income ratio the same as when you got preapproved, or did you go finance a new car after your offer was accepted, and now the debt-to-income ratio has wildly changed? Has your credit score changed for any reason? These are the questions they're looking to answer. Ideally, they want to discover that you are exactly as qualified to pay a mortgage loan as when they preapproved you.

> **Tip:** After your offer is accepted, don't go out and spend a lot of money! Buying new furniture or a new car could jeopardize your financing. After your offer is accepted, think of yourself as participating in the kids' playground game "freeze tag." In that game, when someone tags you, you stop running and freeze in place. That's essentially what you should do with your finances. Getting under contract is the moment when you get tagged—now, freeze! Try not to cause any ripples to your financial picture until your transaction has *closed*.

While certain bank employees are checking *you* out, other employees are checking out the property. Mainly, the appraiser and surveyor: they collectively evaluate the property and make sure it's worth extending a loan on.

The appraisal determines how much the property is actually worth. The appraiser will go to the property, do a thorough examination of its condition, functionality, and quality, and then consider other market factors. They'll do a report similar to a comparative market analysis but to an even greater depth. At the end of that report, the appraisal will determine an amount that the property is worth; they'll tell the bank, "If you loan [this] amount of money, it's a good loan."

> **How are the inspection and the appraisal different?**
>
> **The inspection report is for the buyer** and mainly concerns the condition of the physical property and spotlights needed repairs. **The appraisal is for the bank** and concerns the *value* of the property. Although it

considers the property's condition, it's concerned primarily with what other homes in the area are selling for to ensure this home could sell for a comparable price, in case the borrower had to foreclose and the bank was stuck with selling the property. An appraisal is the bank's own due diligence to ensure that they are comfortable with the risk of the loan amount.

Now, how can the appraisal mess up your financing? Let's say you're buying a house for $500,000, but the appraisal comes back and says it's only worth $480,000. That appraisal value means that the bank is only willing to lend on $480,000—not $500,000. If you still want to buy that house and you know the seller won't go for less than $500,000, you would need to come up with the remaining $20,000 on your own. If you can't, your financing falls apart and you must exit the deal via the financing contingency.

Sometimes, it's possible to negotiate with the seller to close the gap between the purchase price and appraisal. For instance, if the appraisal reveals that the house is on a flood plain, the seller might be willing to drop their price. (Although at that point—do you still want it?) However, if you're in a hot market with lots of buyers, or if there's rapid appreciation in your area that outpaces the bank's estimates—you might simply need to scrounge up some additional cash to make up for the difference in appraisal versus purchase price.

The surveyor examines the land that the building is on and clarifies what you're buying. For instance, the property description tion may note that the lot is on half an acre and will give specifics on where the property begins and ends. The surveyor confirms that the land matches the legal description and that the house sits on the land described. They'll make sure, for instance, that your garage isn't actually on your neighbor's property. If that was the case, you wouldn't end up buying your own garage, and that would be a problem. They're also going to check that none of your neighbor's stuff—fences, their pool, a shed—is sitting on your property. The survey helps clarify what you're actually buying.

The survey is also concerned with property access. Let's say that you're buying a house set back from the street, behind your neighbor's house. The only way to get to your house is by driving on a driveway that's technically on your neighbor's property. So how does that work? You won't be able to buy a house if you don't have access to a public street unless there's some sort of easement that allows that access. The surveyor is in charge of putting all those pieces together.

Okay, so let's say that your credit check has passed. And the appraisal and survey have been completed. Now, all your information is passed onto an **underwriter, aka the information checker.** An underwriter is almost an invisible person, hidden deep within the bank's cubicles. They're invisible mainly because they're supposed to be *neutral.* Whereas you're likely to develop a relationship with your loan officer who gives you your loan and takes all your information, the underwriter is supposed to deal with the plain facts. They check all your information, along with the appraisal report and the title report (we're about to get to that) to ensure that they have every bit of information needed for their closing papers.

Once the underwriter has approved everything, they give the

"clear to close." The loan goes to the closing department, which then produces the final documents and funds the loan. You can think of the underwriter as the gatekeeper at Disneyland. They're going to scrutinize your ticket, make sure you're good to go, and then if they approve—they open the gates, and all the fun begins! As in, now you can start packing up your life into boxes and coordinate moving vans and so on. Yay!

Finally, if you have put less than 20 percent down on your mortgage loan, the bank will require you to get some sort of **insurance** for your loan. Some common forms of mortgage insurance are PMI (Private Mortgage Insurance), usually applied to conventional loans, or MI (mortgage insurance) applied to FHA loans. If you're not able to put 20 percent down on your mortgage, the bank considers you a riskier borrower and therefore wants added protection for themselves in case you default. If they require you to get mortgage loan insurance, this will be one additional fee you'll need to budget into your monthly payment.

THE TITLE TRANSFER

When a property is sold, **the deed, or title, of the property is transferred from seller to buyer.** This sounds pretty straight forward, and it usually is—but sometimes it can get complicated. Here's a real example. (We've changed some names, for obvious reasons.)

Fifteen years ago, the Johnsons bought a house from Bob, who was selling the house with his partner, Shari. On the paperwork, Bob and Shari had both listed themselves as "unmarried." However, at the closing, Bob crossed out "unmarried" and wrote "a married man." It turns out that Bob had a secret wife that Shari never knew about! No one noticed this little alteration to the paperwork, and the property transferred to the Johnsons. However, this secret wife ended up causing some problems for the Johnsons fifteen years later.

When the Johnsons went to sell their house, an issue came up with the title transfer. When the title company dug into the history of this property, we discovered Bob's sneaky little edit that he'd made on the day of closing. In Ohio, if you're married, your spouse also has an ownership interest in the property. For the last fifteen years, the Johnsons hadn't been in true possession of their home—Bob's secret wife owned part of it.

Luckily for the Johnsons, they had title insurance, which protected them against a potential loss. If the Johnsons were not able to sell their home due to the title problem, the title company would have paid out a claim to resolve the issue. The title company did some investigative work and managed to track down the secret wife; she was willing to sign the paperwork to transfer the title wholly over to the Johnsons. The title company is in charge of looking into all the details of the property's history so that if any issues like this come up, they can be resolved, and the title will transfer without a hitch.

As the buyer, *the title contingency* protects you from needing to go through with your purchase in the event there's some issue with the title transfer. Let's say, for instance, you were the one trying to buy the house from the Johnsons, and it turns out the secret wife issue is *not* so easily resolved. Perhaps there will be an indefinite delay while this wife is tracked down. At that point, you are not obligated to wait around for the title to get cleared; you can exit the deal.

So what's the process of getting that title cleared? The title company will take several steps. First, **they make sure they have all the necessary information.** Often, a contract arrives with missing information, and so the work starts with filling in those gaps.

Then, the title company completes a report on the transfer history of the piece of land. They'll note, "It transferred from this person to that person on this date, then from this person to that person on this date..." **This report is called a title search.** It verifies that everything that happened in the past went through correctly and that the person who *says* they own the property actually *does* own the property. (No secret wives? Check!)

Although secret wives are a rarity, it's not uncommon for there to be other issues with a title. Sometimes, people own property without realizing it, like in the case of an inheritance. Other times, people assume they own something but don't, perhaps because the transfer was never correctly processed. If a property owner is delinquent on their child support payments, for instance, that can trigger a lien on their property, which complicates the title transfer. The title company also checks out the buyer to ensure that they are in good standing to receive the title.

If any issues come up, the title company works to **remove any encumbrances** so that the sale of the property can move forward. This extra work is necessary, but it's likely to cause a delay in the closing process. Once the title search is complete and any encumbrances have been removed, the title company verifies that it's ready to go: "Yep, all the liens are paid off, or they are ready to be paid off; all the ownership transfers are clear." Basically, the new owner of the property will get a clean bill of health for their title. The title company also provides a guarantee to the bank, affirming that the property has no title issues and promising to ensure that the property is free to transfer.

A buyer can choose to buy **title insurance** on their new property so that if anything goes amiss when they try to sell it later on (like the Johnsons), they will not be financially responsible for any title issues. For instance, if it were to be discovered years later that there was a lien on the house when you bought it, you would be responsible for paying off that lien before you could sell if you *didn't* have title insurance. If you do have insurance, the title company pays to resolve any issues. You, unfortunately, can't buy title insurance when you go to sell; you must purchase it at the time when you receive the title. We recommend you get this insurance. It could save you some trouble down the road when you'll be dealing with enough on your plate already.

Once the underwriter lets everyone into Disneyland (i.e., gives the "clear to close"), **the title/escrow company acts as the neutral third party to handle all the money and transfer possession.** All the paperwork goes to the title/escrow company to be filed, and all the money goes to the title company to be dispersed. The title/escrow company has everyone sign off on everything, dispenses the money to the appropriate people, and then files it with the courthouse to officially transfer the title. Tada!

The title/escrow company issues a great big guarantee on top of all that, affirming that the money went where it was supposed to go, all the documents were filed correctly, and everyone can trust that everything was done right: the bank, the buyer, the seller, and the agent.

That's what you're hoping for, after getting under contract: you're hoping that the physical inspection works out, the financing goes forward without a problem, and the title can transfer cleanly. Check, check, check. If any one of those phases goes awry, the three contingencies in your contract can enable you to exit the deal.

How common is it for things to go wrong with one of these contingencies?

As a ballpark guess, we'd say that something goes wrong on one of those three contingencies on roughly 20 to 40 percent of transactions. The most common issues come up from the home inspections. (Remember: You are buying a deteriorating building; assume there will be problems and that things will break.) Issues with financing and title come up once in a while, but you might not even hear about it if you have a good team in place. Here's the good news: we'd say that 80 to 90 percent of deals still close when they're under contract. Issues are resolved and things usually work out!

PULLING BACK THE BOW

If you've set yourself up well, then by the time you get to this final stage of contract to close, you should sail right through it. In some ways, you can think of buying a house like shooting a bow and arrow. Your likelihood of hitting the target will mostly depend on how you pull back the bow. Once everything's set up, you simply let go, and the arrow will hit your intended target. But if you haven't pulled the arrow back properly and you try to *will* it to go a certain way while it's sailing through midair, you're far more likely to miss.

We've given you the tools you need to adequately prepare and do your due diligence so that you can hit a bullseye. What does it look like to pull the bow back just right? You carry out each step we've recommended in these chapters:

- You get yourself **ready to buy** strategically, emotionally, and financially, and you commit to learn quickly.
- You **get your mind right**, balancing the concerns of a homeowner and investor.
- You get an **expert team in place**, committing to an excellent real estate agent and finding a mortgage lender who will get you a great loan with top customer service. (This step will radically impact your ease in getting through contract-to-close!)
- You learn what kind of **financial tools** you can qualify for and start examining properties with those tools in mind.
- You learn how to **evaluate a property**, strengthening your understanding of building construction by visiting and comparing a lot of properties.
- You learn how to **evaluate a price** by comparing similar listings and learning how to factor in other market conditions.
- You consider both people and money when you **negotiate.**

If you've done all that, then the only thing to worry about during this final stretch between contract to close is your *own emotional journey*. That's enough—so let's ensure you don't have to deal with more than that.

The emotional journey will be easier and less volatile if you **get yourself well organized**. The more organized you are with your paperwork, the less scrambling you and your team will have to do—i.e., the less panic and stress you'll experience. A good mortgage lender will help you get all that paperwork lined up from the get-go.

And finally, a last word on mitigating stress—**be nice to your spouse** if you happen to be married. Given the high emotions that can come during the contract to close process, it can be easy to vent all your frustration and stress onto your spouse. Although it would be easy to allow these circumstances to drive you apart, they don't need to do that—actually, this can be a powerful moment of marital bonding. Buying a house together can help you understand each other and your values more deeply; it can pull you close as you consider how to make a great decision together.

Your place matters. Your finances matter. *People* also matter. As you go through this process, as you set yourself up well, as you draw the bow back just right—remember to take care of the people surrounding you. Even if you buy the best house at the best price, you won't have a happy home if you trample on your loved ones in the journey getting there. However, by caring for each other along the way, you and your spouse can take this on as a team. You can strengthen your partnership and connection as you make your journey home.

By pulling your bow back well, you'll also help guard yourself against major surprises with the property. Your awesome real estate agent will willingly run interference for you if an unexpected issue comes up so that you don't have to worry about it. Your mortgage lender will have gotten all your paperwork in place so that the financing rolls on without a hitch.

You will have peace of mind knowing you got an accurate price for the property you chose. You'll feel excited about the home you'll be creating with your family. You will have made a powerful decision with open eyes; one you're delighted to live with. You'll hit a bullseye! That's exactly what we want for you.

PART 2

THE TACTICAL FIELD GUIDE FOR *SELLING* YOUR HOME

PART TWO

Selling a House

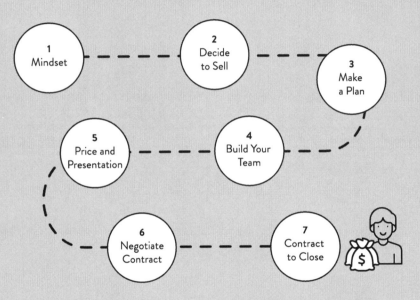

CHAPTER 9

GET YOUR MIND RIGHT

MAKE THE MENTAL SHIFT FROM HOMEOWNER TO INVESTOR

BEN NARRATES: UP *AND* DOWN

The Grand Teton stretches nearly 14,000 feet into the Wyoming sky, and I'd set my sights on the summit. Months before my scheduled climb, I'd started working out like crazy to prepare for the ascent. The preparation paid off. I still looked like a big, bulky guy at the base of that mountain, but my body could keep up. We hiked from base camp at 6,000 feet to 11,000 feet on our first day, then took a day to acclimate and practice maneuvering on the ice. On the third morning, we got up at three o'clock in the morning and began the climb to the summit.

It was a brutal climb, especially the final stage. At one point, we were hanging over a mile drop on a rock face. As soon as I could tuck myself into a crevice, I recorded a goodbye video on my phone to my wife and children, in case I died. It was that terrifying! Still, I focused my thoughts on the summit and kept hustling. Once I'd reached the top, it would be over.

As I finally got the summit in view, I was hit with a realization. It wouldn't be over when I got to the top. *I still had to get down.* The thought made me almost feel sick—I was only *halfway* done.

In one critical area, I had failed to prepare—there had been no mental preparation for the descent, which is actually more challenging than the ascent. That lack of mental preparation nearly ruined the trip for me. At the summit, everyone around me was celebrating, but I felt no joy. We still had to get *down.* "Can we get going?" I urged the others.

Nothing looked familiar on the descent. While hiking up, I'd kept my eyes focused on each step in front of me, but now I was staring out into the whirling snow and open space. It was disturbing not to recognize anything. The danger was real: a fellow climber suffered a bad injury only minutes into the descent, and my guide had to leave us to take him the rest of the way down the mountain.

It took seven hours to get down, and the whole way, every step counted. Visibility was bad, we were physically and mentally exhausted, low on oxygen, and down a guide. The descent was way more dangerous than the ascent. I literally collapsed at the bottom from relief that I'd made it.

I had done a good job preparing physically and mentally to get to the top, but I failed to prepare mentally for the descent. I didn't think through the *whole* journey—and it seriously compromised my experience.

When you get ready to sell your house, it can be easy to make my same mistake. You not only need to get *up* the mountain—finding your new home—you also need to get *down* the mountain—selling your current house. In order to have a good "climb," both up and down, you need to prepare for all aspects of the journey.

Our aim is to help you prepare mentally, emotionally, and financially for this major journey. We're not only going to help you get to the summit, we're also going to help you navigate the entire selling process, so you have a good experience from beginning to end as you make the journey to your next home.

In this chapter, we're going to focus on your **mental preparation**—a critical first step for sellers.

FROM HOMEOWNER TO INVESTOR

When you look at your home, there's a good chance you're seeing it through the lens of all the memories you've made there. The green walls remind you of the painting dance parties you had after just moving in. The kitchen brings to mind all the bits of your life represented on the fridge. When you're out on the patio, you can envision both the before and after of your backyard's transformation. This is *home*.

But now you have to sell it. The real estate agent thinks you should paint the green walls gray, and you're annoyed at the suggestion. Sure, the green is "technically" a little dated, but anyone with decent taste will love it. Won't they? Anyway, you don't want to sell the house to anyone who doesn't love it as much as you do.

Or do you? If someone made an offer for $5,000 *over* your asking price and happened to mention new paint, would you run in the opposite direction? If someone offered $10,000 *less* than your list price but complimented your back patio, would you choose that buyer instead? Is your attachment to your memories worth $15,000? What if you found out that you could increase the list price of your home for close to that amount if you did some of those cosmetic updates yourself? Could you bear it?

We're going to ask you to make a painful mental shift as you prepare to sell your home: move from a homeowner's mindset to an investor's mindset. You need to stop thinking of this property in terms of "your home"—and all the memories associated with that word—and start to think more like an investor. Your property is an extremely valuable product. It's worth getting top dollar for. If you want to get the maximum value for this property, you'll need to market it well, potentially update it, be strategic in how you list it, and negotiate effectively with buyers. You'll need to operate as an objective businessperson.

THINKING LIKE A HOMEOWNER VERSUS AN INVESTOR

Homeowners are guided by ideas of lifestyle and experience. Sellers in the homeowner mindset may dwell on the past experiences they had in the house (either positive or negative), which may unduly influence their perspective of what the property is worth. They may neglect to focus on the structure of the house (like the quality of the amenities, needed updates, etc.), which can hinder their ability to market their property effectively.

For example, if you've had wonderful experiences there, you may have an inflated idea of the property's worth; all those sweet birthday parties and holiday celebrations must surely be worth an extra $50,000, right? On the other hand, if you've had negative experiences there, you may assume it's worth less than it actually is; the fights which led up to your divorce or the long-running argument with your neighbor over their dog might make a beautiful house seem tainted in your eyes.

Investors are guided by ideas of profit. While emotions will still play a role in their decision-making process, their main focus is on how to maximize their returns and minimize their losses. Their decisions may often be influenced by data and financial considerations. The investor sets aside the past—including past memories, past money invested, and past mistakes—and considers what the property is worth *today*, to buyers in the current market. Investors recognize that the factors which impact the value of the home are *only* the ones that impact the market today, such as what similar homes are selling for, economic trends, interest rates, and so on. They understand that none of these market factors have anything to do with what experiences occurred in the house. Investors price their home using the factors that apply to the location, current physical structure, and physical property.

We recommend that *sellers* transition from a homeowner's mentality to an investor's mentality.

Let us be honest: this will not be fun. Whereas buying a home can feel exciting and even romantic, there is nothing sexy about selling your home. Once you decide that you're moving, selling your house feels like a burden. Most people would prefer to simply wave a magic wand and make it all disappear.

For those reasons, selling a house is like climbing a mountain. Sure, it's a worthy endeavor, but the actual experience involves mostly sweat and fear. You're mainly focused on trying to get there and back—to succeed and not fail. There's nothing romantic about it. Still, if you're *mentally prepared* for the challenge, you'll be in much better shape to take it on.

KEVIN NARRATES: THE DANGER OF NOT MAKING THE MENTAL SHIFT

The other day, I had a conversation with some potential clients; I'll call them Liz and Dave. Liz and Dave believe their home should be listed at $700,000, but based on the pricing analysis, it's worth more like $530,000. Liz and Dave are not uncommon in assuming their house is worth more than it is; they've cared for their family there, they've maintained it, and they love it. It *feels* like it should be worth a lot. However—in their case, the pricing discrepancy between belief and reality was particularly large.

Myth: Your house is worth whatever you feel it *should* be worth. Maybe even more!

You might not want to admit this is a myth you'd believe, but we see this assumption falsely guiding many sellers. Your feelings of what something *should* be worth doesn't change what it's *actually* worth.

In an effort to help them see the light, I showed them about ten other homes that were similar to theirs. One house, in my opinion, was nearly identical. The two houses were built only two years apart and had the same woodwork, same carpet, same everything. Liz and Dave disagreed with me. In their opinion, the house I'd found wasn't similar to theirs. "We think our house looks more like *this* one," they said, and sent me a link to a house built three decades later.

Biting my tongue, I asked why they believed their house was similar to the much newer one. The comments they made were fascinating. Liz and Dave did not look at the actual house; they looked at how people could *use* the house to make memories. They said things like, "Well, we remember having our anniversary party in the backyard, and you could do the same kind of party in that backyard. We always had big family dinners on holidays, and you could fit a big table in their dining room." They were partially right, but the cloud of their own memories prevented them from seeing that this newer house had brand new cabinetry, brand new woodwork, and was decorated in all the latest styles. It was a vastly different house and warranted a vastly different price. Their homeowners' perspective made them unable to see the discrepancies clearly.

Liz and Dave were also confused by their own sense of how much they'd invested in their house. They had done a great job keeping their house clean and maintained over the years; in their opinion, they'd invested a lot of money. They believed that their investment should pay off with a higher list price. However, they had done the equivalent of changing the oil and the air filters on a car—they had *maintained* it. But they hadn't bought new tires or put in a new engine—there had been no significant *updates*.

As a result, they were setting themselves up for a disappointing experience selling their house. Again, Liz and Dave's situation is extremely common—we see situations like theirs often. When sellers list at an inflated list price, there's almost no good outcome—something we'll discuss in greater detail in Chapter 13. Usually, it will sit on the market forever, which is depressing. The sellers might get so demoralized that, by the time a buyer does finally make a lowball offer, they wouldn't have the energy to negotiate strategically and might very well lose more money than if they'd listed correctly in the first place. There's a slim chance that an uneducated buyer might overpay for the house and meet the list price, but it's highly unlikely with today's technology, which enables buyers to thoroughly educate themselves about home values.

Your home *is* worth a tremendous value—but understand that the value may not always be represented in dollars. If you've enjoyed, consumed, and lived in your home for years, then you can feel assured that you have gotten your money's worth.

Tip: Stress comes when you think the world should be different than it actually is. If you believe your house should sell for X and then only manage to sell for Y, that can cause a lot of additional stress. However, if you can accurately price it from the start, you're in a better position to make an effective, profitable, and less stressful sale.

THE ART OF NEUTRALITY

The goal is to achieve an informed, neutral stance—to shift your mindset from that of a homeowner to that of an investor. In order to do that, you need to be clear-minded about reality. How do you do that? You start by recognizing *your* reality.

ACKNOWLEDGE THE EXTERNAL AND INTERNAL CHALLENGES

The circumstances which may prompt a move are often emotionally loaded. **Selling your personal home is typically prompted by something happening externally, such as:**

- Job transfer
- A new baby
- Divorce
- Death
- Dissatisfied with your current home

In other words, some of the most common reasons to move are often paired with events that, by themselves, create huge upheaval in your life. When you recognize that you're moving into a time of profound external stress, you can cut yourself some slack. Don't stress out about being stressed—that's just piling on more stress! The external challenges will be a struggle, and you won't always be at your best. That's okay.

It's also okay to recognize that these external struggles are naturally going to create internal struggles. There's a variety of hard and powerful emotions that usually accompany moving. It might be your tendency to avoid those feelings with distractions or by stuffing them down—but we recommend you face them head-on. If you don't, you lose the ability to be objective. Your stuffed-down emotions will leak out during negotiations, or in a pricing analysis conversation with your real estate agent, or with your spouse in the aisle at Lowe's. Rather than separating yourself from your emotions, you'll find those emotions grabbing the steering wheel at all the wrong times.

It's easier to achieve neutrality if you acknowledge the tough stuff happening internally. By allowing yourself to engage the emotions, they're able to pass through you. In other words, you have to start by feeling sad! Grief is a natural and necessary part of making this mental shift. On the other side of those emotions, you're able to achieve the art of neutrality.

You might feel:

- **Confusion**: Selling property is not something most people do every day. You might feel unsure about how to approach it or have some incorrect biases in place. Many people have gotten advice from their relative, friend, or neighbor about how to approach selling their home, which might not always be accurate. People often start this process with a lot of bad assumptions. (We're here to help with that!)
- **Lost**: You might feel lost as to where to begin. Particularly if you've been in your home for a decade or more, it might feel overwhelming to start purging clutter and updating your home. If you feel lost, get advice on the next steps to take.
- **Fearful and distrustful**: You may not know what information to trust or who to believe. Are real estate agents speaking accurately or just telling you what you want to hear? We're going to do our best to help you with this, too, educating you so that you're more empowered with knowledge and helping you pick trustworthy team members.
- **Worry**: You might worry that you'll do something wrong, that you may not get as much money as you need, that people will be critical of your hard work, that you'll miss some key detail.
- **Regret and frustration**: You finally have to deal with all the little property foibles you've been contentedly living with

for all these years. You have to deal with the dead grass and replace the broken outlet cover and clean out the gutters. If one spouse has been urging the other spouse to make those fixes over the years and they didn't, there can be added relational frustration. You might also feel regret that you didn't make the fixes sooner so that you at least could have enjoyed them yourself.

- **Sad**: There's no other word for it when you have to paint over the markings of your kids' heights on the mudroom doorway. When you've seen your home as a place to build memories, have family dinners, raise your kids, and learn about your spouse, it's sad to shift gears into viewing it as a product to sell.

Saying goodbye to a beloved home is like saying goodbye to a friend—it's hard, and you should expect it to be hard. When you give yourself permission to emotionally process, you can more effectively move forward with changing your mindset. By saying goodbye to the home you've known, you are able to step out of your homeowner mindset.

And now, what mindset are you taking on? You're going to take on the mindset of an investor so that you can see your house objectively. You want to evaluate the ways you can minimize your loss or maximize your revenue. Remember: your feelings of what something *should* be worth won't change what it's *actually* worth. Your goal is to become neutral. Separate yourself from the memories. Look at your house for what it is so that you can effectively sell it and move on.

REALITY CHECK

Now that you've acknowledged *your* reality, let's consider the wider reality. These points will help you achieve neutrality!

First, remember that **your home goes with you.** "Home" is not tied to a building. Your home is everything inside the building! It's your furniture, your art, your people, your decor, your bedding. When you move to a new house, you are not leaving your home—you're *moving* your home. You peel everything off the house and put it in a new one. Take your home with you!

Get excited about the next thing. If you've grieved well and can remember that you're taking your home with you, then look forward! Get excited about your new space and how you can make it your own. There will be neighbors to meet, a new area to explore, new opportunities to situate your furnishings in the way you like best. Just as its okay to be sad about what you're leaving, it's okay to move on and be excited for what's next. By balancing the sadness with excitement, you're able to move through the selling process with greater neutrality.

You'll be more effective at thinking objectively if you're thinking of others—specifically, your buyer. **Consider how you can pass this property on well.** Think of your buyers with benevolence: "How can I pass my beloved property on in a way that will bless the next owners, and enable them to enjoy it the way we have?" There's a markedly different feeling when you walk through a home that has been lovingly cared for, compared to one that hasn't. A loved home is viscerally appealing.

But also, **remember that your buyer isn't attached to this house**

in the same way you are. Although buyers will have some emotions involved, they are mainly making a financial decision. Yes, they may want to make memories in a new home, but they're not going to pay a premium to inherit the place of *your* memories versus the house down the road where they could also build memories.

Be self-aware and realistic. Take an open-eyed look at your property. Was it a good investment when you bought it? How have you maintained and/or improved it? If you have been operating as an investor all these years, constantly updating and improving your home at an HGTV level, you can expect to reap the financial rewards now. But if you've simply been living in it and consuming it, don't expect to make tons of money; your gains from this property were primarily made as you lived in it, and that's okay. Form realistic financial expectations about a good list price based on *data* and *market analysis.*

Control your expectations. This is the reason you've dealt with those emotions so that you can take a deep breath and get your expectations in line with reality. Consider what circumstances are prompting your move, and how will those impact your list price? If you're getting divorced and you're eager to get rid of this house as soon as possible, don't expect to get max value. If you've done a beautiful job improving your house over the years, are selling during the summer, and are in a great location, you can expect to get top dollar. Be self-aware, realistic, and mindful of your circumstances so that you can control your expectations.

THE INVESTOR HAT

In summary: when you're getting ready to move out of your current place, seek to set aside the memories that influenced your experience there. Recognize the emotions you feel as valid and allow yourself to grieve, if need be. Give yourself space to be sad about moving on. Then, take a "Marie Kondo" approach: thank the place for serving you and blessing you, then start to purge. Prepare it and repair it so that it's the best it can be for the next person. Form your expectations about list price based off data and realistic information. Be a shrewd, smart, and objective seller by putting on the investor hat.

Many of the following chapters will rely on you thinking like an investor. We're going to teach you how to market your home, how to understand data to inform your list price, give you tips on how to negotiate with your buyer, and so on. In our next chapter, we're going to discuss the pros and cons of renting out your home versus selling it. You will be far more effective at applying *all* of these recommendations if you're able to set aside emotional biases and think like an investor. We want you to **get your mind right so that you can sell your house well.**

CHAPTER 10

RENT OR SELL?

DETERMINING THE BEST
OPTION FOR YOU

BEING A LANDLORD IS EASY (NOT)

Our friend John built a great house for himself. When circumstances required him to move, he decided to rent it out. He wasn't ready to part with the house yet and liked the idea of making some "passive income" by listing it as a rental. Although John already made a salary well over six figures, he figured more income couldn't hurt.

He figured wrong. John's renters were not kind to his house. They ended up trashing it so much so that he ended up spending more than $5,000 to clean it up and do repairs. By the end of his renters' lease, John decided to be done with his landlord experiment and sell the house. Unfortunately, he had enormous difficulty showing it because the renters were still there—and still making a mess. By the time John finally sold the house, we estimate that he probably lost about 20 percent off what he could have sold it for if he'd decided to sell right away and not rent. Although he sold it for $3,000 more than what he'd initially paid, all of his profit was eaten up (and then some) by the $5,000 required to clean up the place, not to mention all the costs of the sale.

Instead of an easy path to passive income, John's rental experience was difficult, stressful, and cost him thousands of dollars in potential profit. Instead of being a way to avoid the emotional discomfort of selling his house, the rental experience ended up resulting in all kinds of emotional discomfort—stress, anxiety, tension, frustration, and anger!

We don't tell you this story to scare you off from renting out your place—we know plenty of people (including us) who have had great experiences renting out their properties. However, we do want to make the point that **being a landlord is not for everyone.** It's more work than it's often assumed to be, and, as John experienced, renting out your property can create unexpected complications.

In this chapter, we're going to discuss the advantages and disadvantages of renting versus selling. Renting can be a great fit for certain people in certain stages of life. For others, selling will be the obvious best choice.

RENT OR SELL? AN INVESTOR-MINDED DECISION

We started Part 2 urging you to *get your mind right*, moving from the more memory-laden homeowner mindset to a more practical investor mindset. Why? **The decision to rent or sell should be made for practical reasons.**

It's not uncommon for sellers to allow negative emotions to drive this decision rather than practical considerations. Let's say you're *sad* about saying goodbye to your first home because of all the memories you've created there. You might conclude you could simply avoid the grief of parting with that home by renting it out. Or maybe you're so *worried* that you'll make a mistake selling, you decide it would be safer to convert it to a rental. Maybe you're *annoyed* that no buyers are offering you the list price you want, so you determine you'll just make a profit by renting and wait for a better buyer. These are all decisions driven by negative emotions, most of which are rooted in the homeowner mindset—but they may not lead to the emotional comfort you want.

Myth: You can avoid all the uncomfortable emotions of selling a property by choosing to rent.

Actually—as we illustrated in John's story—renting can create new problems that cause far more emotional stress than you would have experienced by simply selling your property.

Making the decision to rent or sell needs to be made with a clear head, one that's able to objectively consider finances, practical logistics, and your own strengths and weaknesses.

BEN NARRATES: ARE YOU LANDLORDY?

Rent or sell? Start your consideration of this question by thinking honestly about your own personality. Will you be a good property manager as a landlord? Ask yourself these questions:

- Do you like the idea of being a landlord, acting as the caretaker of your tenants?
- Would you be comfortable treating your renters like business clients, understanding that the relationship would be guided by contractual terms, not friendship?
- Are you ready to be available and responsible for any little thing that goes wrong with the property?
- Would you choose to invest in a rental property today if you didn't already own the property you have?
- Do you consider investing in real estate to be a fixture of your financial strategy?

If you know that your honest answer to one or more of the questions would be a "No," we discourage you from pursuing the rental route. Your life would probably be easier and happier if you sold your property and moved on. However, if the answer to all of those questions is yes, then you might be a great fit to become a landlord and rent out your place.

I'm a landlord, and I like being a landlord. I can remember once being at the beach with my family and getting a call from my tenant telling me that their furnace had gone out. I knew this family had young kids at home and that this issue needed to be addressed immediately. I kissed my wife goodbye and headed back into town to deal with the furnace issue. It was fixed within an hour. As a new landlord, without a team in place, I was essentially always "on call" for my tenants, especially when there were emergencies. I didn't mind that early on—I'd signed up for that lifestyle choice. If that's not something you'd want to sign up for, selling rather than renting might be the way to go.

THE "PASSIVE" INCOME MYTH

But what about the financial considerations? Aren't rentals an easy way to make passive income? In other words, a way to create a stream of cash flow without having to do any work?

Myth: Rentals are an easy way to make passive income.

Wrong. There's nothing passive about it!

This "passive income" view is a common one—but it doesn't bear out in reality. **Remember that when you own a property, you are responsible for maintaining a deteriorating asset.** Every bit of the natural world is hammering away at your structure. Water is trying to get in; tree roots are trying to invade; moss/mold/rot wants to grow; bugs are chewing holes; critters are chewing tunnels; weeds want to choke out the flowers; tree branches are dropping debris. And let's not forget the beating made by the wind, the rain, the snow, the sun, and so on. The laws of physics are battering your house every moment! When you retain ownership of the house—all those issues are still on your shoulders to deal with.

That's just the stuff *outside* the house, though. Let's consider for a second the people *inside* the house. When you're taking care of your own home, you're highly incentivized to maintain it well. You're not only taking care of problems, you're also proactively investing in the property, installing new amenities, or updating the décor. If the sliding door starts to stick, you clean out the track. If the exterior looks shabby after a wet winter, you rent a power washer from Home Depot and go to work.

But renters—even the nice ones—will not have the same level of motivation to care for your place. Most likely, you will hear about problems once they're bad enough to create real inconvenience—not as soon as they're noticed. That, in turn, could lead to more expensive repairs. The renters will choose to live with the dirty carpets; they won't pay for carpet cleaning twice a year the way you would have. As a result, you may end up needing to replace the flooring once they move out, not just clean it. They may be less vigilant about cleaning the bathrooms, allowing mold to grow and proliferate. If they hear scratching in the walls, they may decide they can live with it and not bother asking for a pest inspection. *They* don't want to deal with fumigation. In the meantime, those unseen scratchers are doing who-knows-what to the structure of your house.

And those are the *nice* renters! The bad ones will ruin your property, fail to pay rent, secretly sublet to people you've never met and pocket the profits, refuse to move out, and may even sue you for trying to evict them.[11]

What does that mean for landlords? **You must be an *active* participant in the management of your property.** You need to be vigilant in screening renters ahead of time and making sure your renters are paying rent every month. If they turn out to be lousy tenants, you need to be prepared to take legal action against them.

---

11 Short, Taylor. "3 Types of Bad Tenants—and How to Avoid Them." Software Advice, June 7, 2016. https://www.softwareadvice.com/resources/how-to-avoid-bad-tenants/.

You need to actively supervise the needed maintenance of your property. You also need to ensure the renters are not misusing or abusing your house in any way.

Sounds like a fair amount of work, doesn't it? "But ah!" you might be thinking. "I can just hire a company to manage the property for me. Then I won't have to worry about all that, and my income really will be 'passive.'"

Myth: Property owners can get out of their landlord responsibilities by hiring a management company.

If you hire a *good* management company, this can save you some additional work—but you'll still need to be vigilant about ensuring you've hired a good one, and some responsibilities will still fall to you.

While it's true that a good management company can relieve you of some of the responsibilities of being a landlord, there are plenty of bad property management companies out there, too. A mediocre or sloppy property management company can give you a false sense of reassurance that your property is being well looked after, even while it's falling into disrepair. They also may practice less scrutiny in screening tenants and/or may be less vigilant about ensuring payments are made on time.

In other words, although there's a chance you might have *some* responsibilities relieved by a property management company, you'll still be obligated to manage the management company! Once again, that requires your *active* involvement.

Best-case scenario: let's say you do find a fantastic property management company, and they find you fantastic renters. Your *active* involvement is still required. You're still the one responsible for making arrangements with contractors and handling all repairs. If the management company runs into a scenario where they don't have the authority to make the call, they're going to call you. They still need your final approval on their selected tenants.

Hiring a management company does not enable you to simply forget about this property; you'll still be in regular communication with your property managers. It's also worth remembering that their management comes at a price. You lose part of your rental profits by hiring this company to do the management for you.

Worst-case scenario: if you pick a bad management company, you'll get your house back destroyed. The management company will be able to freely walk away while you're stuck with all the cleanup and repair bills. We've seen this happen—and we know many people who have ultimately had to foreclose because they simply couldn't recover from that.

Here's the moral of the story: don't rent out your property if your main goal is to secure a passive income stream. Being a landlord is not a passive role; it requires your active involvement and time. If you like the idea of passive income, there are other investment vehicles you can pursue that will produce a more truly passive income stream.

FINANCIAL CONSIDERATIONS: HOW MUCH PROFIT ARE WE TALKING?

Let's say you *do* like the idea of being a landlord. You're ready to sign up for the work, and you like the idea of building up your finances through owning rental properties. Good! In that case, we want to make sure you have a realistic idea of how your profits are likely to work in owning a rental.

Rentals create most of their profit for owners in the *long term* building up of equity. As the renters cover most of the cost of the mortgage, they're essentially buying the asset for you. That's where you make the most money. However, there's not as much profit to be gained in the *short term*. Why not?

First of all, some properties can't demand a rent payment that goes well above a mortgage payment. The monthly rent may just manage to cover your mortgage and taxes. "Well—that's not bad," you might think. "At least then I'd be breaking even and building up equity." However—that's not breaking even.

Remember: the house is deteriorating. The roof repair, the window replacement, the tree removal—those repairs all come out of your pocket. Maintenance costs add a significant expense to maintaining your property.

> **Myth: If you can rent out your property for a price that covers the mortgage payments and taxes, you're breaking even.**
>
> That's not "breaking even." Once the renters' payments cover the monthly costs *and* all the costs of necessary repairs, that's when you're breaking even.

You can be a shrewd investor and find rental properties that *will* pay you more than the mortgage payment, taxes, and necessary repairs. If so, then you can build up equity on multiple properties while someone else pays the mortgage. That's a legitimate investment strategy, and one we're both currently pursuing!

However, it's worth remembering that **in the *short term*, each rental property will feel more like a liability than an income stream.** The short-term profits will not be substantial, and ultimately, you may not feel like this avenue of investment is worth your time and effort. The right decision for you will largely depend on your personality, long-term financial strategy, and your interest in being an actively engaged landlord.

YES, YOU SHOULD RENT

We can think of two people-profiles that lend themselves well to renting out their properties. See if either of these sound like you.

One: you have a real interest in becoming an owner of multiple properties. (And if you're married, your spouse does, too.) You plan to think of these properties like a business and invest in properties that make sense as rentals, in terms of their location and structure. You thoroughly research each property's condition, its approximate rental value, and have a plan for how you'll take care of it. However, you're not just interested in doing this for financial reasons—you also genuinely like the idea of being a landlord. You want to be a caretaker of a property so you can bless people with a comfortable place to live. You know there's a lot to learn about how to be a good landlord, and you're prepared to pursue that knowledge.

Two: you need to rent because it's the only way to salvage your credit. This is a legitimate reason to rent, but it may require you to embrace being a landlord in a way you wouldn't have otherwise. Let's say you bought a property when the market was at its height and end up finding yourself underwater as the market takes a downturn. You want to move out but don't want to sell at a loss. In that case, renting out your property might enable you to cover the mortgage costs until the market recovers. You can still build equity, you don't have to foreclose, and your credit won't take a massive hit. We know many people who used this strategy to get through the housing crisis following 2008. Although they were initially underwater, they were able to hang on to their properties and eventually made a great profit selling them after the market had rebounded.

Tip: Time heals all wounds in real estate. If you can hold on to a property long enough and maintain it, it will eventually pay for itself.

If an *external* circumstance forces you to become a landlord because it's the best option among several unpleasant options—embrace it. Learn how to be a good landlord. There are plenty of books that will give you great pointers, and you'll learn plenty from the experience of actually doing it. Embrace the role of caretaker and work to do it well.

KEVIN NARRATES: CHOOSING TO SELL

I remember talking with some friends who were trying to decide whether they should rent or sell. These friends were both doctors and made close to half a million in their combined salaries. However, in spite of all their medical expertise, they'd made a bad buy when they'd moved to a new area. They bought an over-priced condo and, now that they were preparing to move, had to face selling it at a loss. They knew the loss would be substantial—maybe $70,000 to $80,000.

These friends asked us, "Should we just rent it out? We don't want to take the $70,000 loss."

Since they owned the house outright, they could sell it and still recover some of their money. Granted, that was $70,000 less than what they'd originally put in, but the total that they could recoup was still $200,000. I asked them, "Would you choose to take this $200,000 of your money and buy this house to rent out? The obvious answer, for them, was no. They would never choose this particular property for a rental investment.

When the information was laid out for them in those terms, the right choice for them became obvious. They did not want to become long-distance landlords. They did not want to hang on to this property. They mainly wanted to avoid a big financial loss, but that didn't turn out to be as compelling when they considered the math.

Factoring into their mathematical equations was the fact that these people could afford to take that net loss. In their case, their *time* was worth far more in their practice as doctors than it was doing property management. These people could go give a seminar somewhere and get paid $10,000. In other words, there were other ways and *better* ways for them to make a profit than renting their condo. For them, it made the most sense to simply take the loss on their property and walk away.

Choosing to sell will make the most sense for a lot of people—maybe even most people. If you've determined that you want to sell rather than rent, you've got some decisions to make:

- Are you going to do any updates to the house?
- How are you going to sell it? (Will you work with a real estate agent? Will you try to sell first and then buy a new place, or buy a new place and then sell?)
- How will you price the house?
- What is your timing going to be? (What time of year will you sell? Do you have a flexible or a tight timeline?)

These are the questions we're going to answer in the chapters that follow.

CHAPTER 11

TIMING AND PLANNING

DETERMINING WHETHER TO
BUY OR SELL FIRST

KEVIN NARRATES: THE CONDO COLLAPSE

Early on in my career as a real estate agent, I helped some elderly clients who were living on a fixed income. They were noticeably private about their finances, and—not wanting to be nosy—I respected that. However, my experience in helping them sell their house made me realize how important it is to get a clear picture of my clients' finances. I don't want to see any other clients experience the disappointment these two suffered.

This couple was ready to downsize and, with my help, sold their beautiful home. After selling it, they planned to buy a condo. However, when they went to the bank to get a loan for the condo, they discovered they couldn't qualify. Their modest fixed income wasn't deemed sufficient to cover a mortgage loan. As a result, these two needed to scramble to find a rental instead of a place where they could peacefully spend their retirement.

This story kills me because we so easily could have avoided this loss with just a little more planning and communication. If the couple had gone through a loan preapproval process *before* selling their home, they would have discovered that they couldn't qualify and made the decision to remain in their lovely home. That situation would have been far more preferable than needing to scramble to find a rental.

Forming a game plan to get into your next home is one of the most important steps to take when preparing to sell. You need to move *somewhere*. Do you sell and move into a rental, then find a new place to buy? Do you sell and try to find a new place to buy simultaneously? Do you buy first and then try to sell your place, even though that means carrying a massive amount of debt at once? It's a juggling act, and each option has its upsides and downsides.

In Chapter 9, Ben shared his story of climbing the Grand Teton and focusing only on the climb—he'd forgotten to prepare for the descent, and it almost ruined the trip for him. This lesson is critical for sellers: you must prepare for what happens *after* you sell your home. If you want to buy another place after selling your current property, there are often numerous steps to be taken before you ever even list your home. In this chapter, we're going to educate you about the steps you might need to take to form a game plan.

This chapter is only relevant to people who are currently living in the place they plan to list and will need to arrange different housing once it sells. If you're selling or buying a second home, or you *know* you intend to rent for a time after selling, feel free to skip this chapter. This content is mainly focused on helping sellers not become homeless. If you've already got other housing secured, this information won't be as necessary for you.

This chapter is also mainly for people who will be using a bank loan to buy their next home. If you have enough cash on hand to buy your next home without the help of a mortgage loan, you, too, can feel free to skip this one.

For all other sellers: grab a highlighter and a pen. Start taking notes. This is some of the most important information we can give you.

GET YOUR FINANCES IN ORDER

Here's something we've learned over our many years working in this business: this particular area of planning is often not one that consumers think about. If you have a good job with a steady income, you might assume that the bank will definitely give you another mortgage loan. They gave you the first one, didn't they?

But recall what those banks were looking at, way back when you qualified for your current mortgage loan. They were examining:

- Your credit.
- Your access to cash for a down payment.
- Your *debt-to-income ratio.*

When first-time homebuyers are qualifying for a loan, they may have some debt from student loans or credit cards, but the debt is unlikely to be the size of a mortgage loan. However, when you're going to sell a property, you may owe hundreds of thousands of dollars on your mortgage loan.

The bank is going to look hard at that debt before issuing you a new loan. If you make a substantial income, they may determine you *can* juggle two mortgage loans at once. If they do, you have the luxury of finding a new place to buy before you sell, which would be convenient. However, often the bank says, "We don't think you can juggle two mortgage payments at once. You need to sell your current place first and pay back that loan before we'll give you a new one." If that's the case, then you're going to have to sell your place first, then buy. That can be more challenging, and it's often inconvenient. We'll discuss in greater detail how each of those scenarios can play out in a moment.

Now, there are certain financial moves you can make that will enable you to transition more smoothly into your next home. For instance, you could potentially pull cash for a down payment from a Home Equity Line of Credit (HELOC) or even a retirement account—but the feasibility and wisdom of doing that won't be the same for everyone. The timing of when you line those up also matters. For instance, banks usually won't let you take out a HELOC *after* listing your home, but you can *before* listing your home.

How could you use a HELOC to get into your next home?

If you've built up a lot of equity in your current home, you can take out a home equity line of credit (HELOC), utilizing a portion of your equity in the home as a financial asset. Essentially, you can write a check for up to that amount, which works as a cash offer when you buy your next home. Then, after you sell your current home, you would immediately pay off that line of credit.

Here's the tricky bit: it costs banks money to set up these lines of credit, and they're not going to want to create a HELOC for you if they know you plan to sell your home and pay it down within a month. They're hoping you're going to use the HELOC to make some home improvements, and they'll be able to make money off your interest payments. For that reason, it's possible to set up a HELOC *before* you list your house. However, if you ask the bank to set it up *after* your property is on the market, they're likely to say no. At that point, you've lost the ability to leverage your current equity as a financial tool.

It's details like this that make forming a game plan so important. Planning and getting your finances in order is like paving a road: you're setting yourself up for smooth travel. Failing to do either of these is like consigning yourself to bushwhacking your way into your next home. It may work out, and you may eventually get there, but it's likely to be a slow, painful process.

If the planning seems complicated, that's a sign that you're paying attention. Unless you're a financial professional who deals with these tools all the time, this planning process will be challenging. That's why we're going to stress that you **get a good team in place.** Consult financial advisors, mortgage brokers, and experienced real estate agents so that you understand what your options are. Good team members will not only help you avoid potential pitfalls, but they'll also help you see opportunities that you didn't know existed. We're going to discuss more about screening real estate agents in our next chapter; for tips on finding a good mortgage lender, reference Chapter 3 in Part I.

THE THREE SCENARIOS

Most sellers face three options for how to get out of their current home and into their next home. Depending on your financial scenario, you might be able to do any one of these options, or you may be restricted in what you can do.

- **Scenario 1: Buy first and then sell.**
- **Scenario 2: Buy and sell at the same time, via a "simultaneous close."**
- **Scenario 3: Sell and rent, then buy later.**

Let's look at how each scenario works, along with the advantages and disadvantages of each.

SCENARIO 1: BUY FIRST AND THEN SELL

This scenario is generally considered the most convenient for sellers, but it can also be the most financially risky. Buying first enables you to take your time finding the right next house for your family, which can be especially helpful if you're competing with other buyers in a hot market. After getting under contract with your new house, you would then list your current house on the market. You could even wait until you are completely moved into your new house and out of your old one before listing it.

The upsides are many. First, you're more likely to get a new house you're really excited about. You're not under any kind of time crunch, so you can wait until just the right house comes onto the market and then snag it. Moving is also much simpler: your moving boxes go right from your current house into your new house. This scenario also gives you much more control over the timeframe of when you choose to move. If you can carry two mortgages at once, you can choose to give yourself a week to move into your new home, or you could take three years—whatever you determine works best for your situation.

You're also more likely to optimize your investment. If you can buy first and you do your homework to ensure you *buy well*, you're more likely to secure a great new home. You're less at risk of buying a bad house because you were in a hurry. Also, you're more likely to *sell well*. By buying first, you can move all your stuff out, get it professionally staged, and market it like crazy. It's much easier to stage and market an empty home than one that's currently being lived in.

The downside is that you're temporarily stuck with two houses and will have a substantial financial burden until you can sell your current house. If your current house ends up being slow to sell, for whatever reason, that debt could be tough to carry. You're also gambling with what your current house might sell for. For instance, let's say you assume your current house will sell for $250,000 and you buy a new home banking on that amount, but then your house only sells for $200,000. That

$50,000 difference could hit hard. If you were expecting to have an additional $50,000 to pay down on your new mortgage and you don't get it, you might be forced to spend much more per month than you anticipated.

For this reason, buying first is generally an option reserved for those with a lot of financial flexibility and margin—or for those who have a high-risk tolerance.

If you plan to buy first, then sell, one of two things must be true for you:

- You have the spare cash to buy a house first before selling your current one.
- You have some kind of alternative financing mechanism in place, either through a bank that's given you the green light to pursue this option, or through a family member who will lend you the cash needed to buy a new home until you're able to sell your current home.

If neither of those options is true for you, then Scenario 1 is probably not in the cards. Before you dismiss it entirely, though, let us remind you that "cash" can mean several things. Yes, cash can mean money in your bank account. "Cash" can also be money you pull from an investment account, like a retirement IRA. (Keep in mind that borrowing from your retirement may carry some financial penalties; this won't be the wisest move for everyone.) You could also pull cash from a HELOC by leveraging the equity you've built up in your home. (See the previous gray box, a few pages earlier, for an explanation on how this works.)

How do I calculate my equity?

Your equity is the difference between what you still owe on your home and its current market value. You could calculate it using this equation:

[Amount my home is worth] – [amount I still owe on my mortgage loan] = equity

Note: most banks will not give you the *full* amount of your equity if you're pursuing a HELOC. Banks offer a variety of HELOC products that will allow you to utilize more or less of your equity.

SCENARIO 2: BUY AND SELL SIMULTANEOUSLY

Buckle your seatbelts—this scenario involves a lot of close coordination between many different players. In order to buy and sell at the same time, you need to arrange a *simultaneous close*. You might find yourself pursuing this option if the bank has told you that they'll only finance a new loan if you can sell your current home first. "But," the banker might tell you, with a glint in her eye, "We can buy and sell a house on the same day."

Here's how this would work:

- You find a new house you want to buy and get under contract with that seller.
- Either before or after that, you secure a reliable buyer for your current house and get under contract with them. (Preferably before; if you don't already have a reliable buyer lined up, sellers are unlikely to accept your offer.)

- Then, with the help of your team, you would arrange for the closing dates to fall on the same day.

Within twenty-four to forty-eight hours, these two properties would be transferred and paid for in one giant flurry of transactions. As soon as your current house closed with your buyer and the title and money was transferred, the bank would then clear you to proceed with your new loan, and the title company would close on your new house. Is your head spinning? Just wait. We're only getting started.

Generally, if you're trying to do a simultaneous close, you want to include a *home sale contingency* in your contract. In other words, your agreement to buy a new house is contingent on the sale of your current house going through. That way, if your buyer has to back out of the sale for some reason, you're not stuck with two mortgages at once. (Hello, Scenario 1.) Often, the bank won't even let you make an offer on a new house without this contingency because they won't approve your financing otherwise.

These contingencies offer important protection—and they can also create a domino effect. For instance, let's say Amanda and Adam in Akron want to buy a house from Bob and Betty in Billings. Bob and Betty are ready to sell their house to the As from Akron and have found a house they want to buy from Chris and Chrissy in Clairemont. Everyone wants to do a simultaneous close, and all the sellers have contingencies, stating that they don't have to buy their new house unless the sale of their old house goes through.

The day of closing arrives. But—oh no!—there's an issue with

Amanda and Adam's finances! They can't proceed with the sale. They call Bob and Betty, who are crushed. Bob and Betty call up Clare and Chris and explain they can't proceed with the sale. You might find Clare and Chris calling up the owners of the house *they* wanted to buy, saying, "We're so sorry! Our buyers fell through because *their* buyers fell through." The dominos can keep on falling all over the country. (Ben once had a deal go through, which was contingent on *seven* other sales successfully going through as well!)

If that doesn't seem complicated enough, remember all the different people who are attached to every different sale. Each seller and buyer come with their own set of real estate agents, mortgage lenders, title companies, bank staff, movers preparing to come on a certain date, and so on. If something goes wrong with any one of those people—if any mistakes or delays come up, anywhere along the line—the simultaneous close can be jeopardized.

If you are a control freak, Scenario 2 is probably not for you! If you're the kind of person who is comfortable swimming in some chaos and can spare some extra time to shuffle arrangements as needed—go for it.

Having a good team in place can also make or break your success with Scenario 2. If you've got a sloppy real estate agent who isn't on top of things or a mortgage lender who's disorganized in gathering your paperwork, Scenario 2 can crash and burn. However, if you've got a great team of people looking out for you, they'll do a much better job carrying this through successfully. They'll be able to see clearly what's going to happen thirty to sixty days out, and that can save you a lot of trouble in the long run.

The upsides: First, it's convenient—provided it all works out. If you can pull off a simultaneous close, then you may only have to move your belongings once, saving you the trouble of moving into a transitional rental. You'll also get a clear idea of what your home will sell for, which means you're less likely to put yourself into a new mortgage you can't afford. Finally, you're condensing the chaos. All the buying and selling will be wrapped up into one massive transition. Your closing date will be a *crazy* day, but—hopefully—it will just be one day. At the end of it, you can break out the bubbly and sink into a nice, hot bath.

The downsides: Emotional stress and anxiety come to mind! You might think you have a plan in place that's all neatly tied up with a bow, but that nice little plan can very quickly become a disaster scenario. If you're pursuing a simultaneous close, prepare yourself emotionally for something to go wrong. It *might* not—often, everything works out beautifully. But if something does go wrong, that can lead to heartbreak, stress, and major logistical snarls. We've known sellers who had already transferred all their utilities to their new house, and then had to change them back. If you've arranged for all your friends to help you move on Friday, and then the closing falls apart, you need to come up with another plan for your movers.

In the best-case scenario, the simultaneous close goes through, and you're able to successfully coordinate your dates of possession with your buyers and the people selling you your new home. Everyone manages to swap houses successfully within a relatively short time frame, and everyone walks away happy. With a few new gray hairs, maybe—but, happy!

A quick definition: closing date versus possession date

Your *closing* date is the day that the title/escrow company disburses the money after all parties have signed paperwork. After the money is disbursed, then the title/escrow company will file the paperwork at the county, which could be the same day or several days later.

Your *possession* date is the day you get the keys to your new place and are allowed to move in.

These dates are often the same, but sometimes a buyer or seller will request more flexibility with their possession date to give them additional time to move.

SCENARIO 3: SELL FIRST AND THEN RENT

Selling first and then renting can feel the most inconvenient since it requires an extra move. However, there's a lot of wisdom in doing it this way.

The upsides: When you rent, you give yourself plenty of time to find a new house, which sets you up to buy well. You can avoid the pressure of trying to pull off a simultaneous close. You can move into your rental and then stage your house, which increases the likelihood of selling your place for a great price. Selling first and then renting also means there's no guesswork with your finances. After selling, you'll be 100 percent sure of what you have in the bank, which means you have total clarity about what kind of mortgage you can afford when you buy again.

The downsides: Moving twice is, admittedly, a pain. It could require an additional layer of planning as you determine what stuff needs to go into a storage unit and what will come with you to the rental. You'll pay for two sets of movers or two moving trucks. You might need to pay a premium if you do a month-to-month rental. You'll also have to resettle twice. Particularly if you have kids and/or pets, throwing in that extra transition can feel stressful for everyone.

Also, some people just hate the idea of renting; they'd much rather feel they're building up equity with their monthly housing payment than "throwing it away" on a rental. However, this logic might prevent you from fully recognizing the advantages of renting. Remember that, for the first several years after you buy a new house, you're essentially "renting" the property anyway since you're mainly paying down interest. Consider the profit you might make in the long run if you choose to rent and, as a result, are able to get into a much better house by buying well, rather than buying in a hurry. Financially speaking, renting can actually be a much savvier way to go.

> **Myth: Renting is a waste of money.**
>
> Actually, renting can enable you to learn critical knowledge to ensure you buy well. That can save you many thousands of dollars in the long run and give you invaluable peace of mind.

We'd recommend renting for a time if you sell your house in the winter. Because there's so much less inventory on the market during the winter months, you're far more likely to find a great place to move into if you wait until spring or summer, when listings increase.

Also, if you are moving to a new city, we highly recommend renting before buying. Yes, it's inconvenient, but getting yourself this flexibility gives you time to *learn*—and the knowledge you'll gain is invaluable. You'll learn about the neighborhoods, the school districts, the standard market values of properties in this new area, and so on. When you go straight to buying, you risk overpaying or locking yourself into a property that—you may later discover—is in an area you don't love. Renting, on the other hand, gives you the time you need to buy well.

Myth: There's no harm in buying a home in a city I'm unfamiliar with, so long as I work with a local real estate agent.

Buying in a new city before you get to know it is a gamble—and it can turn out badly. Local real estate agents can certainly give you local knowledge, but they won't necessarily lead you in the way you would lead yourself. For instance, a real estate agent can spout off information about the rankings of school districts, but after getting to know the schools, you may decide that you're far more partial to one over another. Also, remember that real estate agents are usually paid by commission. They're not incentivized to help you find a great deal and may not alert you to the fact that a home may be overpriced. We'd guess that overpriced homes are most often purchased by out-of-town buyers who simply aren't aware of the local market.

If you don't have a lot of flexibility with your finances and want to make sure you nail your next buy, selling first and then renting is a great way to go. The temporary inconvenience is often outweighed by the benefits of buying well. Particularly if you have good credit and good financing, you want to make sure you continue on an upward trend. Renting can help ensure you make a great next choice for your family.

OTHER KEY CONSIDERATIONS

The scenario that makes the most sense for you will be probably be determined by your financial flexibility and willingness to take on risk. There are a few other considerations that may impact your game plan as well.

TIME OF YEAR AND MARKET CONDITIONS

The main factor here is inventory: you're trying to determine how easy it will be for you to get into another home after you sell. The amount of homes on the market and the amount of buyers fighting for them will often be determined by the time of year and the market conditions. That inventory, in turn, could impact your timing and planning. Here's an example of how market conditions could impact your game plan:

- **It's summertime, and it's a buyer's market.** There's plenty of inventory and relatively little competition among other buyers. You should try to *sell first* since that's likely to be the bigger challenge, and then take your pick from the houses available to buy. You might be able to easily pull off a *simultaneous close*.
- **It's summertime, and it's a seller's market.** There's a lot of inventory, but there are even more buyers. Sellers are regularly getting multiple offers and seeing bidding wars. If it's in your power, you might try to *buy first*, since that will be the bigger challenge, and then sell—you can probably count on lots of potential

offers, provided you list your home appropriately. You might even pull off a *simultaneous close* if you can secure a buyer for your old house around the same time you get chosen as the winning offer for a new house. If you don't have the financing to buy first, you might want to try to *sell in the spring, then rent;* you could try to buy by the end of the "high season" in the fall.

· **It's winter; inventory is low, and buyers are few.** This is a scenario where we'd definitely advise you to *sell, then rent* until more inventory comes on the market.

Depending on how many homes are on the market and the speed at which they're moving, you might have the ability to maneuver in the current market to achieve the scenario you want.

THE CONTINGENCY FACTOR

If you're in the fortunate position of having cash on hand when you go to buy a property, you're considered a sure thing, and the seller doesn't need to take on any risk with your financing. That makes you a highly attractive buyer and gives you more negotiating power.

Many people, however, aren't able to buy a house with cash. They need to write an offer with a contingency—basically, "I can buy your home so long as I sell mine." Some buyers might want to include this contingency for their own comfort, and others might be required to by their lender. However, **a contingent offer will lower your appeal to sellers because they would need to take on the risk of your house not selling.**

For instance, imagine that it's summertime and you've found

your dream house. Ideally, you would *not* write a contingent offer because there are likely lots of other buyers vying for the same house. If a seller saw a home sale contingency, they might think, "I don't want to risk this deal falling through; I'm going to choose a different buyer who's committing to buy my house, without needing to sell theirs."

But what if you *have* to include that contingency? How can you get the seller to choose you? In that case, you should expect to pay more since you're asking the seller to take on an additional amount of risk.

This is less of an issue in a slower market or in a buyer's market where there's lots of inventory available. However, it's a very big issue in a seller's market, where you're competing with many other buyers who may not have a home sale contingency.

The home sale contingency factor also depends on the person you're buying from. Let's say your seller is also planning to purchase a new house with a contingency. That might make them less willing to accept your contingent offer. They don't want the domino effect of *their* purchase falling through because *your* finances fell through; they're going to want a buyer who's a sure thing.

If you must make an offer with a contingency, understand that you'll have less negotiating power because your offer requires the seller to take on more risk. You might have to make up for that risk by offering to pay more. You could also try making a personal appeal to the sellers. (You can read more about how to effectively negotiate with a seller in Chapter 7 of Part I.)

YOUR RISK TOLERANCE

Your planning will also be determined by your comfort level with risk. Some people might want to go for the simultaneous close in the middle of a busy summer market. They're ready to move at high speed, make assumptions about their finances, and take the risk of finding a buyer and securing a new house at the same time. Other people would feel far more comfortable buying themselves extra time and clarity through renting.

If you know you prefer to operate conservatively, then don't try to force a simultaneous close. The payoff may not be worth the emotional stress and anxiety it causes you. On the other hand, if you have a high tolerance for risk, then ride the adrenaline rush and pursue a riskier scenario.

INTEREST RATES

If interest rates are low, it might be possible for you to buy first, then sell. Low-interest rates will improve your debt-to-income ratio. If you have a more favorable debt-to-income ratio, the bank might approve your financing to carry two mortgages at once.

Conversely, if interest rates are high, that means a higher monthly payment. The bank may determine you can't afford to juggle two mortgages and may require you to sell first, then buy.

KEVIN NARRATES: PREPARE FOR THE DESCENT

I haven't climbed the Grand Teton like Ben, but I have assisted plenty of sellers successfully get into their next home by helping them to mentally prepare for their "descent." Recently, I helped two clients prepare to sell their home; they wanted to move to Florida to enjoy their retirement. In one of our conversations, they let it slip that they were planning to withdraw funds from their IRA to buy their next home.

"Wait—I'd hate for you two to withdraw from your retirement funds, just as you're planning to start your retirement!" I said. "Have you considered a HELOC instead?" Neither of them knew that they could use a HELOC as a financial product until I explained it to them. Fortunately, they'd earned substantial equity in their current house, and we hadn't listed their home yet. They were able to buy a new home using the cash available through their HELOC, and then we successfully sold their home in Ohio. They got the new place they wanted, moved at the pace they wanted, and left their savings intact. Plus, since they essentially paid cash for their new place, they negotiated the list price down and got a great deal. We estimated that they saved about $20,000 in the end.

As you prepare for the full climb that is selling your home and then buying a new one, there are three circumstances that will be a massive help to you:

1. You have the cash to do whatever you want.
2. You have expertise in financial tools and/or real estate.
3. **You're working with an excellent team.**

Given that the people who qualify for number one probably skipped this chapter and the people who fall under number two aren't reading this book let us reiterate this message loud and clear to all you Number Threes: having a great team in place is critical. It's as important as having good guides when you're climbing a treacherous mountain.

As a new real estate agent, I wouldn't have known about helping my clients take out a HELOC, and I wouldn't have saved them that $20,000. However, after years of working in this business, I'm able to provide that expert help. Your team members' expertise can save you stress, help you avoid mistakes, advocate on your behalf, and identify opportunities. Our next chapter is going to cover the different ways you can employ the advice of professionals and assemble the team you need.

CHAPTER 12

BUILD YOUR TEAM

FIGURING OUT THE HOW AND THE WHO

OH THE TIMES, THEY ARE A-CHANGIN'...

The year is 1992. George is getting ready to sell his family home and weighs his options of how to go about it. He could stick a "For Sale by Owner" sign in his window and put an ad in the newspaper. Still, he's not sure what he would write in the posting. He's even less confident that his pictures would do the house justice when printed in grainy newsprint.

Perhaps it would be better, George reasons, to hire a real estate brokerage. In 1992, after all, real estate agents have almost an exclusive knowledge of what's for sale. They know what will be coming available and when, and who's looking to buy. They'll take care of the newspaper ad and control the timing of when it appears. If he wants buyers to look at his house, they'll need to be brought in by an agent. It stands to reason, George considers, that his house would be shown to more buyers if he were to tap into that network of agents. His decision made, George calls a local real estate brokerage and makes an appointment.

Let's jump ahead now to 2020. George's daughter, Jenna, is planning to sell her family home and weighs her options of how to go about it. Transparency in the real estate market has exploded, thanks to the internet, which has led to much greater market efficiency. If Jenna decides to list her home "For Sale by Owner," she can get her listing viewed by thousands of people via an online real estate platform like Zillow. She can communicate with them directly and wouldn't be nearly as dependent on an agent. "That could work," Jenna thinks.

Still, listing by herself on Zillow also means Jenna is trying to appeal to much more educated buyers. Her post will be compared with hundreds of others—could she compete? She's not exactly sure how she should write her posting and even less confident that she could stage or photograph her place in a way that appeals to buyers' high-def expectations. She knows buyers will also have clearer opinions on what her home should be priced—and she's not exactly sure what list price to start with.

Perhaps it would be better, Jenna reasons, to hire a real estate agent. Preferably someone who's internet savvy, knows how to accurately price her home, and can advise her on all the marketing components she feels unsure about. She also knows an agent would list her home on the MLS, which would ensure it shows up on *every* real estate listing platform—not just Zillow. Her decision made, Jenna gathers recommendations, scours online reviews, and takes note of her favorite listings to make sure she finds the best agent possible.

DO YOU NEED AN AGENT?

Frankly, you might not. It has never been easier to sell your house on your own. In the last few decades, the internet has transformed real estate, meaning agents no longer hold all the keys. A platform like Zillow can enable you to list your home, get it seen by thousands of viewers, and communicate directly with potential buyers. You also might be able to get a decent idea of how to price your home by researching comparative properties and considering the pricing recommendations in this book. If you've got access to a great camera, a knack for effective interior staging, and savvy marketing skills, you're in a great position to do this entirely on your own.

However, as both George and Jenna concluded, a real estate agent can still be an enormous help to have around. Good agents will be experts in staging, listing, and effectively marketing your home. They'll help you with pricing and negotiating. They'll help you manage the contract-to-close gauntlet, walking you through the inspection and guiding you through the follow-up negotiation. It can be profoundly reassuring to have someone along to offer guidance, expertise, and advocacy. Most homeowners sell three to five properties in their lifetime. A good real estate agent might sell thousands, making their expertise, confidence, and ability to navigate transactions highly valuable.

For perspective, an article published by the Home Seller's Guide reviewed the pros and cons of doing "For Sale by Owner" (FSBO) versus listing with an agent. Their findings highlight the diffi-culties many owners encounter attempting to sell on their own: "According to Zillow research, 36 percent of sellers attempt to sell their homes themselves, but challenges along the way lead many of them to eventually hire an agent. In the end, only 11 percent of sellers end up selling their home without a real estate agent."[12] In other words, two-thirds of the people that attempted to sell on their own ultimately concluded they would be better off going with an agent.

It's worth weighing the pros and cons of both options: selling on your own versus selling with an agent. In this chapter, we're going to give you a clear idea of what you should consider if you plan to do it alone. We're also going to give you a clear idea of what services an agent can—and should—provide to you.[13]

FOR SALE BY OWNER (FSBO)

Congratulations—you're the boss! You're going to do everything related to selling your house, which means you'll need to answer these questions:

- How do I prepare my home to showcase its best features for a buyer?
- What type of work do I need to do on my home to prepare it for sale?

---

12   "For Sale by Owner (FSBO) vs. Real Estate Agent: Zillow." Home Sellers Guide, December 23, 2019. https://www.zillow.com/sellers-guide/for-sale-by-owner-vs-real-estate-agent/.

13   Full disclosure: Given that we are part of the real estate community, you will naturally see a bias in this section toward working *with* real estate agents. If we didn't believe that we were providing a valuable service, then we'd probably find something else to do with our lives. With that said, we do attempt as much as possible here to be neutral.

- What is the value of my home? How much should I list and sell my house for?
- How do I market it, and where do I advertise it?
- How do I interact with potential buyers and real estate agents?
- How do I negotiate my deal and make sure it's a good deal for me?
- How do I navigate the sales process and all the various steps between contract to close?

You need to be an expert in all of these points in order to ensure the sale goes well. Unfortunately, we're not exaggerating when we use the word "expert." You might *know* how something is supposed to work, but that knowledge is different from actually being able to *do* it at a professional level. For instance, maybe you've watched enough episodes of "Fixer Upper" to know that the color gray is super trendy and farmhouse style is in. It's one thing to *know* that—and another thing to actually transform your house into a Fixer Upper "after" photo.

We both have seen a number of successful FSBO transactions. Admittedly, it's a small number—and many of Kevin's clients come to him after their FSBO attempts have flopped—but some people really can pull this off. If you have the right skills and the right knowledge, selling your home on your own is more doable than it's ever been.

"For Sale by Owner" will make the most sense for these scenarios:

- You deal with real estate often and fully understand all the nuances of the selling process, and/or you know someone who has expertise in this area and will provide you with free advice.

- You want to sell your home to a family member or friend. If you already have a buyer and are less concerned about getting top dollar for your listing, FSBO could make sense for your situation.

If you don't find yourself in either of these categories, this might not be the best option for you. You might want to skip to the next section, or—if you need more convincing—read through the pros and cons to follow.

THE PROS

There's one main pro when you sell your house by yourself: **you don't have to pay a listing agent's commission.** A seller's agent will typically make around 2.5 to 3 percent commission on your home. If you're selling a $250,000 house, that's going to be between $6,000 and $7,000—a substantial chunk of change.

Keep in mind, you're still going to pay all the other transaction fees. You're still going to pay the title company. You will probably still have to pay the buyer's agent's commission. But you won't be on the hook for a listing agent's commission, and that appeals to many sellers.

THE CONS

Selling on your own is challenging to do *well*. Although doing FSBO will save you money on the listing agent's commission, **you might end up *losing* more money than you save if you handle the listing process poorly.** People doing FSBO are often nagged by doubts that they're doing it wrong, or at least not doing it as well as they could. Here are some of the specific questions that might keep you up at night:

- Did you price your house accurately?
- Did you bring the listing to the market in the right way so that you got the max competition for it?
- Did you get expert advice about what you needed to do to clean up your house to get max price for it?
- Do you know what the pitfalls are that can jeopardize real estate transactions and how to navigate them?
- Did you handle the negotiation as well as you could have to get a great deal?
- People that are inexperienced with the real estate contracts often have a hard time making the words and numbers match up on an agreement.

When you're working through all these questions on your own, **you might never have a feeling of emotional assurance** that you're getting it right. Even if you spend hours on Zillow, collecting pricing data and doing your best to apply what you've learned to your listing, you still might come up short. Zillow often gets their "zestimates" wrong because they're entirely based off of algorithms; they can't factor in property nuances like what the neighbors' houses look like or the grade of the land. If you rely solely on Zillow's zestimates, you might commit to the wrong price and ruin your introduction to the market.

Myth: Zillow knows.

Zillow is not always a reliable source of information on pricing. It can't show nuances, like how a neighborhood might change drastically within a couple of blocks. Given its limitations, Zillow should not be your only source for coming up with a list price.

There's also a possibility that **buyers' agents won't want to show your home if they can detect anything amateurish about a listing.** Buyers' agents know that FSBO sellers can be more challenging to work with. They may be unfamiliar with real estate contract wording, which means they might say or do things that communicate the wrong thing to the buyer. Those mistakes can result in lost trust and even cancel the deal, especially if the numbers work out differently than what the seller or buyer had planned on. Often, a buyer's agent might assume an FSBO listing means they're going to end up doing twice the work for half the pay. That doesn't sound great, so they may steer their clients elsewhere.

Another con: it's hard to change hats between real estate agent and homeowner. Let's say a buyer's agent calls the number on your listing, expecting to talk to a real estate agent—but you're not in "agent mode" when you answer the phone, and their first impression is that you don't know what you're doing. Sometimes you'll talk as a homeowner and give insider knowledge of the property; in other moments, you need to talk like a real estate agent and get the deal closed. It can be very easy to confuse those two hats. If a buyer notices some stains on the outside of the house and asks about the gutters, it can be easy to take offense: "Are you implying I've been neglecting needed repairs?" If they muse that the local school has gotten a lot of negative reviews online, well, that's *your* kids' school. Are they suggesting your kids are getting a bad education? It's hard *not* to take these sorts of comments personally, which makes needed neutrality tough.

Likewise, **at the negotiation table, it can be challenging to function as an objective expert.** Whereas a good real estate agent will be skilled in navigating contracts, contingencies, and adjusting their negotiation strategy for different buyers, you may not know all those dance moves. Once again, it may also be challenging to keep your emotions out of the discussion.

Myth: I will save money if I sell my house on my own.

Actually, you might end up seeing a net loss if you inadvertently make some clumsy mistakes in the listing or negotiation process.

HOW TO DO IT WELL

FSBO probably makes the most sense if you're selling to a friend or family member and aren't necessarily looking to sell at max value. However, if you haven't already secured a buyer, we recommend these additional steps to help you sell well.

- Hire a professional to stage and photograph your home. One of the surest "tells" of a FSBO listing is bad photographs or photos of weird things. (You just couldn't resist five close-ups of the new bathroom tiling.) A professional can help you avoid those mistakes.
- Find an expert friend who can help you with bringing your listing to market and assist you during negotiations.
- Consider paying for a professional pricing analysis to be done on your home. Alternately, do extensive research, consulting multiple online databases and people familiar with real estate in your area.
- Look up a good title/escrow company that specializes in FSBO

transactions and can help you more fully understand the transaction process. Since you'll have to pay the title company anyway, you might be able to get some advice from them about navigating the contract-to-close process.

It is possible to do FSBO well, and you'll learn much of the information you need in this book to do it successfully. However, remember that you should consider this book to be a field guide, providing you with tips and information to navigate the trek of selling your home. This field guide can offer you generalities and tips on how most treks will go—but we won't be on hand to tell you what to do if a tree has fallen on the path and obscured the way forward, figuratively speaking. That's when you need an in-person guide—to guide you through the challenges of your unique situation. If you want reassurance that you're listing your home in the best possible way, you might decide it makes the most sense to work with an expert listing agent.

WORKING WITH A FULL-SERVICE REAL ESTATE AGENT

Any real estate seller's agent that's worth his or her salt will offer you seven different services:

1. How to prepare your home objectively for a buyer.
2. Advise you on a listing price and how your house fits into the current market.
3. Market your property and bring it to the open market.
4. Present you with buyers' offers and offer insight on the pros and cons of each.
5. Help you negotiate a contract.

6. Manage the inspections, appraisal, and all the moving parts of the transaction.
7. Interact with all parties to facilitate the closing process and help double-check everything.

It's important to note, these seven services will be performed by a *good* agent. A bad real estate agent will generally go MIA once your house is under contract. A good agent, on the other hand, will work with you from start to finish. They'll meet with you and offer advice before you even list your house, and they'll stay connected until you're settled into your new home.

As you sell your home, you'll eventually gather a team of people around you—your agent, the title company, potentially a mortgage lender, and so on. **Think of your agent as your team's quarterback**: they're the one leading the rest of the team, the one tasked with taking you down the field. A good agent will often be connected with other great team members, just as the best quarterbacks usually play on great teams. If they run into challenges on the field, they'll have the skill and flexibility to run a different play. A great agent means you're going to have a much better chance of a victory.

THE PROS

A good real estate agent basically does everything for you, acting as a buffer at every stage. **They'll be a source of reassurance, expertise, and hand-holding** from the moment you meet with them until you've totally closed on your house sale and settled into your new property. They'll offer clarity: when details or complications come up, a good agent will boil the information down to present you with a simple decision.

The agent is your marketing expert. They're going to tell you exactly what you need to do to update your house and prepare it to be seen. They'll handle the open house and interface with your potential buyers. They'll write your listing and present your home to the world.

The agent will also handle all communication. They'll communicate with the other agent and manage any potential potholes that might come up on the horizon. They'll handle every phone call and every inquiry. They'll lead you during the contract-to-close process and ensure every step goes smoothly.

What do we mean by "manage potential potholes"?

A good agent will anticipate a transaction's weak spots and will work to mitigate them. For instance, if the physical property has some issues, the agent might suspect that the inspection might turn up some bad surprises that could jeopardize the deal. That agent will show up to the inspection and help keep the experience positive. They'll communicate with the other agent: "We know that this isn't a perfect house. Let's come to an agreement that is fair." They'll *manage* that potential pothole.

Another situation: let's say a deal goes through lots of changes from start to finish and has gotten messy. The agent will make a point to ensure the final document reflects all the changes correctly.

Another one: let's say you sold the house at max value, and there's a risk that the bank's appraisal will come up short of the sales price, once again jeopardizing the deal. A good seller's agent might voluntarily send the appraiser information on other comparable sales, pointing out other similar houses that sold for a comparable value: "Here's how we priced the house. Just wanted to provide this to you for your reference." Those efforts could end up bringing in a more favorable appraisal value, causing fewer problems down the road.

These are all "potential potholes" that can jeopardize a deal's success. An agent wouldn't be *required* to make any of these efforts, but good agents will do them voluntarily. They'll spot potential problems ahead of time and work to manage them as needed. If they're good, you'll probably never know about all of the work they did to make that bumpy road smooth.

THE CONS

If you hire a seller's agent, you'll have to pay a listing agent's commission. A good agent will make up for that cost by getting you a better sale in the long run. Still, at face value, getting an agent is more expensive than doing a FSBO.

If you hire a *bad* seller's agent, the results could be disastrous. It's extremely common for people to work with the first agent they meet, particularly if that agent is an acquaintance. However, it takes very little effort to get licensed as a real estate agent, and there are many poor practitioners out there who would love you to pay them—even if they don't have much expertise to give you, and even if they don't plan to work very hard on your behalf.

Working with a bad agent can be incredibly frustrating. Think of how awful it feels when the quarterback of your favorite team is playing badly. Now, imagine that quarterback is holding all of your money as he runs down the field. Every time he messes up a play, he tosses thousands of dollars—*your* dollars—into the air to be blown away in the wind. That's how maddening it can feel working with a bad agent.

A bad agent will botch the list price, meaning your home will be either priced too high or too low. If it's priced too high, you won't get offers; if it's priced too low, you'll get paid much less than you should be—or, worse—people might assume there's something wrong with it and avoid your listing altogether. Their marketing might be bad. They might communicate poorly, messing up conversations with potential buyers, and offering you confusing rather than clarifying information.

The difference between working with a good agent versus a bad agent is significant. In fact, we think it would be better to attempt to do FSBO than work with a bad agent who's leading you badly. So, let's make sure you pick a good one!

HOW TO FIND A GOOD SELLER'S AGENT

Real estate agents are some of the least-trusted professionals in the United States—their trustworthiness ranks just above car salespeople and politicians.[14] Why? Because there are a lot of

---

14 "An Era of Eroding Trust: National Study Reveals Occupations Americans Find the Most – or Least – Trustworthy." An Era of Eroding Trust: National Study Reveals Occupations Americans Find the Most – or Least – Trustworthy | Business Wire, September 18, 2018. https://www.businesswire.com/news/home/20180918005181/en/Era-Eroding-Trust-National-Study-Reveals-Occupations.

bad real estate agents out there, and plenty of us have had bad experiences with them.

Many of these poor-performing agents are doing their best—they're simply inexperienced. Unfortunately, even if their intentions are good, they might still play a terrible game. Other agents may take advantage of you, using tricks of the trade to ensure they benefit from the deal more than anyone else. For instance, a bad agent might tell you that your home is worth more than it actually is so that you hire them, even though they know it's going to sell for less.

Myth: I should hire a seller's agent that I'm personally acquainted with, because I can trust them.

You might trust in someone's good intentions toward you—but can you trust their expertise? It's very easy to become a real estate agent, which means there are plenty of agents who don't yet have the experience or expertise you need in selling your home. You need an *expert* to sell your home. Remember: this is one of the biggest financial and life decisions you will experience in your lifetime. Find someone who will do it well.

If you're acquainted with an agent who has years of experience and excels at selling homes—that's ideal. However, if your acquaintance *isn't* a proven expert in selling homes, we'd advise you to prioritize expertise instead.

Selling your home will be stressful. If your agent ends up performing badly, that could actually ruin a relationship—not strengthen it.

A good real estate agent, on the other hand, can save you thousands of dollars and an untold amount of stress. We devoted an entire chapter to how to find a good real estate agent in Part I—and it's even *more* important to find a good seller's agent than it is to find a good buyer's agent!

Selling a home successfully requires very different skills than what makes a good buyer's agent. Buying a house is relatively easy for an agent—it's fun and exciting, and the buyer's enthusiasm may help gloss over their agent's mistakes.

Selling a home is different: you need someone who is committed to protect you. You're getting ready to sell one of the biggest financial assets you have, and you need someone who will go to bat for every last dollar on your behalf. They need to be strong, technically knowledgeable, and relationally intelligent.

So here's how you find a good one: meet with a few agents; interview them. Walk through your house with them and invite them to share their observations about its selling points and detractions. Get their suggestions on various ways you could prepare your house to sell; see if they can explain how those suggested updates would impact a list price. Ask them for a ballpark pricing estimate.

Tip: Beware of the real estate agents who give you the highest pricing estimate! Those numbers will feel good to hear, but there's a good chance that the agent is just telling you what you want to hear in order to get hired. An inflated estimate is a sign that the agent is either clueless about pricing or not a straight shooter. In either case, you want to steer clear.

As you interview potential agents and walk through your home together, you're asking questions to determine whether or not they have these recommended qualities:

1. **They need to accurately determine the pricing of your house.** Ask a potential real estate agent to explain their pricing process to you. Their answer should thoroughly convince you that they're consulting data, market trends, and their own years of experience.

2. **They need to be a team player.** Selling a home requires a myriad of skills, and it's rare that one person can do everything well. You want to find somebody who can clearly identify where they excel and name other team members who help fill in their deficits. For instance: "My assistant Alison is going to stage your home, and we have a professional take the photographs." If they're collaborative and candid about their own strengths and weaknesses, that's also a sign that you're dealing with someone who will be honest with you on a number of levels.

3. **They have to be comfortable talking about money.** This is the person who's going to advise you on what financial tools to use in listing your house, guide you through your negotiations in which you are dealing with *many thousands of dollars,* and may even weigh in on your planning for getting into a new home. You want someone who is clear-thinking and pragmatic when it comes to finances. They should have financial conversations intelligently and objectively.

4. **They have to be willing to potentially offend you and tell you when you're wrong about your house.** Homeowners famously have inflated ideas of what their home is worth. You don't want to hire an agent who flatters you by agreeing

with that inflated price—your house will not sell well if you go with flattery over reality. You need an agent who will tell you exactly what your home is worth. This agent needs to fight for you during negotiations, which means they have to fully believe in the product they're offering. They won't be able to do that if they know they're marketing a fantasy—therefore, they have to be able to tell you when you're wrong.

5. **They have to be great at standing up for you.** They should show conviction in their beliefs about the quality of your house and have enough of a backbone to defend your property in negotiations. They have to be strong.

6. **They should be experienced.** Ballpark, you're looking for someone with a minimum of three to five years of experience or more who sells around forty to sixty homes per year. If they sell less than twenty-five homes a year, that's a yellow flag to ask more questions. You probably don't want a part-time agent who does real estate as a side hustle; you want an *expert* in the field who is constantly honing their craft and will guide you through this enormous financial and life decision with excellence.

7. **They should interview *you*.** Good agents won't work with everyone; they'll have specialized areas of expertise. They should recognize that they would be a good fit for your needs.

8. **They should educate you.** An agent should justify their opinions with evidence and good rationale. They should genuinely want to help you understand things. You don't want someone who asks you to simply "take my word for it."

After the agent leaves, do a little extra homework. Look up some of their other listings. How do they look? Do you like how they wrote the property description? How is the quality of the photographs? Look up their referrals and read reviews; if those aren't easily found online, then ask the agent for the numbers of their past clients and call them.

We also recommend that you show your potential agent our list of seven services that a good agent will provide, listed a few pages earlier. Ask them to describe their approach and experience with each step; ideally, they will fully convince you of both their expertise and their commitment to their clients.

Does this sound like a lot of work? It's certainly more work than signing up with the first real estate agent you encounter, which is how most people do it. Still—if you want to end up working with an expert over a Joe Blow—the work is going to pay off.

JOE BLOW VERSUS EDDIE EXPERT: A CAUTIONARY TALE

Let's say you don't want to bother doing such a rigorous search for your seller's agent. You meet an agent named Joe Blow through a friend, and Joe seems friendly enough. You ask him a few questions: "How many transactions do you do per year?"

Joe has a reassuring answer: more than thirty. "And," he boasts, "I specialize at selling homes *fast.*"

That sounds pretty good to you: he's experienced, he sells homes fast. Great! You decide to go with Joe. However, if you had done a bit more homework, you might have discovered some red flags. If you'd looked at Joe's other listings, you would have discovered their subpar quality. Joe doesn't like hiring other team members to take photographs or help him stage; he'd rather make as much money off of his deals as possible, which means doing all the work himself—even if it doesn't look great. When he presents your house to the market for the first time, he ends up doing a bad job.

If you had asked Joe to explain his pricing method, he would have given you a confident but vague answer. He would not have tried to reassure you by providing supporting data and evidence; he would have asked you to take his word for it and trust his experience. The truth is, Joe consistently *underprices* his homes—that's how he gets them to move so fast. He's not thinking about how to get you the best price for your home; he's thinking about how soon he can get his commission check. As a result, he lists your home at an inaccurate price. You're going to end up losing thousands of dollars that you had worked hard to earn.

If you were to ask Joe to do a walk-through of your house and offer recommendations on what you could update or rearrange, he'll blow that off. "We're just not going to show buyers the hole in the attic," he says. "We'll just show them the good stuff." He's not interested in helping you make improvements that will improve the market value—that would take too long. He knows he can get buyers in the door if he underprices your home, regardless of what updates you do or don't make.

During negotiations, Joe will not advocate for you; he will deal for himself. He's going to recommend negotiation strategies that will serve *him* well, even if it's not great for you. For instance, let's say Joe's girlfriend is also a real estate agent and brings a buyer who's interested in your home before the listing ever goes live. Joe is likely to advocate you go with that buyer, even if he knows there are likely to be more offers and *better* offers if the home hits the market in the traditional way. Sellers put an enormous amount of trust in their agent's recommendations—which makes things problematic if your agent is pushing a certain buyer not because it's good for *you* but because he wants to score points with his lady.[15] You deserve an agent who will objectively go through all offers with you, highlighting the advantages and disadvantages of each *as they impact you*—one who makes the right recommendations for the right reasons.

Some bad agents are just clueless—they'll do their best for you, but it won't be a good job. Joe is smoother and slipperier than that. He *seems* like he really knows his stuff, but it's because he's a manipulator. He's been around long enough to tell you what you want to hear. It would only be through careful digging that you'd discover the truth about Joe: he's totally in it for himself and will not serve you well.

Now let's say you do your homework, you read reviews, you ask around, and you do a really thorough interview of several different agents. You end up hiring Eddie, the expert. How would Eddie do things differently than Joe?

First of all, Eddie would educate you. He'd walk through your home with you and make recommendations of different updates you could make, giving you a range of small-scale to large-scale changes to consider. He'd sit down with you and educate you about your local market. He'd provide data on what other homes

---

15 Unfortunately, it's not uncommon for real estate agents to want to help out their friends in the business by matching one's buyer with another's seller. If those two agents are bringing together an ideal buyer and an ideal property—that's great. However, if your agent is not being above board, they might push their friend's client as the best option, without highlighting the advantages of a different, better offer.

have sold for in the area, current market inventory, and price ranges correlating to time of year. He'd go over the strengths and weaknesses of your particular home and give you a recommended list price. He'd be able to explain clearly why that price makes the most sense for your home.

He'd bring in team members to help him with the listing. They'd work with you to set your home up to maximum effect, and they would take beautiful pictures. When Eddie brought your home to market, he'd write an eloquent description of it and show it off at its best.

During negotiations, Eddie would advocate on your behalf. He's not just going to be thinking about getting himself through the deal; he's going to consider how best to get you into your next home. For instance, if you get a great offer and you're ready to jump on it, Eddie will ask you to slow down. "This offer only gives you two weeks before you have to be out of your home. Is that going to be enough?" If you haven't found a new place yet, he'll ask for an additional two weeks for you to rent back your place from the new owners, giving you extra time to find a new house and sparing you the trouble of moving twice, saving you between $3,000 and $4,000. If there are multiple offers, Eddie will negotiate with several of them to ensure you have an excellent first deal *and* an excellent back-up deal if anything goes wrong with the first.

None of this is required or expected of a seller's agent; they're responsible for helping you *sell* the home, not buy a new home. But a good agent like Eddie will look out for you and help you spot potholes ahead, ensuring you make it all the way to your comfy La-Z Boy in your new home. They'll use their skill to work for *you*, not just for themselves.

AUCTION AND LIMITED SERVICE

It's worth mentioning two other less common ways to sell your home: auction and limited service.

An auction would be a good option if you need to sell your house in a hurry and don't really care how much you get for it. Auctions make much more sense for dilapidated properties that need a lot of work, because they're sold "as-is." If your house is in mint condition, you'd never want to risk selling it through auction; you could end up losing thousands. Often, the children of a deceased parent will choose to put their parent's house up through auction because it's a fast way to liquidate the estate and doesn't require repairs.

- *Auction Pros:* Auctions are fast and will resolve your selling process quickly. If you sell your home at an "absolute auction," you will be guaranteed to sell your home on that given day. Auctions have the potential to turn out great for you. If you end up getting two people that are both excited about your house, the live-action atmosphere of an auction can whip up their emotions and cause them to compete to the point that one of them ends up committing to a generous offer for the house. That would be ideal! But...

- *Auction Cons:* Auctions can just as easily turn out badly. You're limited to the people that are there. If the auction happens to be scheduled on a day with a terrible hailstorm, fewer people might show up, and you might get a disappointing price for your home. It's a gamble.

Limited service is a good option for people who have some expertise in real estate but still need help in a few areas. Limited service is basically an "a la carte" option for using a real estate agent; it enables you to pay for *some* services, but you're not paying for full-service. For instance, you might put together your listing, but then you pay an agent to post it on the MLS. Or, perhaps you find your own buyer, but you hire an agent via "limited service" to help walk you through the negotiations. You can find a limited-service real estate brokerage by doing a Google search for one in your area. We're guessing these types of brokerages will become more and more popular in the years to come, as technology continues to make it simpler for people to handle many aspects that an agent can now.

- *Limited Service Pros:* This option could enable you to experience the best of both worlds: you pay less for a real estate agent but still get help where you need it most. If you feel relatively confident in your ability to handle most aspects of selling your home but not all, this would be a great option.

- *Limited Service Cons:* With limited service comes limited reassurance. You may find yourself wishing you had an expert on hand to walk you through all parts of the process.

YOUR BEST APPROACH

The right approach for selling your home will be different for everyone, depending on what you prioritize most in selling your home. Although a great full-service real estate agent can do wonders for your home-selling experience, it's also easier than it's ever been to do FSBO, given how technology has changed the real estate market. What matters most to you?

- Consider doing **FSBO** or **Limited Service** if you care most about saving costs and don't feel the need for expertise.
- Consider doing **Auction** if you care most about selling a home quickly.
- Consider doing **Full Service** if you care most about selling at max value and ensuring your home is listed well. (And make sure you find a good seller's agent!)

Regardless of whether you're selling on your own or using the help of a real estate agent, **it's crucial that you have a clear understanding of what your home is worth** so that you can control your expectations and be strategic in negotiations. That's what we're going to talk about next.

– 🔑 –

CHAPTER 13

PRICE AND PRESENTATION

HOW TO PRICE STRATEGICALLY AND MARKET SUCCESSFULLY

EXPERTISE MATTERS: KEVIN NARRATES

I met Jim when he hired my company to do a professional pricing analysis. Jim was attempting to do For Sale by Owner to save $15,000 on agents' commissions, but it wasn't going well. Jim had spent years building himself a gorgeous home. He's a professional tile installer, so the home's construction was beautiful and meticulous. The house was in a great school district, had a big backyard, and was in amazing condition. Jim had a great product to sell. Still, although he'd had several open houses, no offers came in. He couldn't understand what the issue was. That's when he came to us.

I determined that the house should be priced somewhere between $335,000 or $340,000, which was well *over* Jim's list price of $325,000—one of only two instances in my career when an owner has *under*valued their home! What's more, he had been getting ready to drop the price down to $310,000 because it wasn't selling. But Jim's low list price was only part of the problem—the rest of the issues were in his presentation.

The marketing of Jim's listing was terrible. As a result, his property had taken on "stale dud" status after sitting on the market for weeks. All of his pictures had clearly been taken with his phone, and many pictures seemed random—like a closeup of the fireplace mantle he'd hand carved. He was showing the property from his perspective rather than from a buyer's perspective. In Jim's opinion, the quality of his house should have spoken for itself, but—especially given the questions raised by his home's low list price—it wasn't.

Because of Jim's low list price and weird photos, he was attracting the wrong buyers to his open houses. The buyers showing up were looking for a fixer-upper that they could flip and profit from—why else would it be listed so low? When they discovered that Jim actually had a beautiful home in mint condition, they left to go find a better investment opportunity. Meanwhile, the buyers that Jim needed—those who wanted a beautiful home and would be willing to pay a premium for it—were turned off by his poor presentation.

When I sat down with Jim, I brought along some pictures of bad tile jobs I'd found on Google. He was immediately able to recognize the amateurish work. I said, "This is what you've done with your listing, Jim. Your house is worth more than you've listed it for, and there are a bunch of amateur mistakes. Now—what would you think if you walked into a bathroom with this kind of tile work?" We looked at one of the pictures.

He said, "They should have called a professional from the beginning. I could have saved them thousands. Now it's going to take more time and work to clean up the mistakes."

"Right," I said. "That's the situation we've got here. We need to fix some of these amateur mistakes." That resonated with Jim. He understood the analogy perfectly—and he hired us to sell his home.

We pulled Jim's listing off the market and kept it off for several weeks so that people would forget about it. In the meantime, we completely redid his listing. We took new professional photos, bumped *up* the list price to the accurate number I'd determined, and reintroduced his home to the market at $340,000. Over fifty people came to our open house, and we got three offers on the first day. Jim finally sold it for $342,000—$17,000 more than his original list price. Although Jim had been trying to save money by doing FSBO, we ended up making him more money than he would have saved. We also managed to get his house sold!

Here's the moral of the story: **pricing and presentation work together.** One supports the other, and they both need to be done well. The wrong list price can cause your listing to stagnate and raise questions in buyers' minds. It can also cause you to attract the wrong buyers who will end up feeling confused and disappointed by the mixed messaging. It is critical to nail your property's introduction to the market. One of the biggest ways you do that is to ensure you price your home correctly.

For that reason, this is a particular area where **expertise matters**. Pricing will be determined by the state of your home but also from factors *outside* of your home. Both need to affect your pricing strategy. Unfortunately, there isn't a simple equation that you can plug all those factors into and churn out a number—it is both an art and a science. The people who are best equipped to do it will have years of experience and will be emotionally detached from your property.

GET YOUR MIND RIGHT, TIMES TEN

Emotions can cloud objectivity—a theme we've revisited several times in this book. It's okay and healthy to be emotional. Selling your home *is* an emotional process—but that's all the more reason you should consult professional advice when selling your home.

You must objectively understand the product you have if you're going to market it effectively. Are you selling a fixer-upper project, which will attract people looking for discounts? Or are you selling a home, which will attract people looking for abundance and willing to pay a premium? If you're selling the Taj Mahal, you need to market it like the Taj Mahal. If you're selling a turd, be honest about the fact it's a turd and price it to be the most appealing little turd on the market.

To be clear, **here's what *doesn't* impact the value of your home:**

· How much money you've put into it.

- How many memories you've created there.
- What you think it's worth.
- What your real estate agent says it's worth. (Sometimes agents will make an off-the-cuff guess that's not accurate or may even give you an inflated price just so that you hire them. We recommend that you pay someone to do a third party price analysis for you.).

The only thing that matters is: **how much is a buyer willing to pay for your home?** In order to think clearly through that question, you'll need to disconnect from all the personal associations you have with this home. Embrace the fact that you enjoyed it; recognize that you benefited from all the hard work you invested. Now, it's time to view the property as a financial asset. Price and present it to maximum effect, so that it can profit you one last time.

PRICING: THE SCIENCE AND THE ART

There are several factors that impact the *science* of how you should price your home. We're going to briefly touch on those here, but **pricing factors are discussed in much greater depth in Chapter 6 of this book, "Evaluating the Price."** If you haven't already read that chapter or need a refresher, we'd encourage you to go back and review those major pricing factors. Much of the pricing information for buyers will also be relevant to you as a seller. Here they are again, briefly.

THE SCIENCE: EXTERNAL PRICING FACTORS

- **Interest rates:** Low-interest rates mean you can sell for a higher price. High-interest rates mean you should sell for a lower list price. Why? Your target buyers will generally be limited by a monthly payment they can afford. If they have to pay higher interest, they'll look for a less expensive house.

- **Trends in the local area**: If your neighborhood is growing in popularity, that should cause your list price to swing upwards. If the neighborhood is in decline, your list price should go down. Consider what local trends are making your location either more appealing or unappealing to buyers.

- **Time of year**: There are generally far more buyers looking to buy in the warmer months than in the winter, which may mean you can list higher in the summer.

- **Number of buyers and market inventory**: If there are lots of buyers looking for homes like yours, you can list high and negotiate for the terms you want. However, if there are more homes like yours than there are buyers, you might need to drop your price and negotiate to work with the buyers' terms.

- **Comparative Market Analysis (CMA)**: We recommend hiring a professional third-party company or an appraiser to complete a CMA on your home. A CMA will provide data telling you what homes like yours have sold for in your area. The more alike the houses are, the smaller the range of error will be. For instance, in a development where all the houses are the same, it's very easy to see what your house should sell for. The more unique a property is, the wider the potential pricing range will be.

Several of these factors will be easily determined by a quick Google search. Getting a CMA done for your home will take more time, effort, and money—but it's one of the most important steps you can take to price it accurately. This baseline data will give you a clear range to work with. From that platform, you're better informed to consider how some of the intangible factors—"the art"—should sway the price toward the lower or upper part of that range.

THE ART: ALL THE INTANGIBLES

In addition to some of the more data-based pricing factors, there are also intangible factors that should inform your pricing. We're going to categorize those under "the art" because they need to be navigated with nuance and thoughtfulness. Some of these factors will have to do with your buyers, some of them will have to do with the property, and some of them—believe it or not—will have to do with you.

Your Buyer: What They Ate for Lunch Today

Your potential buyers are real people, with real moods, emotions, and good days and bad days. Sometimes, a potential buyer will have a fantastic lunch just before coming to view your home and will be feeling great. Maybe they just rocked a presentation at work; maybe their kid just scored a game winning goal. For whatever reason, they feel amazing. That buyer might see your house, decide it's the one, and make a very generous offer. This seems random and unpredictable—and it is, but we still see it all the time.

As a seller, you should pounce on that offer and then proceed with caution. That buyer may easily start questioning their emotional decision when the mood has passed. They will want assurances through the rest of the negotiating process that your house *is* actually as good as they first thought, and they weren't making a reckless decision. Although your buyers' intangible moods will not impact your decision on the list price, it's an important intangible factor to be aware of during the rest of the negotiations.

Your Property: What Are the Neighbors Like?

What are the neighbors like? Do they have rusted cars parked in their front yard? Do they have a terrifying dog? Or do they have nice landscaping, with a green, freshly mown lawn? **These intangible environmental factors will shape buyers' impression of your home and should also impact price.**

Consider: what does the street look like? Are there sidewalks and hanging baskets of flowers—or is trash littered everywhere? What does the air smell like? Do your neighbors have roses in their front garden, or twenty cats marking up their territory and causing it to reek? What is the grade of the ground? If it's on a very steep hill, that property will be less useful and therefore less valuable. What are the traffic patterns on the street? What is the noise level? What amenities are nearby? Does your building have amazing craftsmanship, or was it built on the cheap?

In addition to the environmental vibe of your neighborhood, **your property has unique pros and cons that will also affect the price.** For instance, we recently listed a home that had a certified ADA-in-law suite (Americans with Disabilities). Without that certified suite, the home would have been worth around $260,000, but the suite made the list price jump up about $50,000. Houses with these kinds of amenities are rare, even though there are many families with ailing relatives that could use them. A family with the financing to afford a property like that will readily pay $50,000 more to take care of their family's health.

So, what unique features does your home have? You'll know these better than anyone: the kitchen drawer that only opens if you also open the oven door; the delightful loft hideaway that's a perfect place for kids to play; the hard-to-access storage space; the pipe in the backyard that needs to be cleared of roots every three years. Which of these features should raise the price of your home? Which should lower it? What, if anything, should be dealt with before you list your home?

Consider your own biases as you evaluate your home's subtleties. You may think your backyard shrine of garden gnomes should hold universal appeal, but it might actually turn some buyers off. Once again, it can be incredibly helpful to have a more objective third party to consider how the intangibles of your home should impact its price. These intangible qualities are hard to quantify but undoubtedly make your property either more or less appealing.

Your Needs: What Strategy Should You Pursue?

Lastly and most importantly, **your own needs and motivations as a seller should impact how you list your home.** Any third party pricing analysis will generally give you a range of low-end pricing to high-end pricing that would be appropriate for your home. The number that you ultimately go with will be heavily informed by your selling strategy—and your selling strategy should be informed by your needs.

What do we mean? Let's say that Kevin came to visit your home and tells you, "If you do nothing to update the home, my recommended list price would probably be between $125,000 and $135,000. But if you decide to put in new countertops in the kitchen, that would raise the appeal considerably. It would also be great to hire some professional landscapers to clean up the yard and increase the curb appeal. With those updates, we could comfortably list your home around $145,000 or $150,000."

Do you have the time, space, and extra cash on hand to make those updates? Is the potential payoff worth the effort? If it is, then go ahead and make the updates; list your home at max value and present a dynamite product.

However, if you don't want to bother with the inconvenience and expense of doing those big updates, that's a legitimate need. In that case, your strategy should prioritize your family's convenience, and you should list your home on the lower end.

We're about to explain three different strategies of how you can price your home along with the range of data provided to you. As you consider which strategy to go with, keep your own needs and motivations in mind. Here are a few common seller motivations that would directly impact a list price strategy:

- **"I don't want to invest any time or money into updating my home, but I still want to sell quickly."** This motivation is common among sellers with dilapidated homes who don't want to invest the time and money into updates; these sellers should price their home to attract cash investors—i.e., on the lowest end of the CMA data.

- **"I'm willing to invest the time and energy to maximize the profits."** In that case, take the time to do improvements. Invest in an agent who will do top-notch marketing to fuel competition among buyers. List at the high end of the CMA data and hold your line during negotiations. Don't overprice it, or else you'll scare off most buyers. Competition among buyers is the main reason homes sell above the asking price; if you ruin your opportunity to create competition, you lose out on your best buyers.[16]
- **"I have a nice home, but I don't want to invest any more time and energy into updates."** We see this motivation often in people who have relocated and are still waiting to sell their old house. Every day that they maintain ownership of their (now empty) house, they're paying holding costs: the insurance, the mortgage, the taxes, etc. They're also dealing with the opportunity cost of not being able to invest that money elsewhere and the emotional cost of not being able to move on while they're dragging that burden behind them. For sellers like this, they need to do a balancing act with their list price. We'd recommend listing at the low to middle range of the CMA, and ensure you market it well.

Start with the science: gather all the numbers determined by a CMA, interest rates, market trends, time of year, and so on. That will help you determine an appropriate range of pricing for your home.

---

16 This recommendation would change if it's a seller's market versus a buyer's market. In a buyer's market, listing on the higher end with good marketing will hopefully stir up enough competition that you get your asking price. In a seller's market, listing in this manner could create so much competition that you get beyond your asking price and "press the market forward," meaning your home could be the new highest price home sold in your area and increase the value of your neighborhood.

Then, apply the art. Consider your home's intangible qualities, the relative appeal (or detractions) made by its surrounding environment, and your own needs as a seller. Once you have all that information gathered, it's time to choose the best strategy to list your home.

THREE STRATEGIES TO PRICE

There are three ways you can choose to price your home along the range determined by "the science and the art" factors we just discussed:

1. **List it low, watch it go.**
2. **List it right, sell it tight.**
3. **List it high, never say goodbye.**

Let's think of a real example to help us consider the pros and cons of each strategy. Jerry and Lois are getting ready to sell their home, and they think it's worth $400,000. However, after Kevin completes a CMA for them, he determines it's actually worth closer to $360,000. Jerry and Lois have cared for and maintained their home well, so they want to get a good price for it. However, they also need to sell it quickly. Other agents have told them it's worth $400,000—so, how should they price their home? Let's discuss.

Keep in mind that all of these strategies should still occur within a reasonable range. If your list price goes way *below* its appropriate range and is marketed badly, buyers will assume there's something horribly wrong with your home and avoid it; you may also attract the wrong kind of buyer, like Jim in our opening story. If it's listed way *above* its appropriate range, buyers will ignore it entirely and go look for a different listing.

LIST IT LOW, WATCH IT GO

Listing low would make sense for Jerry and Lois if they decide their main motivation is to sell in a hurry or if it's a strong seller's market. If they're selling a great home and there are a ton of buyers on the market competing for every available house, their low list price could attract lots of potential buyers and result in a bidding war. In that case, they're not only going to sell quickly; they're also going to end up getting much more than their low list price. They might list at $360,000 and end up selling for $375,000. That strategy, however, depends heavily on lots of buyer competition.

If it's a slower market, this strategy won't work as well. Listing low would probably result in *selling* low. If your home could have potentially sold for tens of thousands more, this is a major drawback. However, if Jerry and Lois' main motivation is to sell it quickly, listing low might still be the appropriate strategy for them.

LIST IT RIGHT, SELL IT TIGHT

This is what we'd consider to be the ideal option because it's most consistently the best way to get the max price on your home. Here's why: the day you introduce your home to the market is like your "grand opening." Everyone is excited to see the new homes on the market, and if you've listed your home right, you'll present it as a high-quality product at an appropriate value. That's going to attract buzz, lots of interested buyers, and likely multiple offers. **We see houses most consistently selling for their max value when the seller nails the introduction to the market and sells on day one.**

Let's say that Jerry and Lois decide to factor in the CMA data but also recognize that, due to the intangible and environmental appeal of their home, they can pitch it slightly higher than the data. In other words, they're combining the analytics with the human element to make a wise decision. They take some time to do a few cosmetic updates, which will heighten the appeal of their photos and list it at $380,000.

The message Jerry and Lois send out with this listing is that their property is unique, it's quality, and they're confident that they've got a great product. They're going with the high side of the data, and that's okay because they've got something great to offer. They get multiple offers on the first day and end up selling for $387,000.

Listing right will take a little more care and effort, but it's consistently the best way for sellers to maximize their profit.

LIST IT HIGH, NEVER SAY GOODBYE

Now, let's say that Jerry and Lois want to ignore the CMA data entirely for emotional reasons, and they throw the analytics out the window. They love their house. They think it deserves a high price—at least $400,000, heck, why not $410,000? In this case, Jerry and Lois are doing the equivalent of attempting a half-court shot. Their list price is a wish and a prayer; likely, they're setting themselves up for disappointment.

Here's why: if you don't list your house right, you *lose* your best chance to get multiple offers from all that first-day buzz. **The longer your house sits on the market, the less attractive it becomes.** All the shiny, buzzworthy, novelty appeal that was with you on day one goes away, and your home now becomes the wallflower of the real estate market. That's a bummer.

Typically, when sellers want to list with an **inflated price**, we see one of three scenarios play out:

- **The house sits on the market forever.** As the "days on market" number rolls into weeks and months, buyers may start to assume there's something terribly wrong with the house. The sellers might get so demoralized and tired, that they'll negotiate badly when they finally do get a buyer and, once again, lose money. In other instances, the sellers may remain determined to get their top price. When they can't, they give up trying to sell it and decide to rent it out instead, which introduces a new set of potential problems.
- **The sellers do some necessary work to update the house and increase its appeal so that they *can* command the higher list price they want.** However, rehab fixes can be stressful, and there's no guarantee that the house will sell for enough to make the financial gains worth the stress of the updates. This can sometimes be a savvy investor move, but the juice isn't always worth the squeeze.
- **You get lowball offers that are hard to negotiate.** For instance, let's say Jerry and Lois' home is worth $380,000, but they list it at $410,000. After sitting on the market forever, they finally get an offer for $340,000. The difference between that offer and their list price is so vast that

negotiations are extremely difficult to navigate, and tensions ride high throughout the process. They finally sell for $350,000—far below what their home is actually worth and an embarrassing amount lower than their asking price. Their selling process turns out to be a depressing and demoralizing experience.

If you list it high, you're also going to attract critical buyers. People will come in looking for the reasons why your home is listed at such a high price. If there's not something obvious to justify that high price, like a waterpark hidden in the backyard or a rooftop patio that you forgot to mention, those buyers are going to scrutinize every bit of your home. "I guess it's a nice kitchen, but is it really *that* nice of a kitchen? Look! This tile is cracked. Totally not *that* nice of a kitchen."

On the other hand, if you've listed your house accurately, people are crowding into the kitchen saying, "Wow! It's a nice kitchen! This home is a great deal." When you lose out on that grand opening buzz and inevitably create critical attitudes in your buyers, you're most likely going to be forced to sell for less than you would have if you'd listed it right.

Although listing *low* can work well under certain market conditions, and listing *right* almost always results in the greatest success, listing high is basically never a good idea. If you go way beyond the analytics' recommendation, you're banking on finding a buyer who's just had the best lunch of his life, has money to burn, and/or is clueless about appropriate market values. That's a gamble that has slim odds for success.

PRESENTATION

So, you've picked your list price! Now, how do you make sure you actually *get* that price? That's where marketing comes in. The following strategies will help you present your home in the best possible way and nail that introduction to the market.

BE SMART ABOUT UPDATES

After walking through your home, your agent will likely make a number of observations. "It's a great backyard, but the shed is an eyesore. You might want to consider tearing it down. Your kitchen is roomy but will be perceived as dated. This couch has been well-loved; we might want to move it out before the open house. Great master bathroom! What do you think about taking down the wallpaper? Wait—and how old is the roof?"

In preparing your home to be listed on the market, there are probably any number of updates you could do to spiff up your property. Some updates are costly, time-consuming, and may not ultimately increase your selling price as much as you'd hoped they would. It can also be frustrating to make updates to your home, which you've always wanted, just as you're preparing to leave. So what updates are actually worth the effort and money?

We recommend easy, aesthetic changes—a "mini flip." Paint color on the walls and trim is a quick way to update your home with current trends. Furniture arrangement can also help boost appeal. You might even consider buying new, cheap furniture that's aesthetically appealing; the effect will lead most people to assume this is enormous value added. Instead of replacing the cabinets in your kitchen, consider painting them. Instead of redoing the landscaping for your front yard, consider investing in a few hanging plants for the porch.

Regarding bigger updates: weigh the potential payoff against the time, effort, and expense of the update. A kitchen remodel probably won't make sense for someone about to sell; it's a massive, expensive, time-consuming undertaking, which will cause huge inconvenience to you. Your potential buyers would probably prefer to do their own kitchen design anyway. If your kitchen is dated, drop the price. On the other hand, a furnace replacement could potentially be done quickly and inexpensively. You can find a decent furnace in our area for around $3,000, but most people will assume that's around $7,000 in value added to the home. That new furnace gives your agent an easy selling point for very little effort on your part.

If there's a real problem, solve those material problems so you can stand firm on your price. If you don't want to deal with them, that's okay—but in that case, be honest with your buyers about the issues and recognize that those problems will necessitate a lower price. It's not okay to hide the issues; in fact, in many cases, it's actually illegal.

Consider what *could* be updated and what *should* be updated to maximize your value. Is the juice worth the squeeze?

PREP YOUR HOME FOR ITS CLOSE UP

Now that the big updates have been sorted out, it's time for the **finishing touches**. Get everything clean and well organized. Put out some flowers or a few new potted plants. Clear out clutter and personal stuff. Take the kids' art and the family photos off the walls. You want people to envision living *their* lives in your home, not see how *you* lived your life in that home.

Consider hiring a professional to help you with staging, unless you have a great sense of current trends and an intuitive knack for furniture arrangement. Less is more when it comes to staging. Rooms look larger when they're not full of furniture, but a few pieces here and there can help people envision how they could enjoy a space—for instance, some Adirondack chairs on the patio, or barstools at the high-top counter. You want neutral colors and neutral pieces so that buyers can envision themselves in your home. (It's probably best to put Aunt Jana's red antique Chinese sideboard into temporary storage.) A professional will know how best to arrange the furniture to flatter the space.

Once your home is ready for its close-up, it's time to take your pictures. **We recommend hiring a professional to do your photos.** Most websites only show the first five photos of your listing in their preview pane, so always put the best pictures first. You have less than twenty seconds to catch someone's attention; with a real estate listing, that attention-grab will be accomplished by your pictures. So, make sure they're good ones! There's a big difference between photos taken by a $75 professional and a $400 professional, and it's worth it to spend the $300 extra on something this important. (That could translate into tens of thousands of dollars gained if you get multiple offers!) A high-end real estate photographer will not only take high-quality photos, they'll also know how to best capture the feel and possibilities of your house.

The better the pictures, the more buzz your home is going to get. The more buzz, the more people will show up at your open house—and if you can pack that open house, you're almost guaranteed to get multiple offers. There will be a feeling of competition among the various buyers, which will create a sense of demand, driving bids up.

Myth: I should use filters to make my home look brighter, bigger, and more attractive.

Actually, no! You don't want buyers feeling disappointed with the real thing when they arrive with inflated expectations based on your highly edited pictures. Your photos should be inviting but not unrealistic. You want buyers to conclude, "This home looks pleasant and I could see myself living there. I want to see more!"

BEN NARRATES: TELL YOUR PROPERTY'S STORY

Every home has a story—and with each new buyer, there's a new potential story that could unfold. In your listing, you want to tell that story. There will be a spot in your listing where you can include a brief paragraph describing the home. This description can make or break your introduction to the market; it can either give buyers a vision of how they could enjoy your home or it can land completely flat. Here's an example.

I recently found a ranch property that looked as though it might be a diamond in the rough. However, the property description was terrible—it was basically an apology:

Ranch on large parcel with a pond. This home features three bedrooms and one bathroom, one set up as a master with a kitchen area. Home does need repairs. Value is mostly in the land, but the home could be redone and make a good investment for the right buyer. This property is eligible under Freddie Mac first look initiative; "as is" sale. Buyer needs to verify all information. Buyer or buyer's agents responsible to check all building codes.

The description makes it sound like this home is a tear-down that should be purchased by investors only—but the "Freddie Mac first look initiative" is for homeowners. So who are they gearing the description toward? As it stands, both investors and homeowners are likely to be turned off. The pictures were also all wrong. Although the listing states that the value is mostly in the land, there wasn't a single picture of the land!

When I went to look at the property, it was beautiful. The properties around it were also beautiful. The house had been listed at $49,000 but would probably be worth $175,000 after being renovated. I estimated that it would need between $50,000 and $70,000 worth of work, but that's still a bargain for what you could gain. You could have easily written a story that gave people an idea of how they could enjoy it:

> *Spacious three-bed/one-bath family home in desirable neighborhood on a beautiful two and a half acres with fishing pond. The house is every DIY homeowner's dream: with TLC, this diamond in the rough will make for a fantastic investment and you'll have plenty of room in the budget to renovate to taste. Property is incredibly versatile and ripe for use—plant a garden, build a treehouse, build memories fishing in the pond, build a garage for your RV. The sky's the limit![17]*

With a story like that, along with professional photos of the land,

---

17   Property description based off a listing by Erick Salgado, with Palisade Realty, Inc.

the pond, the views—this property could have been presented as the gem that it is.

When you list your home, your photos and description should give buyers a vision of how they could enjoy your property. Tell *their* story back to them: the story of how their lives could pleasantly unfold in the home you're selling.

When you're writing this story, it's important to **consider your buyer's profile.** If you know you're selling a fixer-upper, then you're going to want to target your story to people interested in doing a home flip. If you're selling a beautiful home for max value, you want to write your story to people who want a move-in ready home, with lots of fantastic amenities to enjoy. Think through the people who will be most interested in buying your home. What do they care about most in buying a home? With that in mind, write the story for them.

OTHER MARKETING TIPS

Here are a few more tricks of the trade:

- **Be mindful of buyer search bands.** Buyers will typically enter a price range they're looking for: "$150,000 to $200,000." If you price your home at $205,000, you're going to miss all those buyers who have identified $200,000 as their upper limit. On the other hand, if you price your home at $199,000, your listing will be seen by all those buyers. If it's a great home for that price, there's a good chance you'll get multiple offers and may end up walking away with the $205,000 you were hoping for.

- **The day of the week matters.** Homes listed on a Thursday will attract more interest than homes listed on a Monday. A home that pops up on a Thursday will get people's attention as they're heading into the weekend. You're giving people enough time to get excited about your home and adjust their plans to show up to your Saturday open house. On the other hand, a home listed on a Monday is competing with everyone's back-to-work distractions. By the time their weekend rolls around, they may have forgotten about it.
- **Days on market can be a killer.** Your home will sell for the best price if it sells within its first few days on the market. Let's say you list your home at $375,000, and a hundred people who are looking for a house between $350,000 and $400,000 see the listing. Those people will either decide they're interested and try to nab it before anyone else does—or decide they're not interested. If the second week rolls around, and those hundred people have decided they're not interested, you're now banking on *new* buyers showing up. Your showings may drop from twenty-five in the first week to two in the second week. The longer your home sits on the market, the more buyers will be wary of your product, and its perceived value will decrease. In the end, you're going to end up getting lowball offers from bargain hunters.

HAPPILY EVER AFTER

Have you caught on to the weirdness of what we're asking you to do? We're asking you to *disconnect* from the story of your home so that you best *tell* the story of your house.

Your home has a feeling and a vibe and a story—a great story of people who have lived there, thrived there, and made memories there. However, in order to tell that story effectively, with all the tricks that will make buyers perk up and pay attention, you have to disconnect from that story.

As a seller, you need to switch from the homeowner mindset to the investor mindset, where you see your home as an asset. Take down your kids' framed art; repaint the walls in a neutral color; swap out your comfortable La-Z Boy recliner with a smaller, sleeker armchair. Price it accurately, stage it effectively. You're seeking to become neutral toward your house in order to objectively assess how it fits into the current market.

Ironically, those shifts and changes away from the "personal" enable you to provide signals to buyers that will more effectively share your property's story: this is a good house. This is a loved house. This is a place that could house *your* memories, that could benefit *your* family.

When you nail the story, the pricing, and the presentation, your home is likely to attract lots of buyers in its first few days on the market. If you get great attendance at your open house, buyers will feel an increased sense of confidence that your home has great value, that it's a desirable product, and that *they want to live there.* That's going to result in multiple bids, great offers, and delighted buyers who want to continue the good story of your house.

And guess what that means for you? A satisfying conclusion, a great new beginning, and a story that looks a lot like happily ever after.

CHAPTER 14

NEGOTIATING
THE CONTRACT

HOW TO CREATE A WIN-WIN
SITUATION FOR ALL

KEVIN NARRATES: HOLDING YOUR LINE

Rebecca hadn't just completed basic maintenance on her house—
she had consistently *updated* it at HGTV-worthy standards. When
she put it on the market, she had full confidence that anyone who
ended up buying her house would get a gem. My pricing data put
her house around $450,000, which was the recent selling price
of a bigger home in the same neighborhood. Rebecca wanted to
list it at $495,000. We weighed the pros and cons of listing it
so high, but she was firm on that price. She believed her house
was at such a high quality, she could push the market forward.

Rebecca got an offer for $450,000 on the first day and didn't entertain it. She got a second offer for around the same price and began negotiating with those buyers. For *two weeks*—basically an eternity in real estate terms—she negotiated with those buyers, increasing their bid by $35,000. Ultimately, however, that deal fell through. I started getting nervous for Rebecca but she was not deterred. She believed in her house.

Finally, Rebecca's perfect buyers came along. Their grandchildren lived in Rebecca's neighborhood, and they were wealthy. They wanted to find a nice, comfortable home to live in near their grandkids and were willing to spend a premium. Those were exactly the kind of buyers that Rebecca's listing attracted: she was marketing it as a premium product at a premium price, and that's what these buyers were looking for. When they did the walkthrough, Rebecca's house did not disappoint. It was every bit as immaculate as we'd marketed it to be. Rebecca ended up selling for $490,000, and everyone walked away feeling great.

Most people could not have gotten away with listing so high, but Rebecca was able to pull it off for this reason: she knew what she had and was confident about her home's value. Because of all the time and money Rebecca had invested in updating her home, it was as close to "brand new" as a used house could ever get. She knew she had resolved every one of her house's issues. She knew she had updated it with quality materials in fashionable ways. She had evaluated market prices and was deliberate about choosing a high listing price. When other lower offers came her way, she unflinchingly held her ground. She was confident she had done the hard work to warrant a better offer—and her ultimate buyers were happy to reward her for it.

CREATING A WIN-WIN

The negotiating process can either be one of the most stressful episodes in the home-buying journey or one of the most gratifying. It will be stressful if you view the negotiation as a win-lose scenario, where your buyer is an adversary that you need to beat. That's going to be hard, frustrating, and exhausting. However, if you view your buyer as a partner in a transaction—someone who is *giving* something to you even as you *give* to them—you can pursue a scenario where everyone wins. **Negotiations should be understood as agreements.**

> **Myth: During negotiations, my main focus should be to get as much money as I can out of my buyer.**
>
> Negotiations are about much more than money. If you focus solely on money, you're almost guaranteed to walk away from the negotiation feeling lousy. Negotiations are about timing, convenience, your property's condition, your motivations, your buyer's motivations, and everyone's needs. When you enter into the negotiation with the whole picture in mind, you're going to have an easier time getting your needs met, getting your buyer's needs met, and making sure you all walk away feeling good.

In the best negotiations, no one's trying to swindle someone else and get something for nothing. Instead, the negotiation should center around how best to affect a *trade*: the buyer is giving you an accurate amount of money, and you're trading them for the accurate house. Along the way, you want the trade to go down smoothly by arranging timing that works for everyone and including contingencies to make sure everyone's protected. You conduct yourself with truth and transparency; you don't have

anything to hide. *This* is how selling a home can become a gratifying, meaningful experience: you bless your buyers with a home
that you've loved, and you do it right.

Maybe you're thinking to yourself, "Actually, I'd really rather
have a few extra thousand dollars than that warm fuzzy feeling.
Other people can prioritize the moral high ground, but I'd prefer
the money." We don't blame you if you think that—we are not
strangers to that rationale.

But here's what we've discovered: when you gouge someone, it
follows you. It haunts you. We know a real estate agent who was
getting ready to sell a house that he'd fixed up. It was a cute
house, but one of the foundation walls was at a massive slant.
This agent—we'll call him Ray—could have spent $5,000 to *claim*
he'd had the wall fixed or could have spent $15,000 to properly
fix it. He opted for the first option and ended up selling the
house to a young woman who believed him when he told her
the foundation had been dealt with. Almost immediately, she
started experiencing problems. She's either going to need to
spend $10,000 to $15,000 to fix her house, or she'll have to
eventually sell for much less than she got it for.

Ray, in the meantime, can't forget this. Sure, he walked away with
that $10,000, but his reputation is now in question because the
young woman has a legal and ethical suit against him.

There's a way to ensure you get a good price for your home while
still maintaining a positive rapport with your buyers. That's what
this chapter is all about.

THREE CHARACTERISTICS OF SUCCESSFUL NEGOTIATION

So how do you negotiate effectively? There are three pieces to achieving a successful negotiation. We're going to talk about each one, along with some additional tips:

- **Know your product.** If it's solid, keep the price high; if it's crappy, lower it.
- **Know your primary motivation in selling.** Take the steps necessary to achieve that goal and work toward that primary motivation in negotiations.
- **Know the other person's motivation** and gear your negotiating style toward their goals.

BEN NARRATES: KNOW YOUR PRODUCT

In order to successfully bring about a win-win scenario during negotiations, the most important thing you can do is to **know the quality of your product.** If you know your home has lurking issues, like a thirty-five-year-old roof, or a leaky kitchen pipe, or a dead tree out back, you will not be able to stand your ground on a maximum price as Rebecca did. You'll need to make appropriate concessions to your buyers. However, if you know you've invested thousands of dollars over the years into updating and maintaining your home and are selling a premium product, you're going to feel much more confident holding firm.

Confidence in your list price is huge when it comes to negotiating—that's why we just spent an entire chapter going over how to price your home accurately. **Negotiations are based on an internal fortitude regarding your list price.** Before you negotiate with a buyer, you negotiate internally with yourself. You're thinking, "Is that dropped price reasonable? Is this the only buyer that will make an offer? Is my house worth less than I think it is?" When you confidently know the worth of your product, those questions won't bother you; you'll have the internal fortitude to stick to your guns during negotiations. But without that inner confidence, your resolve is likely to weaken.

Here's an example: I once helped remodel a home that had a small section with a flat roof. In the area under the flat roof, I noticed a stain: clearly, the flat roof had issues with leaking. Rather than just patch the leak and clean up the stain, my partner and I decided to go the extra mile. We replaced the flat roof entirely with a rubber roof that would never have issues with leaking. We didn't have to do this—none of our potential buyers would think to scrutinize that one section of roof. But we knew we were saving the future homeowners trouble down the line.

When it came to negotiations, we didn't hesitate to say no to buyers who wanted to offer beneath our asking price. I knew that I was selling a great house and I wanted to wait for the buyer who could recognize and appreciate that. My internal voice was thinking, "I know I've done right by these future homeowners, and I'm not okay with someone treating me poorly. I did the hard work, and I deserve to be rewarded for that."

Sure enough, we got that buyer willing to pay top dollar, and she was delighted to get a house that had been restored so well. If I had left that roof as-is, I would have gotten nervous and dropped my price. That inner voice would have doubted that the property was worth my asking price, and I would have caved.

I know this because I often buy dilapidated properties to restore, and I can see the sellers weaken during negotiations. All I have to do is ask them questions about the property. I can see their wheels turning as they self-negotiate, and eventually, they acknowledge that the property has many signs of neglect. It's easy at that point to come to the shared conclusion that their price should drop to reflect the cost of that neglect.

Here are some pointers which will ensure you know your product, know its worth, and can bring that internal fortitude to the table.

- **Be objective.** Get a Pricing Analysis done for your home and use the data as your starting reference point. Remember to shift from the homeowner mindset to the investor mindset so that you're not unduly influenced by your emotions during negotiations.
- **Recognize the updates you've done and the updates that are still needed.** What property problems have you resolved for your future homeowners? Did you fix them permanently, or only temporarily? Have you left some issues unresolved? Is your home updated in the most current trends, or will your buyers likely want to invest some money into remodeling? During negotiations, these considerations should cause you to either make concessions to the buyer or hold your line.
- **The market will tell you quickly what your home is worth.** If your home is on the MLS, the market will work efficiently and tell you whether you got it right. If people are excited about your home, you'll get lots of interest quickly along with multiple offers; negotiate with that bargaining power. If your home is still on the market after three to four weeks, that's a pretty clear sign it's overpriced. If you get an offer, under-

stand that you may need to make some painful concessions in negotiations.

- **Control your expectations.** Remember that nothing is free in life. Your property's issues will cost you one way or another: either you invest the money to fix them while living there, or you sell at a lower price. If you've put in the money to resolve those issues while living in your home, then that investment should pay off when you sell: hold your line during negotiations. If you've held off on making repairs, you'll need to sell your home for less. Price it accurately, be honest about the issues, and then hold your ground on that accurate price.
  - If your home is nice (it's been maintained, updated, and there are no major issues), expect full offers.
  - If it needs work, expect offers to take this into account. Be logical and give a discount.
  - A "mini flip" will help increase your home's value but won't substitute for bigger updates. Be realistic about what future costs you're passing onto homeowners when you negotiate (e.g., a new roof in the next five years; a new furnace in the next two years), and then sell for an accurate price.

Myth: If I've done a good job maintaining my home, I should expect top dollar.

Maintaining is different than *updating*. Maintaining is like changing the oil in your car; you're doing what's needed to prevent problems down the road. Updating is like getting a new *engine* for your car or totally replacing the interior with newer designs. If you've done a good job making repairs on your home, then you've done good maintenance; that should be reflected in a solid list price. However, if your home still needs updates—if it looks dated—you should not expect top dollar.

In sum: negotiate from a place of reality. If you need help clearly seeing what that reality is, bring in some professionals to give you objective advice. Negotiations go well when the seller knows what they're giving, and the buyers know what they're getting. This requires you to be self-aware about your product and transparent with the buyer.

KNOW *YOUR* MOTIVATION

What's most important to you as a seller? During negotiations, it's important to identify your primary motivation and negotiate strategically to achieve that goal. Are finances most important? Is timing your biggest need? Do you want the convenience of selling as-is or do you want to do work? It's unlikely that you will get *everything* that you want during negotiations, but if you understand your primary motivation, then you can focus the negotiation on achieving that goal. You'll also have an easier time accepting the results if you need to concede on some less important points.

Here are a few ways your primary motivation could lead you in your negotiating style. (Note: these tips are generalities. In your own negotiation, there will probably be more nuance and complexity.)

- **Motivated by profit:** Wait for a buyer who shows real appreciation for your home and is willing to pay top dollar. During negotiations, you might also want to push for the buyer to pay most of the closing fees and prorated costs.
- **Motivated to sell quickly:** If there are multiple offers, you should go with the buyer who has the surest financing, even if it's not the highest bid; that way, you're less likely to get

stalled during escrow. You also want a buyer who is willing to do their own repairs, and you should expect to drop your price rather than do the needed repairs yourself.

- **Motivated by timing**: If your main motivation revolves around timing, you need a buyer that will work with you on convenience. You might go with a lower bid on the condition that they give you an extra two weeks to remain in your home after the closing date, for instance. Perhaps you need to pull off a simultaneous close, so you go with the buyer with the most reliable financing to do that successfully.

Motivated by the buyer: Maybe you're getting ready to sell your beloved grandfather's home and you really don't care how much you get for it or when the deal closes—you just want to make sure it goes to homeowners who will enjoy it, rather than investors who will demo it and build two new houses on the property. That's fine; look for the buyer who will help you achieve *that* goal and understand that you should expect to make concessions in other areas. **When people are unclear on their motivation, they can easily get stuck.** Let's say James wants to get the maximum profit on his home, but he hasn't identified that as his main motivation. He doesn't do the updates needed to bring his home to max value. He goes with a less experienced agent who does a sloppy job with his listing. James hasn't done the *work* to achieve his motivation. When James gets lowball offers, he gets jammed up. He's frustrated and disappointed with the offers he's getting— even though the lower offers are an accurate reflection of how he brought his home to market. He doesn't want to accept those low offers and ends up getting stuck with a house he can't sell.

Conflicting motivations can also jeopardize your ability to

stay neutral during negotiations. Your own inner conflict can cause you to get confusing—for instance, if you want max price *and* want to avoid doing repairs: "I'm not going to accept that low price! They keep bringing up the roof issue. So what if it's thirty years old? It's in good condition! Why should I replace it?" When you're consumed by the emotions stirred up by those conflicting motivations, you can't think about the other person; you're too busy thinking about yourself. At that point, you might easily offend them and lose the deal.

When you're *clear* on your motivation, you can match your goal with the next logical steps. During negotiations, you can prioritize that goal and feel good when you get it. You don't need to feel bad about concessions you make which are outside of that goal. You might even feel greater appreciation for the buyer who's helping you achieve your main motivation, which will help negotiations go smoothly.

COMMON POINTS SELLERS CAN NEGOTIATE

Just about anything can be negotiated when you're selling your home—even that Big Green Egg grill in your backyard! Here are some of the more common points to negotiate:

- **House price:** You've determined your best list price but expect offers to bounce around that number. Consider how much you're willing to bend on that price in order to sell and/or whether or not you'd be willing to drop your price to secure other points of negotiation.
- **Closing costs:** Determine who will pay them and/or at what percentage.

- **Repairs (negotiated after inspection):** Sellers can either make the repair themselves or offer to drop the price for buyers. Generally, it's easier and more convenient to simply drop the price; however, it will be more strategic to complete the repairs for certain buyers. (We'll explain more about this later in the chapter.)
- **Home warranty premium:** Sellers can purchase a one-year home warranty for the buyer that covers items such as appliances and small homeowner repairs that homeowner's insurance doesn't cover.
- **Closing/Possession dates:** Flexibility on when the new buyer takes possession of the house can be helpful for both sellers and buyers. Sellers may need a few extra weeks to get into a new home, or buyers may want to finish up a lease or close on their former house first. Buyers may also ask sellers to pay the penalty for breaking their lease early.
- **Furniture, cosmetic updates, etc.:** You might have furnishings that work with your home's unique space and don't want to take them to your new home. A buyer may choose to buy some of the seller's furniture and/or amenities. They can also ask for certain cosmetic updates to be made, like paint colors or new flooring.

KNOW *YOUR BUYER'S* MOTIVATION

Different buyers will bring different goals to the table, and therefore different negotiation styles. If you can identify your buyer's motivation, you can be smart about how you proceed. You're less likely to be taken advantage of, and you'll be able to speak to the buyer's needs in a way that leaves everyone feeling good.

There are generally three types of buyers: the investor buyer, the homeowner buyer, and a rare few who are a combination of both. Here's how we'd recommend negotiating with each:

- **The Investor Buyer (approximately 45 percent):** It's all about the money. These are people looking for a deal. They'll nit-pick your house and do everything possible to make you feel bad about your product—and even yourself! They'll often know more about financing and the market than you and will come across as informed, savvy, and intimidating. They will be well-practiced in their rationale to get you to lower your price. (This is why you need that internal fortitude!) They know they're likely to make money on your house.
  - *How to negotiate with investor buyers:* Regardless of how they scrutinize your home, these investors see your property as a diamond in the rough that they can profit from. So **spell out the future they're envisioning:** "I'm asking $150,000 for my house. I know that once this home is all redone, it could easily sell for $270,000, and it only needs $60,000 worth of updates. I'm offering you the right price. I'm not going to give you a dime more." Give them the *vision* of how they stand to profit. They might try to distract you by complaining about your home's current condition, but internally, they're looking ahead to what your home could be—so meet them there. Don't bother offering to do repairs for investor buyers; they'd rather do the repairs themselves.
- **The Homeowner Buyer (approximately 45 percent):** It's all about the experience. These buyers, aka "retail buyers," are mainly thinking with a homeowner mentality. They're considering what the house will be like to live in; generally, they're not thinking about profits. They usually buy properties for what they're listed for. They are consumers; often, they don't know much about real estate.
  - *How to negotiate with homeowner buyers:* Experience is everything

for these buyers. They're looking to buy a home for their family, and they want to have a meaningful story about how it all worked out. Be affirming and encouraging. Offer to do any repairs identified during the inspection so that they have a perfect entrance into their home. In fact, you can expect to devote approximately 1 percent of your list price toward requested repairs for these buyers.

Myth: The best offers are the biggest ones.

Actually, sometimes those offers will be the least reliable. One particular type of homeowner buyer is **the emotional buyer,** and they're often the ones making offers way above the asking price. The emotional buyer makes their offer in the midst of an emotionally charged moment—maybe in the middle of a packed open house. You might be excited by their enormous offer, but proceed with caution! That emotion will wear off, and these emotional buyers are prone to buyer's remorse, especially if they overpaid. If any issues come up with the inspection or appraisal, they may look for an excuse to back out of the deal or get the price down. Particularly if buyers overpay, they want everything to be PERFECT. So, do your best to give them the best experience possible. Respect the fact that you're giving them a story and make it a nice one. A positive experience between contract to closing will help assure the emotional buyer that they made the right decision.

- **The Homeowner/Investor Buyer (approximately 10 percent):** It's all about making a wise decision. These are the buyers who have learned to think like both a homeowner and investor—in other words, anyone who has read Part 1 of our book! They want to secure a nice place for their family but also don't want to put themselves into a bad investment.

Generally, they know themselves well enough to identify whether or not they lean more toward homeowner and investor. They're educated, savvy, and may be able to spot material problems in the building.

- ○ *How to negotiate with the hybrid buyer:* Negotiate by giving them options: "We can drop your offer price by $8,000 so that you have that money to fix the septic system, or we can put that money in escrow and have a contractor fix it for you after closing."[18] Respect the fact that these are more educated buyers and allow them to do the driving.

- **No buyers:** If your home isn't getting any offers, that means something has gone terribly wrong. Your list price might be way off, or the presentation to market might have been bungled, or perhaps there's a glaring issue with your property that you don't have the objectivity to see. There's usually a logical reason why homes sit on the market; if you're not able to understand why you're not getting any offers, bring in an expert. They should be able to identify the issue quickly and help you resolve it.

THE ART OF NEGOTIATING: MORE TIPS

When you list your home, your list price is the starting point of your negotiation. The warm chocolate chip cookies you serve at the open house is part of the negotiation. Your hard line on what repairs you will complete is part of the negotiation. Your final words of encouragement and advice to your buyers after giving them the keys help conclude the negotiation. Negotiation isn't just a quick and dirty conversation over terms—it's how you

---

18 "Escrow" refers to a neutral third-party who handles all the money exchanged in a real estate transaction.

shape and influence your buyer's experience from beginning to end. You want them to feel happy about how much money they're handing over so that *you* feel good about handing over your house.

In sum: you want to find the best scenario for all people. Here are a few final tips to make sure you provide a great negotiating experience to your buyers and make sure *you* get the price that your house deserves.

- **Be neutral; see your home with the investor mindset.** If you've got a critical or irritating buyer, it can be easy to get emotional and end up losing the deal. Don't let those emotions cause you to make a bad decision. Allow yourself to be emotional about saying goodbye to your house—but try not to get emotional about what your buyers are saying. They're simply doing their best to achieve *their* goals.

- **See the other people as fellow human beings.** The buyer and buyer's agent are not your adversaries; the inspector is not your enemy; the appraiser is not your foe. These are all people who have their own motivations, their own dreams, their own favorite Netflix shows. Do your best to show them respect, understanding, and meet their motivations. In turn, they'll be more inclined to meet yours.

- **Expect to pay 1 percent of your list price in doing repairs.** There *will* be issues discovered during the inspection, and you'll need to either fix those or drop your price. Expect that you will have to pay out-of-pocket anywhere between 0.5 percent and 1 percent of the listing price. So, if you get under contract with a $500,000 offer, expect that you will ultimately sell at $495,000. If you can expect this 1 percent expense, you won't get frustrated when the costs arise and can plan accordingly.

- **Negotiate right up until you close.** New variables may continue to come up during escrow as each contingency is managed. Handle your contract as a living document and keep your game face on until everything has closed.
- **Don't be penny-wise and pound-foolish.** In other words, be smart about the offer you accept. One buyer might offer you $3,000 above your list price, but their lender is notorious for bad loans made with people who have bad credit. There's a high likelihood that the offer would never make it through escrow. Another offer might be made at asking from a buyer with great credit. Go with that second buyer and use the first offer as leverage to negotiate a slightly higher purchase price.
- **Negotiations are where you can make or lose your return.** Most properties have about a 5 to 10 percent swing, from where their list price starts to where they finally end up at closing. If you've done the hard work on your home to bring it max value, you can expect that swing to go upwards, landing over your asking price as you get multiple bids. If there are areas of your home you've neglected, your list price may swing down, dropping by the time you're through negotiations.
- **You have the unique thing.** The buyer has the money, yes, but lots of buyers have money. By the time someone puts an offer on your house, they've decided that they want *your* unique house. Don't be afraid to lean into that; buyers will usually be inclined to move up more than you might expect.
- **Don't negotiate alone.** The two of us—although experts at buying and selling homes—still consult one another regularly when we're negotiating over a property. An additional expert or smart friend will help you see more nuance in the negotiation; they're likely to be more objective and less emotional. Particularly if they can help balance your natural bias toward

either homeowner or investor, these additional people can be instrumental in helping you see the whole picture.

Here's the good news: if you've done all the hard work to get your house in great shape, *you've done* the hard work. Selling it will be the easy part! Particularly if you've got a great listing, effective marketing, and a lovely product to offer at the price you've assigned, buyers will line up to make you offers.

THE COST OF SELLING YOUR HOME

Let's say you listed your home for $390,000, got multiple offers, and settled on a great one with reliable financing for $400,000. Now: how much of that $400,000 will you get to keep?

Psst: the correct answer is *not*, "All of it."

Selling your home comes with a number of costs—and the full extent of them is sometimes an unpleasant surprise for sellers. We want to make sure you're well aware of those costs before getting under contract with a buyer so that the final stretch goes as smoothly as possible.

Ready? Take a nice, deep breath and light a scented candle. Grab a favorite beverage. We're about to talk about lots of dollars leaving your bank account, but there's no reason why it shouldn't be as pleasant an experience as possible.

First, let's state the obvious: you have to pay off the rest of the mortgage you still may owe the bank on the property you're selling. If you still owe $300,000 on your mortgage, there's a

$300,000 bite taken out of that $400,000 pie. (Maybe you've paid your house off. Hooray! More pie, all for you.)

Next, there are the seller's closing costs:

- **Real Estate Agent Commissions**: Sellers are responsible for paying commissions to both the seller's and buyer's agents. These commissions usually total between 5 to 6 percent of the sale price, usually split in half between the two agents.
- **Title and Escrow Fees**: There are lots of people and processes involved in transferring a property from one party to another. The processes cost money, and the people would like to be paid. That's what these fees cover. They include:
  - *Title insurance*: Sellers typically pay half of a title insurance premium for their buyer. The cost of title insurance will be based on the price of the property and the rules prescribed by the state it's in.
  - *Escrow fees*: Sellers should expect to pay half of the escrow fees for the entire transaction, typically somewhere between $250 to $700.
  - *Title search*: This fee pays the title company for doing the title search. The cost will range between $300 to $750. (The range in most of these costs are mostly dependent on the going rates in your location.)
  - *Deed preparation*: $50 to $150 for the deed, please.
  - *Miscellaneous Fees*: There may be various other charges that need to be covered, like a charge for overnighting a wire payment or document prep; plan to pay somewhere between $150 and $400 for these miscellaneous fees.
- **Government Taxes**: Wait—you sold your very valuable home?

Uncle Sam would like a bite of the pie, too, please. You should expect to pay:

- *Transfer taxes:* Think of this as the sales tax, also known as the "county conveyance fee." This cost of this tax is levied by county; for instance, in our county in northeast Ohio, it's $4 per thousand (so, for a $400,000 home, the cost of transfer tax would be $1,600.) In our neighboring Wayne County, though, it's $2 per thousand ($800 for a $400,000 sale).

- *Property tax prorations*: You will need to pay your property taxes up to the point you lived in your house. Usually, this means you need to pay your buyer a credit toward the property tax bill they will receive in the future, covering the cost of the period when you were still living in the home. Huh? How does that work? Property taxes are paid for the *previous* year, not the current year. In other words, when you receive your property tax bill in January and July, those bills are for the first half of *last* year and the second half of *last* year. So, when your buyer gets their first bill for property taxes, they're being asked to cover the payment for when *you* were still living there. You will kindly give them another portion of your $400,000 pie, and they will put that pie in the freezer, and when the tax man comes to collect property taxes, they will take it out of the freezer and give it to him.

- *Water hold*: Since the water and sewage utility is attached to the property, not the person, the final water bill must be paid. The title company will hold money to ensure that the final water bill is paid. Once you show the title/ escrow company proof that you paid it, this money will be returned to you.

- *County assessor fees:* In some rare instances, the county may have done work to your property that they require payment for when you sell your home, like if they fixed the sidewalk in front of your home. You would cover this fee in a payment to the county assessor.
- **Miscellaneous:** You may be asked, expected, or required to pay other miscellaneous costs. These might include:
  - A one-year home warranty for the buyer.
  - A termite/pest inspection.
  - VA/FHA fee.
  - Any outstanding liens you might have, such as: child support liens and/or any judgments against you; sales tax liens; delinquent taxes.
  - Other (It's amazing how many ways the universe can come up with to charge miscellaneous fees!).

So what's *your* takeaway going to be? You won't know for sure until you get all your details in order, but we can shed light on how it might play out for you through an example.

Let's say Dahlia Brown just sold her lovely brick home for $400,000. Her original mortgage was for $330,000, and she's lived there for seven years.

- She still owes the remaining balance of $300,000 to off her mortgage.
- She hires Kevin at Exactly to sell her home, which means she pays a flat fee of $4,800 for his commission; she pays the buyer's agent 2.5 percent, which works out to $10,000. The total for agent commissions comes to: $14,800.
- Her county charges a $4 transfer fee, which means she owes

$1,600 for transfer taxes. She pays average costs for title and escrow fees, working out to about $750.

- She pays for half a title insurance policy, which costs approximately $1,150.
- Dahlia owes $6,500 for nine months' worth of prorated property taxes.

When all those fees, taxes, and costs are added up, Dahlia pays $24,800 to sell her home, plus the $300,000 to pay down her mortgage. With a sales price of $400,000, her net proceeds total $75,200.

That means, after seven years of homeownership, Dahlia walks away with a check for roughly $75,000, lots of memories, and is in a great position to move on to her next home.

FINAL PEP TALK

Maintain inner fortitude during your negotiations by being totally clear about the product you're selling, working to achieve your primary motivation, and understanding your buyer's motivations. Work to achieve a win-win scenario for everyone by showing respect and holding your line. Invite expert advice from more than one person.

By the end of this, you and your buyer can both walk away feeling satisfied. You've traded an accurate house for an accurate price, and you did it in a way that was mindful of everyone's needs. This can be an incredibly meaningful experience that will set you all up for future success—that's the goal!

CHAPTER 15

CONTRACT TO CLOSE

LEAP THE FINAL HURDLES AND AVOID BREAKDOWN

IT'S NOT OVER 'TIL IT'S OVER

Offer chosen! Under contract! It's over! Right?

Well...not quite. Almost! But not quite.

If you've gotten your house under contract, that's worth celebrating! But remember the story that we opened Part 2 with: you've summited the mountain. Now you still have to get *down*. Between contract to close, you're going to want to step carefully and stay alert—there are a number of ways this can still go sideways, and you want to stay on your guard.

We heard of a nightmare scenario of a deal breaking down which involved a real estate agent acquaintance—we'll call him Fred. Fred's clients were preparing to sell their home and had made the plan to sell first, move into a rental, secure their financing, and then buy again. Under Fred's leadership, they got the house under contract and moved their four kids out of the home into a tiny rental. They also sold a bunch of their furniture and loaded everything else into a storage unit.

There was one major problem: Fred hadn't ensured that the buyers had solid financing. During the underwriting process in escrow, the deal fell apart. The buyers backed out, and the house had to be put back on the market. The family couldn't afford to pay both their mortgage payment and a rental payment, so they had no choice but to move *back* into their former home. They had to cancel their rental lease, pay the penalty, get their stuff back out of storage, renew all the utilities that they had cancelled, and move back into their house.

Can you imagine the stress? The kids' confusion? The anxiety-induced arguments between the husband and wife? All the money they lost from putting the first and last month's rent down, the moving trucks, the storage unit, and so on? And let's not forget the awkward conversations with the neighbors: "Hi, we're back! Yep, we thought we were moving, too, but...nope." What a nightmare!

It doesn't have to be this way, and it shouldn't ever be this way! With this chapter, we're going to make sure that you know exactly how a deal commonly breaks down so that you can ensure your deal *doesn't* break down.

Step One: make sure you're working with a great real estate agent who will ensure nothing like this ever happens to you.

Step Two: understand that the deal's not over until it's *over*. We call the final stage of selling your home "contract to close." Most real estate contracts contain a number of *contingencies*. Any one of these contingencies can serve as an exit point, enabling your buyer to freely back out of the deal. That means until you close, there's potential for flux.

In this chapter, we're going to discuss the five common points where a deal can break down so you can understand how to navigate them successfully. By leaping over these final hurdles, you ensure the agreements in the contract are kept, the title is successfully transferred, and you're able to cross the final finish line of selling your home.

THE FIVE COMMON POINTS OF BREAKDOWN

Between contract to close, there's a lot happening behind the scenes. Much of the activity will be out of your control, but you will be able to influence some of it. Start by setting yourself up for success: select the offer that's best in line with your primary selling goals.

1—ACCEPTING THE OFFER

There's a danger in accepting an offer that *you don't thoroughly read.* When a contract is written up, there's complicated language that can be tempting to gloss over. You might see confusing phrases like, "seller pays prorated taxes," or "rent will be prorated as of the date of closing." You might assume that your real estate agent will explain those to you later, thinking, "If they didn't bring it up, it must not be an issue." However, that assumption banks on the fact that you have an extremely motivated and experienced agent who will take the time to closely review your contract. That's not something they're necessarily required to do.

Here's the thing: all those little phrases relate to cold, hard cash. The words directly correspond to numbers, and those numbers determine *who* is paying *how much*. If you don't closely read and understand your contract, you're likely to be surprised later in the escrow process when you realize you "agreed" to pay the fees for x, y, and z. When sellers are surprised by subtleties in the contract that they signed, there's often frustration and arguments. That, too, can lead to break down.

Myth: My agent will ensure the contract is all good.

No—the contract is on you! The agent should help you navigate the negotiation, but it's your job to ensure the contract writing correctly reflects everything you decided on. You should solicit your agent's help if you have trouble understanding the wording, but *you* will need to take the initiative to ask those questions. Your agent is not required to go through all the intricacies of the contract with you. Many of them don't have time to do that; other, newer agents may not even fully understand the intricacies of a contract. At the end of the day, it's your job to ensure the written contract correctly reflects the agreement you made.

One last point to keep in mind when you're writing up the initial contract: **contracts can be written up in a thousand different ways.** If you don't love the way your contract is written up, you can ask for it to change! Also, make sure your real estate agent is thoroughly familiar with all the different ways a contract can be written. If they don't, ask your agent if they can bring a more experienced team member to negotiations with you. There are countless possibilities that can help you maneuver in all sorts of ways to ensure everyone's needs are met. If you have good people helping you shape the contract, you're far more likely to get through the escrow process smoothly and successfully land in your next home.

Tip: Many sellers would benefit by including a **Date of Possession clause** in the contract. How does this work? A seller can request that the date of possession come *after* the scheduled closing date, during which you would essentially rent your house from its new owners. Creating a buffer between closing and possession is one of the best ways sellers can protect themselves. Let's say you're scheduled to close on April 1, but you request April 14 as the date of possession. You're giving yourself an extra two weeks to ensure the deal successfully closes, secure the money in the bank, and arrange your move. A space between closing and possession also provides a time buffer in case there are any delays in closing.

2—INSPECTION AND REPAIRS

Once their home is under contract, most sellers want to minimize expenses and race to the finish line—however, the inspection will force you to pause and make some hard decisions. We're going to ask you to accept a few hard truths to avoid breakdown during this phase:

- **Your home almost certainly has a few things wrong with it** that the inspection will reveal, which you didn't know about.
- **It is natural and normal for your buyers to ask you to fix those things.** They're getting ready to spend an enormous sum of money. In agreeing to make repairs, you're giving your buyer an important affirmation that you will take care of them. That reassurance will help ease their anxieties and ensure they continue with the sale.
- **Resolving those issues will require you to either drop your price or spend money on repairs.** As a reminder: sellers should expect to spend roughly 1 percent of their list price on doing post-inspection repairs.

If you don't go into the inspection phase of escrow with these expectations in place, things can once again get dicey. We worked with some sellers recently who accepted an offer for $5,000 above their list price. They were thrilled with that offer! However, the inspection revealed that the home needed a new furnace—likely an expense of around $2,700. The sellers dug in their heels. They did *not* want to replace the furnace and deal with this cost—even though they would still be coming out ahead! It took a lot of coaxing and cajoling for them to finally agree to fix the furnace and move on. You can save yourself some heartache by simply going into the inspection with these expectations in place.

Also: remember that **your buyer is a different person than you and will want different things.** For instance, you may have had all your electrical work done by your neighbor, a retired electrician. His license may have expired years ago, but he knows what he's doing, and he gives you a great discount. Your buyer, however, might insist that the electrical repairs be completed by a licensed electrician. This could make you grumpy: your guy would be way cheaper, and he would do just as good a job. However, we were once in this exact situation with a seller and buyer and ended up discovering that the buyers' son had died years ago in an electrical fire. No wonder they wanted to insist on using a licensed electrician.

You may not know where your buyers are coming from as they insist that certain repairs be done a certain way. They might be willing to compromise, but if they insist on their own terms—go ahead and flex. Give them the reassurance and encouragement they need by going with their request. You'll get through the inspection phase more quickly and avoid breakdown.

With that said though, **you don't have to fix *everything* they ask you to fix.** Consider your own needs, your buyer's motivations, and the market when choosing what to repair.

Although the issue at hand may concern building materials, **dealing with inspection repairs often stirs up strong emotions.** You might feel indignant that a problem which you've happily lived with for ten years strikes the buyers as a deal-breaker issue. (It never bothered you. What's wrong with these people?!) But remember that your buyers are emotional, too: at this stage in the game, buyers usually need reassurance. They're feeling some trepidation over spending so much money, and they need to feel like they've gotten a "win"—whether that's through a dropped price or a completed repair. Consider where your buyer might be coming from and respond to their repair requests in a way that shows them you genuinely want to bless them with a good home.

One final note: all of the issues you *knew about* should have been reflected in the list price already. The only repairs you should be negotiating during this phase of escrow are the issues you *didn't know about*. If you've been transparent from the beginning about your home's known issues, then the discoveries during the inspection are more likely to seem minor rather than major.

3—APPRAISAL CLEARING

If you've made it through the inspection and repairs phase, give yourself a big pat on the back. The bulk of your responsibilities as a seller are behind you! In this appraisal stage, you're passing the baton to the folks at the bank who will continue the race forward.

If you're in a market that's stable or taking a downturn, you don't need to give the appraisal a second thought. (Feel free to skip this section.) However, **if the current real estate market is in an upswing or you have a unique home, the appraisal could pose a challenge.**

Here's how appraisals work: the bank hires an appraiser to come evaluate the fair market value of the house. The appraiser will go through the home and consult past market data of what similar homes have sold for recently in the area. Finally, they'll issue their appraisal value. Let's say the bank appraises your home for $400,000: that's what they think your home would sell for, in a fair market.

This can get problematic if you're in a hot market, when bidding wars can cause homes to be sold for well above their list price. Let's say, for instance, that someone offers you $430,000 for your home, but that's $30,000 over what the bank has determined it's worth. They will *only* finance a loan up to the amount of the appraisal value, minus the minimum requirement for a down payment.

If the bank appraises the property for *less* than the purchase price, one of four things will happen:

1. The buyer chooses to cancel the deal, and everyone walks away.
2. The seller reduces the price to the appraisal amount.
3. The buyer will pay the difference in cash between the purchase price and appraisal price. (The money required to make up the difference would not count toward their down payment.)
4. The buyer and seller each make concessions to meet somewhere in the middle.

The appraisal could also be an issue if you have a unique home, or a home with valuable updates. In either case, the bank won't have a large pool of comparative data to pull from, which means they could easily get the appraisal wrong. In our area, for instance, we know some Amish contractors who do an incredible job restoring homes. They're well known for their quality, and buyers are often willing to spend much more to buy one of those homes, because they know they're purchasing an incredible product. However, if a bank is comparing a three-bed/two-bath in Ramona Heights to another three-bed/two-bath in Ramona Heights, they're not going to consider which builder did the renovations. They might give those two homes an identical appraisal, even if one is considered much more valuable to buyers.

As a seller, how should you respond to an appraisal issue? That will likely be determined by your market. If there were multiple offers on your home, you might simply go with a different buyer who can put more money down. However, if there *aren't* multiple offers, you should consider dropping your price or doing something else to help your buyers come through, like offering to cover the closing costs.

If you have a good seller's agent, they might be able to predict issues with the appraisal and get ahead of it. For instance, they might research other homes with *pending* offers to provide proof that market values are rapidly increasing in that area. With their advocacy, you might be able to shrink the gap between the appraisal value and purchase price, saving yourself some trouble.

4—TITLE CLEARING

Contract, check. Inspection and repairs, check. Appraisal cleared, check. Now let's deal with the title.

When a person sells a house, there's a title transfer: Joe Johnson transfers the deed of ownership to Sheila Shelby. Ideally, the title is "clean"—in other words, it meets the following three standards:

1. There are no unknown liens against the property.
2. There are no issues with accessing the property. (e.g., The driveway doesn't cut across the neighbor's land.)
3. The seller has the legal right to sell it.

The title company is in charge of researching the title and ensuring it meets those standards. Sixty to 70 percent of the time, it does. The title is given a clean bill of health, and the sale continues to move forward. However, 30 to 40 percent of the time, there are complications.

What kind of complications? Here are a few:

- The person selling the house doesn't actually own it because a mistake was made in the title transfer when *they* bought the house. In other words, the prior title company missed something.
- There is a lien against the house, like a federal tax lien or a child support lien. In that case, the seller doesn't own the home outright; a credit agency or the federal government has a claim to it until the debt is paid off.
- Someone besides the seller has a claim to ownership. For instance, if a widower wants to sell his house after his wife passes away, but her name is still on the title as co-owner; that title typically must be transferred through the probate court. Or perhaps a couple is separated but not officially divorced; both spouses would need to participate in the sale.

Title issues are becoming more and more common because technology has increased the speed at which these deals race along. When a deal moves fast, it's much easier to make a mistake. You might assume the people processing titles on the county level would catch any mistakes before officially transferring the title, but they can miss key details, too. In our area, we've seen an entire generation of title experts retire and be replaced by newer employees who might more easily allow mistakes to slip through.

Unfortunately, sellers won't know if there's a title problem with their property until they go to transfer the property. Only at that point will a title company discover if there are title issues. Here's the good news: title issues are usually very solvable. It might take extra work and extra time—you may have to rearrange some logistics because the closing date will likely be pushed back. However, a title company can typically solve the issue and get the title clean.

If a title company can't easily solve the issue with some research, phone calls, and elbow grease, the title issue may turn into a **title insurance claim**. Title insurance is something you can choose to buy when you initially purchase a house, and it will protect you from any consequences that might arise from a title transfer issue.

Here's an example of when that insurance might come in handy. We recently worked with a couple who had bought a house twenty years ago. The previous owner of their home had a federal tax lien against the house, which no one caught before the title was transferred to the new owners. The new owners never knew about the lien attached to their property and it continued to accrue interest over the twenty years they owned it. When they went to sell, they thought they had built up $450,000 in equity. Unfortunately, they also had a lien against their property worth $1.1 million! Before they could sell, they had to deal with that debt. Fortunately, they had title insurance and filed a claim. The title insurance dealt with the debt, and the couple was able to successfully sell. These scenarios don't happen often, but when they do, they can be devastating if there's no title insurance.

Once your title is given a clean bill of health, the bank is notified, and the final obstacle is removed. You've leaped over each hurdle—now it's a sprint to the finish line!

5—FINAL BANK APPROVAL

Now it's time for a sprint to the finish—or maybe a slow crawl. **Depending on what lender your buyer is using, the final "clear to close" may come quickly or be maddeningly delayed.** Particularly if you're dealing with a large bank, your property sale may simply be treated as a piece of paper in a large stack of papers. No one in those back rooms will necessarily be incentivized to make your life significantly easier and hurry the deal along.

Ideally, you will have chosen a buyer with a good, efficient lender. However, sometimes those variables will be out of your control. If your house doesn't close on time, you'll unfortunately just have to deal with it. No one can make it go faster.

Myth: My house will close on its closing date.

Banks view the closing date more as a goal than a deadline. If your house does happen to close on its actual closing date, that's something to celebrate! Unfortunately, it's just as common for a snag or inefficiency along the way to cause a hold up. We recommend having the expectation that it will probably *not* close on the actual closing date and have some contingency plans ready.

Given how often closing dates are pushed back, you might be wise to have a contingency in your contract that you can keep possession of the house until after it closes. That could save you a great deal of stress, hassle, and heartache.

LESS COMMON SCENARIOS

Those are the five common hurdles to leap over between receiving an offer and making it to close. However, there are other less common scenarios that can trip you up as well. Here are just a few ways "life" could intervene and cause a deal to breakdown:

- There's an "act of God," like a tree falling on the house or an earthquake.
- Someone dies.
- Someone gets into a car accident and becomes handicapped.
- Someone loses their job.
- Someone gets pregnant, and their perceived needs suddenly change.
- A pandemic like the coronavirus hits; everything is upended.

Buyers' remorse is one of the more common "less common" scenarios that threaten a deal's completion. Someone could simply wake up and decide that they don't want to keep their agreement with you anymore, for whatever reason. Maybe they're sensing instability in their job, or they see a new house listing that looks better than yours—who knows. Human beings are unpredictable.

That's why it's critical to remember when you're selling your property that it's not over until it's *over*. Every decision you make during this selling process should have a back-up plan. Choose a back-up offer; develop some back-up negotiation strategies; get a back-up moving plan in place. Where you can, get these contingency plans in writing, so there's added protection. And as much as possible, offer your buyer reassurance throughout the process, so they're as motivated as you are to see it through.

At some point, you'll have to move forward in good faith; for instance, you may have to move out of your house before it sells so that it can be successfully staged and marketed. Decisions need to be made, and actions need to be taken, even before it's all a sure thing. Still, some contingency planning will go a long way in helping you guard against the consequences of possible breakdown.

Plan for the worst, hope for the best, be flexible and keep taking deep breaths. Eventually, it will all work out!

SPEAKING OF BREAKDOWN...

You may have picked up on the fact by now that selling your home is a stressful, hard process. Think of what a normal day might consist of: you wake up, shower, go to work, come home, make dinner, hang out with your kids, take them to soccer practice, then watch TV, and go to bed.

When you sell your home, you're packing up your entire house. You're potentially moving to a different area. You're changing school systems. You're leaving your friends and neighbors. You're making arrangements with movers. You've got a headache from too much adulting, dealing with the contracts, the schedules, the logistics, the fees. Also, you're dealing in *hundreds of thousands* of dollars. That's stressful!

We'd like to help you avoid an *emotional* breakdown at least as much as we want to spare you a deal breakdown, so we want to give you a heads up about the emotional rollercoaster you can expect to ride in these final few weeks. It's normal and appropriate to experience these different emotions at different phases of the process:

- *Deciding to sell*: emotional high and excitement. Here we go!
- *Preparing your home to list*: depression. Updates are expensive, and you might have a lot of work to do. The updates might also make you sad: "Why didn't we do this earlier so we could have at least enjoyed it?" You might also feel fear for what's next or worried that you're making mistakes.
- *Bringing your property to market*: anxiety and stress. You hope people like your home; you may feel like you're putting yourself out there only to risk rejection. It's also stressful to keep your house clean all the time if you're still living there.
- *Receiving offer(s)*: excitement, surprise. If the offers aren't what you wanted, you might be disappointed.
- *Negotiating repairs*: offended, insulted. If your home holds up well under inspection, you might stay excited.
- *Release of contingency (get through inspection)*: relief, hope. You're nearly there!
- *Final closing*: frustration if you encounter unexpected costs; fatigue at dealing with this long process. It's common to get to the end with a feeling of, "I'm so over all of this. I just need to get my money so I can buy my other house."
- *Back at buying!* A new emotional cycle begins...

If you find yourself currently within any of these stages, cut yourself some slack. It's going to be hard until you're on the other side. Selling a home is one of the most stressful experiences in life, and if anything goes wrong, the stress can go through the roof. However, you're not the only person who's experienced this ordeal and made it through. Keep breathing—and keep going.

CROSSING THE FINISH LINE

We want to assure you: you will make it past that finish line! Once you get there, you might feel like you've just completed the 200-meter hurdles—sweaty, red-faced, exhausted, and ready to collapse—but you've *done* it. Particularly if you've read our previous chapters and you've assembled a good team, you're going to make it through these final hurdles like a trained athlete.

Eventually, the lender's final approval will come. Swap the keys, call the movers, and pour the champagne! You've made it!

THE HEART OF THE MATTER

You are worth more than the plus or minus of money; the hard moments during negotiations or escrow do not have anything to do with your personal worth. Do what you need to keep your head clear and maintain your sanity. Expect this to be a long and expensive process. As much as possible, try to be flexible on the details and don't try to save every penny—that can create unnecessary anxiety. Trust your team. Run the race with perseverance!

CONCLUSION

There's a memorable scene at the climax of the movie "Indiana Jones and the Last Crusade," when Indiana Jones must get through a gauntlet in order to reach the Holy Grail.[19] Indiana Jones, played by Harrison Ford, is looking out over a gaping abyss. Somehow, he has to cross over to the other side, but as he stares down into the gaping hole beneath him, he can only see darkness. He reminds himself of the instructions he's been given: "It's a leap of faith." Closing his eyes, he steps out into the void—and steps onto something solid.

Beneath his feet, a path of rock stretches forward in a slim bridge across the abyss, totally camouflaged against the walls of rock stretching downward. Although the path is nearly invisible, it's there, holding Indiana up as he walks across. After he reaches the other side, Indiana gathers a handful of dirt in his hands and scatters it across the bridge so that he will see it more clearly on his return.

19 *Indiana Jones and the Last Crusade.* Paramount, 1989.

Indiana must have felt enormous anxiety and fear before stepping out into the void—two traits that we often see characterizing people who are preparing to buy or sell their home. When the path is unknown, it's scary. The way forward seems dangerous. The correct route feels invisible. The risks seem enormous.

But what if the path was more readily seen? What if someone helped you see its outline, its breadth, its trajectory? Your steps would be more confident and sure. Suddenly, it wouldn't feel so scary—it would feel more like an adventure.

That's what we've tried to give you with this book: the knowledge you need to walk this risky path with confidence. The two of us are guided in our careers by our values for truth and transparency. We want to give our clients and readers all the information they need to make wise decisions. In these chapters, we've given you a comprehensive review of how to wisely navigate the processes of buying or selling your home, and we've included stories of real experiences along the way to help illustrate the importance of our recommendations.

The transition between where you live now and where you end up living doesn't need to be scary or miserable—it can be one of abundance and joy. We know that people want to make a joyful decision, one that enables them to move from one home to another while experiencing abundance. This joy can come when you have the information you need to make wise decisions that will bless your family—not just in the near future but for decades to come.

For both buyers and sellers, there are key principles and phases to understand, which will help you step surely:

- **Get your mind right.** Buyers need to think with a *balance* of a homeowner's and investor's mindset. Sellers need to *transition* from a homeowner's mindset to an investor's mindset. It's important to make a smart financial investment *and* to commit to a property where you'll enjoy living.

- **Plan and prepare.** Buyers need to think through whether they're ready to buy strategically, emotionally, and financially; they also need to prepare to learn as much as possible about their desired neighborhood, market trends, and building construction. Sellers need to consider whether it makes more sense for them to sell or rent out their property as they prepare to move. If they decide to sell, it's critical to get a plan in place about whether to sell first, then buy; or buy a new place first, then sell.

- **Assemble a good team.** It's critical to have the right people around you when buying or selling a home—just as crucial as selecting a good guide to take you up and down a treacherous mountain. The right real estate agent and mortgage lender will make a world of difference in the quality and success of your experience.

- **Get your finances teed up.** Buyers have a range of financial products available to them; by learning what tools are available, buyers can avail themselves of more opportunities. Similarly, sellers need to tee up their own financing so that they know exactly how best to approach getting into their next home. There are important financial tools that they can take advantage of as well, like a HELOC, which can help pave the way for a successful transition.

- **Learn how to evaluate building construction and property value.** Remember: everything in the natural world is slowly causing buildings to deteriorate! Part of being smart in real estate is learning how to properly assess the level of deterioration. Buyers need to learn how to evaluate the quality of a building so they can ensure they're making a smart buy. Sellers need to be aware of the building and property they're offering to buyers so that they can price it accurately.

- **Learn how homes are priced.** Both buyers and sellers benefit when they learn how to assess property value. Understanding market variables like local trends, CMA data, time of year, interest rates, inventory factors, and the emotional "x factor" will help both buyers and sellers make smart decisions about the fair market value of a property. Additionally, sellers need to learn how to present their home so that it has a successful introduction to the market.

- **Negotiate well by understanding the other party's motivations.** Buyers and sellers are likely to be more successful during negotiations if they have a clear idea of their own primary goals and can recognize the main goals of the other party. Ultimately, buying and selling a home is not just about getting the best price; it's about trading an accurate property for an accurate price and blessing the other person while doing so.

- **Successfully get through the final stages of contract to close.** Buyers and sellers will navigate the inspection, appraisal, title investigation, and financing of their deal after getting under contract. Although much of these steps will be outside of their control, there are ways buyers and sellers can help smooth the process. The team you've assembled at this point will play an invaluable part in keeping things running smoothly. This phase is an emotional one for both buyers and sellers. Anticipating that stress can help you stay focused on the light at the end of the tunnel and the hope that's coming.

We've passed on our tips, expertise, and stories regarding each of these principles so that you feel empowered to walk forward on solid ground. Perhaps at one point you felt worried that you might get tricked by a questionable real estate professional, or embarrassed, or that someone might try to hide something from you. Perhaps you worried that one bad decision could be catastrophic—that you would fall into that abyss.

In passing on this knowledge, we've tried to dispel those fears and replace them with confidence. We know it's possible to make a decision with your eyes open and see all the different factors you're committing to. Our goal has been to illuminate both the potholes and the possibilities on this path—both the dangers and the opportunities. By passing on what we've learned, we hope you feel empowered to make wise, accurate decisions.

To all the potential buyers reading this book: go shop! Go learn. Walk through a ton of buildings and shape your understanding of what you're looking for. You know what you need to know now to make a smart decision.

To sellers: thank your home for what it has provided you and get ready to pass it off well to its next owner. Find the right people to help show off your home to its maximum advantage and advocate on your behalf. In fact, if you live in northeast Ohio, give Kevin a call at Exactly. He will take care of you!

CONNECT WITH US

Kevin Wasie: https://exactlyusa.com/. Hire Kevin for expert real estate help to buy a home or sell your home.

Ben Walkley: https://smallerproblems.com. On Ben's website, you can find free educational resources like a home evaluation worksheet, For Sale by Owner tips, a monthly payment calculator worksheet, and others, along with an opportunity to sign up for classes about investing in real estate.

Whatever real estate decisions you make now, you can trust that you're making them with wisdom and objectivity. Don't hesitate to reach out to us if you have additional questions or need more depth. We'll give you truth and transparency—our real answers and our real experience. You can count on it.

ABOUT THE
AUTHORS

BEN WALKLEY has been involved in more than ten thousand real estate deals as an active investor and the owner of The Fireland Title Group. A mentor and speaker, Ben is passionate about real estate and the impact a positive experience can have in his clients' lives. Ben lives with his wife and their six kids in Medina, Ohio.

KEVIN WASIE is the founder and CEO of Exactly Real Estate, a company with a unique consumer-centric business model and one of the fastest-growing brokerages in northeast Ohio. An expert in residential real estate sales and marketing, Kevin has an economics degree from John Carroll University. He's a northeast Ohio native and lives in Akron with his two kids.

Made in the USA
Monee, IL
03 March 2022